SPIRITUAL JOURNEYS

twenty-seven men and women share their faith experiences

FOREWORD BY
BERNARD CARDINAL LAW

EDITED BY
ROBERT BARAM

St. Paul Books & Media

Library of Congress Cataloging-in-Publication Data

Spiritual journeys.

    1. Converts, Catholic—United States—Biography.
I. Baram, Robert.

BX4668.A1S65   1987   248.2'4   87-6668

ISBN 0-8198-6877-9 c
     0-8198-6876-0 p

In this collection of essays—for the most part—each author's preferences regarding capitalization and italics have been followed.

Second printing, revised, 1988.

Printed in the U.S.A., by the Daughters of St. Paul
50 St. Paul's Ave., Boston, MA 02130

The Daughters of St. Paul are an international congregation of women religious serving the Church with the communications media.

CONTENTS

FOREWORD

Reading these "spiritual journeys," I was reminded of St. Augustine's remarks about his own tormented pilgrimage of faith: "Late it was that I loved you, beauty so ancient and so new, late I loved you! And, look, you were within me and I was outside and there I sought for you.... You were with me, and I was not with you.... You called, you cried out, you scattered my blindness, you breathed perfume, and I drew my breath and I pant for you: I tasted, and I am hungry and thirsty; you touched me, and I burned for your peace" (*Confessions*, X, 27).

What these spiritual journeys have in common is not how relatively "late" or "early" conversion took place, but how from the very beginning the Lord was "within" each one of these writers all along their pilgrimage of faith while they were, in varying degrees, "outside." It was through the Catholic Church's clear and unchanging conviction about doctrine and morals that He "cried out" for them and "scattered their blindness." It was through the sacramental life of the Church, especially the celebration of the Eucharist, that they "breathed the (divine) perfume" and "tasted" the goodness of the Lord, becoming "hungry and thirsty" for more, "burning" for His peace.

May our reading of these spiritual journeys awaken our spiritual senses to the Lord's presence in the Church and His call to daily conversion to Him through the

Church's teachings and sacraments. For whether we are born Catholic or become one later in life, our spiritual journey is never over. Every day we must put to death our old selves and live in the Spirit that newness of life that Jesus gives each day until the journey is over in eternity.

"When in my whole self I shall cling to you united, I shall find no sorrow anywhere, no labor; wholly alive will my life be all full of you" (St. Augustine, *ibid.*, X, 28).

May it be so for these pilgrims whose testimonial in this book so encourages us, as well as for each one of us, with God's grace.

Bernard Cardinal Law
Archbishop of Boston

PREFACE

Herein are the heartfelt stories of individuals whose souls were troubled by uncertainty, by confusion, and even by pain and suffering until they discovered the miracle of immaculate faith, and were themselves found and embraced by Christ and Catholicism.

For many of us, the seemingly impossible journey to the moon is regarded as the most incredible extra-territorial adventure of humankind. But that was only a small step when compared to the infinitely varied and remarkable discoveries that have taken these men and women not merely to the moon, but far beyond to heaven itself, where the ultimate stars of peace and of love and of faith burn forever brightly and are waiting there to be shared and treasured by those who are willing to seek, and those who are eager to be found.

Robert Baram
Professor of Journalism
Boston University
College of Communication

ruggle—A Gift

Wick Allison

The bored clerk in the processing center at Fort Polk, Louisiana, had already typed my name onto the form. Using the hunt-and-peck method, he was finishing up the last digits of my new identification number.

"Religion?" he asked.

I hesitated. I understood why the Army would want to know someone's religion. Well, then, how did I want to be buried?

The clerk drummed his fingers.

"Catholic," I answered.

Some people forge their conversions in the heat of great intellectual encounters. Others wrestle with demons through dark nights. A few are struck as if by lightning on the road to Damascus. My moment of conversion came while I stood on a dirty linoleum floor in front of a green metal desk on the day I was drafted.

Of course, it happened earlier and it happened later.

Two years later I returned from my tour of duty. In my old bedroom my father was helping me unpack my duffel bag. He pulled out my set of dog tags, looked at them, then suddenly sat down on the bed. On those tags, next to a name as familiar as his own, because it was his own, were two words that had been anathema to the generations of Southern Protestants who had engendered and raised him.

"Are you a Roman Catholic?" he asked.

"Kind of," I answered, sheepishly.

He stared at the floor, he stared at the wall, and finally he stared at me.

"From what I know about Catholics," he said in his slowest, most thoughtful Texas drawl, "you either are one or you aren't." He paused. "I think you'd better see a priest."

And so it was that four months later, on a beautiful December afternoon in 1972, I was received into the Roman Catholic Church. My proud Methodist father stood behind me as I knelt.

The profession I had made first to an anonymous clerk, then to my father, and finally to the Church itself had roots more difficult to trace than the events are to remember. After more than a decade's reflection, I've concluded that the digging out of each tiny tendril would be an exercise in irrelevance. Because conversion is not an act of psychology, or of the will, or even of comprehension. It is a gift.

It is a gift that can easily be refused. At a party some weeks after my Catholicism became known, an old family friend came up to me to congratulate me. He talked of his great admiration for the Church and said that once he had almost converted himself. I asked him why he hadn't. "Because in those days," he said, "the only Catholics were Mexicans in our part of the country. If I had converted it would have ruined my family. In small-town Texas at that time it just could not be done." He said this wistfully, as if it were a regret he had learned to live with. A few months later, before we could talk about it again, he was dead. So conversion is a gift, but it is a gift that requires action. The convert has taken an action against the myriad of actions he could have taken. Unlike the born Catholic, he is not impelled by a familial or cultural tradition to accept the faith; more often, family and culture are obstacles in his path. The convert has made a choice, and it is such an important choice there is no good reason to be bashful about it. And that, I guess, is why the words "Catholic convert" are synonymous with "zealot" the world over.

Born Catholics harbor a stereotype of the zealous convert which turns out to be true ninety-nine times out of a hundred. The convert plunges into his new faith, diving as deep as he can, relishing every drop. Often the best topic for a parable is money. In most cases, inherited money is quiet and unassuming. It does its best to live simply, in comparative normalcy, and to safeguard itself for future generations. New money, on the other hand, is most often open and gregarious. It is a little dumbfounded by its own good luck, a little humble about its success (if not about the accomplishment that brought the success), and determined to enjoy itself to the fullest. New money is perhaps more willing to advertise. So is the convert.

I think it is important for born Catholics to understand the convert's strength of conviction. It might even be more helpful for the Catholic clergy to understand this. Most religious grew up in the faith; they are inheritors. I've known some personally and have found them to be people of deep faith. But only in rare and justifiably famous cases (I'm thinking here of Monsignor Eugene Clark in New York and of Mother Angelica in Birmingham) have they shown they understand why on earth anyone would want to become a Catholic. It is a question they have never had to answer, although it is the one question that is more basic than the question of why anyone would want to become a priest.

For years my dear maiden aunt, a loving woman and devout Baptist, refrained from referring to my conversion. She would follow me along to Midnight Mass (the family must stick together), she would joyfully send along news clippings about various matters of Christian interest, she would cluck her tongue at me conspiratorially over some niece or cousin's pagan ways, but she would never say a word about my new faith.

One evening we were sitting side by side on her couch after dinner. As if some irresistible urge had been suppressed too many times before, she finally blurted out:

"You're such an independent person. I just don't see it! How could you let the Pope in Rome tell you what to do?"

How indeed?

I had come to the Church out of admiration for one of its great insights, an insight that I now realize is of its essence. That insight is about human nature, and the insight is that it is unchangeable.

How simple that seems! Yet in the modern age, between the Nietzschean call for the Superman and the Marxist promise of the New Man, how many millions have been slaughtered in the ideological quest to prove the opposite. It was this insight, found over and over again in Catholic writings, that had led me in search of their source. I had come to the Church fathers, who, by the logic and force of their arguments, had brought me right to the front door of the Church.

It seems a shorter journey now than it did then. But I'm older now, more settled in, more comfortable with the nooks and crannies. Right then, it was all discovery, hard argument, contradiction and refutation. Because, embracing as I did these insights and arguments of the Catholic fathers, I found myself confronted at last with their claim: that the Roman Catholic Church is the one, true Church.

At the core of the conversion experience stands Christ himself. Sometime in his life any thinking person who comes of age in the Western world must confront the idea of Christ. The believing Christian is the person who moves beyond the idea to reality. But the essential, whether it occurs in a flash or through the struggles of a lifetime, is the act of confrontation. Once we confront the idea of Christ, we reject or accept the claim He made about His Godship. It is our reaction to this claim that defines who we are.

The encounter of a stranger with the Catholic Church takes place at a different stage, but on a similar plane. Sooner or later every thinking Christian confronts the claim of the Catholic Church. And to the thinking Christian, that claim is as outrageous as it is unavoidable.

This is precisely the point that most priests—in my experience—do not understand. In working with converts, they attempt to soften the blows, to gentle the troubled waters of controversy. This is the great mistake, for the act of conversion, to Christianity and to the Church, is an act of confrontation. This is the struggle a prospective convert faces, and it is a struggle he must face. It is a mistake to downplay the struggle; the struggle is the gift he has been given.

In my case, the struggle was this business of the "one, true Church."

The phrase does not ring with resonance to Protestant ears. But it is the very outrageousness of the claim that leads one to ignore its implied sting and grapple with its content. If I loved and embraced all that the great men of the Church had taught me, could I then turn a deaf ear to their claim that what they taught is the Truth? In their minds, it was the Truth not because they were great men, or because I embraced what they taught me. Their authority, they said themselves, came neither from their own insight and intelligence as teachers nor from mine as student, but from their authority through the apostolic succession from Christ. It was their duty as teachers to teach the magisterium of the Church, and it was my duty as student to accept. For the magisterium is exclusive. There is only one. It comes from Christ. It comes through the apostles to the fathers and the bishops. It is, in a phrase, the Roman Catholic Church.

As my father had said, sitting sadly on that bed and fingering my dog tags, "From what I know about Catholics, you either are one or you aren't." I think he knew that sometime in the long-ago past, one of our ancestors had forked off the main road and that I was going back.

There are things I would like the friends and family I left behind to know about what I've found on my journey. For the Protestant it is an article of faith that one's relationship with God is a personal relationship, and in a sense then it becomes an isolated relationship, for a conversation between self and God is by necessity a very private conversation. For the Catholic the relationship is more private than the Protestant realizes, but it is also communal. I don't mean communal in the sense of some celebrant's believing that people should hold hands during the singing of the Our Father to "feel community." I mean in the sense that Chesterton defined tradition, as the democracy of the dead. I can walk into a Catholic Church and feel the accumulated prayers on earth, almost hear the ongoing prayers in heaven, and sense the power of the generations caring for one another—dead, alive, yet to come. It is a rare and beautiful thing for the drop in the river to be cognizant of its flow.

The other fact I have to mention is the Eucharist. This is harder to speak of because, once again, it is a claim, and for any person who thinks seriously about Christian religion it is a claim that must be confronted. But for me it remains a mystery. I can only recall the moment when I knew it was a mystery that animated my understanding of my faith.

My brother lives in England. On a visit over there years after my conversion he told me he had a treat in store for me. Knowing my interest in religion (he's an agnostic) and my love of history (which he shares enthusiastically), he had arranged to drive me to see the oldest standing Saxon church in England, reputed to date in part from the sixth century. When we arrived, we wandered for a while through the graveyard, then finally entered, stooping through the doorway into the tiny church. It was bare stone, damp and cold. But all I felt as I stood there was a startling sense of loneliness. For some reason that feeling overcame all other sensation. After some minutes of looking up at that lonely grey stone altar I understood. The Eucharist was not present. The little church no longer contained life. The chain of community that should have tied me, a 20th-century New York publisher, to the peasant laborers who once knelt on these hard stones, had been irrevocably broken.

It was in recognition of the lost that I discovered most of what I've found in the mystery of the sacrament. It is only when one knows what is missing that one understands what one has found.

In other times people were attracted to the Church because of the beauty and dignity of its liturgy. In most places those qualities have been dissipated now; some new liturgists have wreaked havoc on the Mass. There is more Latin—and more connection to the ancient Church—in the average Methodist service. But the Catholic view is a long-term view, and there have been worse moments in the history of the Church. There are worse moments right now in the prison camps of Vietnam and Rumania and countless other places. Beauty will return because the human aspires to beauty in expressing his deepest-felt beliefs. I am a post-Vatican II convert, and hold no nostalgia for another time I didn't know. But I see glimpses of the rare power a beautiful liturgy can bring to a deepening reverence in worship, and these glimpses show that restoration of the liturgy is not far away.

My father died over ten years ago, and I remember him in my prayers. My children will know through family stories that it was an act of his that stimulated the act of mine that made them Catholics. They will be inheritors. They will never know what it is to wrestle with the outrageous claims of the Catholic Church. They will accept the Church as their heritage, as what they are, as how they define themselves. They will be Catholics, pure and simple.

And, lucky as they are, that's why I think I'll always have one up on them.

Wick Allison *is editor-in-chief and publisher of* Art & Antiques *Magazine, as well as president of his own small publishing company. He resides in Manhattan with his wife, author Christine Allison, and their two children. He is a native of Dallas, Texas.*

With the Heart Alone

Leonie Caldecott

It was the middle of the Holy Year, late summer 1983. I had set out with my husband on a driving vacation across Europe. Our destination was Rome. Our intention was to soak up the sun, take in the sights and visit friends. In that late summer, however, I found something far more substantial. By the end of the trip I had become a Roman Catholic.

This turn of events came as something of a shock to many people who knew me at the time. Friends who were involved with me in ecology and the women's peace movement, whose spiritual bent might broadly be termed "new age" rather than traditional, never expected me to plunge myself so thoroughly and abruptly into the arms of the Church. If I had told them of travels to India in search of Enlightenment, or apprenticeship to a shaman in the desert of New Mexico, they might have listened with respectful interest. But when I tried to explain (somewhat nervously, being rather taken aback myself) that I had found, not a guru or a goddess, but Jesus Christ, it was another matter altogether. For this wasn't the archetypal Christ of a Jungian "collective unconscious," nor yet the Christ of a sophisticated esotericism which the Church had forgotten or suppressed. No: this was the Christ whose mystical body is "one, holy, Catholic and apostolic"—and very, very Roman.

Looking back now, I realize that I had, in fact, been preparing for this step throughout most of my life, however sudden the final commitment. Or rather, I was *being prepared* without being fully conscious of what was happening to me. On the one hand, I had always been religious, in the semi-dilettantish, church-going manner so prevalent in England. On the other hand, as the child of a failed marriage, I suffered from profound internal conflicts as to which values and beliefs to embrace, and for a long time this prevented me from setting my vague religiosity on a firm personal and doctrinal footing.

My father, who was an Anglican, though strongly marked by the strict Scottish Presbyterian ethos of his own father, would pray the Lord's Prayer with me each night, patiently explaining what each part of the prayer meant. It was from him that I derived a sense of moral order: a sense which, had it not been for the manifest breakdown of this order in the very fabric of our family life, might have saved me from the mistakes I was later to make.

Since his first marriage ceremony had not been conducted in church, he was able, after his divorce from my mother, to marry a Roman Catholic, a Frenchwoman, who came like a breath of springtime into our lives. It was thanks to her that I first tasted the security of Catholic family life. Although in some sense I remained a perpetual outsider, still spending most of my time with my mother and feeling internally the lack of legitimacy that was inherent in my condition (a feeling that has never fully left me), my stepmother did everything in her power to counteract this feeling. She treated me exactly as she was to treat my three half-brothers, combing the tangles from my hair and from my heart, and taking me to Mass with her, where the liturgical magic of pre-Vatican II Catholicism made a profound impression on my youthful imagination.

My mother, with whom I had an intense, half-adoring, half-anguished relationship, was not religious at all. However, she so resented all the "popery" I was being exposed to whenever I visited my father's household, that one day she seized me by the hand and dragged me round to the nearest Anglican church. "Kindly do something about this child," she said to the vicar. "She's being turned into a Roman Catholic."

And so I began going to Protestant-style Bible-Class, and singing in the church choir on Sundays, elements in my education for which I am extremely grateful. I enjoyed the Bible study, in part because it enabled me to show off a precocious propensity for metaphysical interpretation. Occasionally the curate's wife, who also took the class, would seem a little perturbed by my antics. This was a somewhat fundamentalist church.

It was here that I first formed an unfavorable impression of Christian womanhood: drab, quiescent pea-hens eclipsed by the ecclesiastical and social plumage of their male counterparts. Since I was not mature enough to see beyond the obvious, this model set up something of a tension within me. On the one hand, I wanted to be a good Christian. On the other hand, as I entered my adolescent years, I was surrounded by values and images which spoke of a different, more exciting way to be female. Finally, in my late teens, I became more interested in sex than religion.

Tension continued throughout my college years and early twenties. It's hard to describe myself during that period. I explored whatever avenues seemed to promise comfort or self-fulfillment, social relationships, political ideas or spiritual paths. At the same time, I was obsessed by the idea of goodness. I wanted to be moral, I wanted to be wise. I wanted to save the world. My propensity for emotional self-indulgence and my high-minded purpose strangely co-existed together. I was a volatile mixture of confusion and arrogance.

When the fancy took me, I would go to high-Anglican church services. I knew that there was something vital in the sacramental aspect of Christianity. But I felt, increasingly, that my native religion was too narrow, too oppressive vis-à-vis women, ignorant of a whole dimension of human experience which I vaguely categorized as containing the natural, the creative, the esoteric, the ecstatic. Though my objections didn't reduce themselves to this one point, a large part of them evolved from my reluctance to live up to the Christian sexual ethic. Though by no means wildly promiscuous, I still sought refuge in physical love as a means of intimacy, an intoxicating draft to dull, temporarily, the aching void at the center of my being.

In the midst of this period, grace nonetheless was preparing a new dimension in my life. I made the one unreservedly sensible decision of my early years, marrying a man of unusual integrity, who like me was searching for a spiritual path to which he could adhere. The carefully considered, open-minded manner in which Stratford approached everything from Carlos Castaneda to Zen Buddhism, came, over the years, to have a great influence on my own more erratic search. Yet when he himself began, in 1979, to gravitate towards Roman Catholicism (influenced, ironically, by my abstract enthusiasm for Christian sacramental "symbols"!), I found myself unable to follow him. By the time he was baptized (having been brought up an agnostic), in November, 1980, I was so deeply enmeshed in my personal and political turmoil that pride would not let me consider that I might be in need of some serious conversion myself.

I should explain that, for us, the issue of to-be-or-not-to-be never seriously revolved around any church other than the Roman. This was partly due to Stratford's understanding of the importance of unbroken tradition in religious matters, an understanding derived initially from "traditionist" writers such as Fritjof Schuon and René Guenon. The only other option, under these conditions, was the Eastern Orthodox Church; yet though we loved its liturgy and its devotions, it seemed somehow culturally alien to us. As for Anglicanism, it had ceased to be a player in the all-or-nothing realm in which our conversions were to take place, perhaps partly because of the very lack of challenge contained in its theological plurality. It would have been very easy for me, in particular, to fall back into being a practising Anglican (for by this time I hardly ever went to church), to find a niche where my misconceptions would not be too badly disturbed, where I could settle without struggle. But for some reason, and not because of integrity (which in many other matters I sorely lacked), I was never tempted to do this. Perhaps my indifference by now just ran too deep. It was to take more than the convenient institution of Henry VIII to bring me to myself.

As Stratford turned to the Church, I was turning to the peace movement, the burgeoning alliance between feminism and ecology, and the New Age-cum-Jungian notion of spiritual "individuation" as signs of a vital spiritual force trying to incarnate itself in human society. I was also serving my apprenticeship as a writer, trying to write inspiring tracts about these phenomena, as well as a book about women and Christianity.

Although I didn't go along with Mary Daly's uncompromising stance on the hopelessly patriarchal character of the Christian tradition, I was nonetheless affected by feminist grievances against the Church. They chimed with my own doubts about my true nature as a woman, my sense of being an outsider whenever I stepped through the door of a church, relegated to the subservient side-lines along with the women who, I believed, could only approach the altar-steps with a scrubbing-brush in hand.

Strangely enough, it was not the doctrines and beliefs of the Church that I had problems with. The Incarnation, the Passion and the Resurrection made complete sense to me. In the teachings of Christ—with His special compassion for those whom others despised, be they lepers, tax-collectors or fallen women—I tasted food that could

sustain me. Having gleaned something about the importance of polarities and their interplay from my interest in
Taoist, Kabbalistic and Jungian ideas, I didn't have too
many problems with a God conceived of as male, incar-
nated into a male body and represented by male priests.
This, after all, was only one side of a mysterious equa-
tion. The other side, represented by Mary, who opens
herself up so completely to God that she not only con-
ceives Him in her heart and mind, but in her body as
well, was unequivocally female to me. That is to say that
we are all, women and men, feminine in relation to God,
and it is specifically under the aspect of this relationship,
this great love affair between Creator and creation, that
God is revealed to us as masculine.

The two events, the icons that embodied this for me,
were Mary and Jesus offering themselves up, in an act of
unconditional love, during the Annunciation and the Passion. By turning themselves into living Grails, they were
accomplishing (each of them at a different level, given
Jesus' divine nature) the miraculous turnaround whereby
an alienated humanity could be reconciled with its Creator. I had only to meditate on the wound opened in the
side of the crucified Christ by the centurion's spear, with
its sacrificial outpouring of blood and water, to sense the
profoundly feminine mystery this act of divine self-giving
and human self-surrender represents.

My problems with the Church had more to do with its
human, its mundane, its institutional nature than with its
central teachings. Was this, I asked myself, the Church of
the poor and the oppressed, the last who shall be first in
the kingdom of heaven? Or had it indeed been hijacked
somewhere along the way by what Simone Weil called the
Great Beast, the conquering, one-sidedly masculine face
of humanity which invariably consolidated itself with
wealth and worldly power? And, at a more personal level,
were women really respected within the Church, or was

the basic agenda merely to keep us barefoot and pregnant and thoroughly, thoroughly ostracized?

How does one find the truth? In my case it was certainly not an intellectual matter, as it was, in large part, for Stratford. I had to undergo a conversion of the heart, a reorientation of the will, before I could shift my perspective on the Church. And in order for this to happen, my heart had to be broken, my will crushed, by events beyond my control, events I was not capable of rationalizing away whilst they were happening. My radical need of God and His Church had to be overwhelmingly demonstrated to me. I had to go on a journey of no return.

Here is what happened. I was growing disenchanted with the world of political activism in which I had immersed myself. My personal problems, most notably that of coping with an alcoholic mother, were far from being resolved by analysis, meditation or mere good intention. In fact, my life had reached a crisis point. Everything I touched, from friendships to professional commitments, was turning to dust. I had ceased even trying to be a "good person" and was talking more and more in terms of my rights, of protecting myself, of "finding myself" no matter what the cost. And yet I hated myself for this, felt guilty and full of despair. For all my attempts to develop a sophisticated understanding of the human psyche, to unearth the secret of the universe, I was increasingly collaborating with, rather than standing up to, the dark forces of the confused and dangerous times in which I lived.

That summer of 1983, setting out on our journey across Europe, I no longer knew which way to turn. I longed for truth and integrity, but I mistrusted my capacity for self-deception. My feelings echoed those of Dorothy Day at the moment of her own conversion: "I was tired of following the devices and desires of my own heart, of doing what I wanted to do, what my desires told me I wanted to do, which always seemed to lead me astray."

On the second morning of our travels, I accompanied my husband Strat to Mass in a beautiful Gothic church in a French village called l'Epine (the thorn). Hearing the liturgy spoken in French triggered childhood memories of attending Mass with my stepmother. Suddenly, in the midst of that tranquil building, with its delicate stained-glass light, its paving stones worn with the passage of time, its exultant architecture dancing between field and sky, I longed to come home to the garden I knew to be hidden behind the walls of illusion with which I had surrounded myself. I longed to be part of this Church, to partake in her life and sacraments. Yet after Mass, when I tried to pray in front of the statue of the Blessed Virgin, I was aware only of my own inner devastation. In the book reserved for the intentions of the faithful, I scrawled: "Oh, Mother, teach us how to heal the world." The political animal I had adopted so passionately still prevented me from personalizing my request.

By the time we reached Rome, I was in real torment. My feminist aloofness was crumbling fast, as I was forced to confront the powerful feelings that were sweeping over me. Time and time again, as I had stepped into a church in Domrémy, Pisa or Siena, an image had flashed onto my inner eye, Mary, leaning from out of that vastness, handing me a chalice, asking me to accept it, no matter what it might contain. And still I demurred. It was as though I had fallen in love with a person who to all intents and purposes was an appalling character—and Rome, with its Baroque excrescences, its evocations of Borgia corruptions, Inquisitions and other shameful passages of history, pressed these associations all the more forcefully upon me.

Something more was needed. A Tibetan lama we had admired, perhaps the closest conduit to holiness I had known before my conversion, had talked of something called "guru yoga," a process whereby the contemplation of an exemplary human being acts as an almost subliminal beacon for the seeking soul. I was later to find this notion echoed in the writings of Don Giussani, founder of the Catholic renewal movement Communion and Liberation. "Richiamo" is the word he uses, a word which is hard to translate, but which means a recall, almost an admonition or warning, something which brings one to oneself, wakes one up.

The person who fulfilled this function for me was, naturally enough, a woman. Although several people, including Strat, had prepared the ground, it was this woman, a Vietnamese many years older than I, and herself a convert, who was to unlock the part of me that was capable of making a true leap of faith.

She was the friend and mentor of a close friend of mine, an Italian woman I had got to know whilst researching the part of my book which concerned orthodox Catholic women. In fact I had already been introduced to her by my friend, and held her in a certain amount of awe. I think I was even a little afraid of her. Anyhow, soon after our arrival in Rome, we all went to lunch at this woman's house. It was the feast of St. Gregory the Great, and before lunch, a priest celebrated Mass in the exquisite chapel this Vietnamese family had created from a kind of conservatory area, full of plants and muted light. I, of course, was the only one who could not go to communion.

After Mass we ate lunch in the garden. It was a beautiful day. The family was extraordinarily warm and welcoming, and I found myself feeling more at ease in the company of our hostess. And then, to my amazement, she began to talk exactly about the problem that was still keeping me from the Church: the question of authority.

"You know," she said, but without seeming to address me directly (I had mentioned nothing about the direction my thoughts were taking, even to our mutual friend), "the main difference between Catholics and Protestants is that Catholics are prepared to accept a fallible human being as their infallible representative before God. Why do they do this? For one thing, because it is an exercise in humility. And from humility there springs a multitude of graces."

Humility. That was something I hadn't thought about very seriously before. Yet, how I lacked it, with all my hasty judgments about the world, my defensive need to be in "the right." For a few moments I experienced a kind of double vision. There were two fields of perception operating around me, the one I was familiar with consisting largely of a wall designed to prevent me from even knowing the other one existed. The doctrine of original sin, which had always made me feel uneasy before, suddenly became an experienced reality. It had been the numbing, deadening field into which I'd been locked all my life.

A little later, she said something else. It had to do with the dangers that lay in wait for anyone who wanted to change the world for the better. Her own experience, in Vietnam and then in the West, had shown her only too clearly how important it is to be protected by the Church, with her unbroken tradition of prayer and sacrament, the spiritual power accumulated over centuries of experience, no matter how human corruptions had affected and troubled it along the way.

That was it. All my objections crumbled under the tidal wave of clarity that flooded my heart. She had converted me, not just to Roman Catholicism, but to the first *deeply* felt Christian sentiment of my lukewarm life. I wanted to weep. I wanted to shout. I wanted to dance.

Being English, I did none of these things, but waited until we were on our way home to confess to Strat and to our friend Cristina that I wanted to be received into the Church as soon as possible. My benefactor, who was, with Cristina, to become my sponsor, later admitted that she had known, whilst at prayer that morning, that this would be the day of my conversion. Yet she had lacked the courage (this most formidable and courageous of women) to speak to me directly about my relations with the Church, knowing how reserved we English are about our personal lives!

Since I had already received instruction three years earlier, things moved fast. Three days later I made my first confession and was reconciled with the God I had tried so hard to ignore for so long. Two days after that, on the feast of Our Lady's birth—September 8th, 1983—I was received into the Church. It was as though a great weight had fallen from my shoulders. Here, in the small chapel where five days earlier I had been unable to approach the most sacred Body which was now to become my daily bread, I participated for the first time in that ultimate liberation which is communion. I wore red, the colour of the repentant Magdalene, also the traditional wedding colour in Vietnam. I was to wear it again when Stratford and I finally renewed our marriage vows eighteen months later, having at last come to understand our marriage as the vocation it is.

If this were a commercial for the Roman Catholic Church, I would end now by saying that of course I lived happily ever after. But this would be a distortion of the truth. If you want a quiet life, I say to perplexed friends and relatives who question me on the subject, I don't recommend this religion. Its fruits are not the sweet Californian ones of instant enlightenment or self-fulfillment. Never have I been faced with so many harsh truths about myself as I have during the last few years. Those seven devils didn't let me out of their grasp so easily. The year following my conversion was a veritable purgatory, during which I was stripped of many old habits of body, mind and soul which I wouldn't have had the courage to drop any other way. In the short course of my development as a Catholic, I have quickly realized that the old wine could not be mixed with the new, and the wisdom of tradition has held far more interest for me than more recent theological experiments.

St. Paul was struck blind after his vision of the Light on the road to Damascus. I was in some sense struck dumb after my encounter with the Word on the road to Rome. Certainly, I have found it much harder to exercise my vocation as a writer. I hope that this is God's way of giving me a new voice, just as He gave St. Paul new eyes.

The very fact that I am not very good at explaining my new-found faith, fitting it neatly into the picture I formerly had of myself, feminist ideals and all, is a sign of its authenticity for me. And authenticity is what I now seek, with the desperate thirst of one who has lunged after many a mirage. As Antoine de St. Exupery, another wanderer in the desert of the modern world, wrote: "It is with the heart alone that one can see rightly. What is essential is invisible to the eye."

Leonie Caldecott *is the author of numerous essays and articles on topics ranging from women's issues to the arts and religion. She has also written a book entitled* Women of Our Century, *which accompanied the BBC TV series of the same name. After her conversion to the Roman Catholic faith in 1983, she spent some time in Boston, Massachusetts, with her husband Stratford, a writer and book editor. There they both had the opportunity of deepening their experience of the Church through the lay movement Communion and Liberation. They have now returned to London with their growing family.*

Who Are These People Called Catholics?

**Our Search Leads Us
to Christ's Church**

Christopher Canwell

My personal story of conversion begins in my earliest years, continues through my adoption of Catholicism as my religion, then through my wife's experience of finding the Church, and finally in our marriage and raising of a family. I will tell that story in a chronological order, begining with my best recollections of my earliest years.

In the case of my family, it is particularly interesting to know that my father's brother married my mother's sister and that together they bought a former estate in the country near Spokane and established their homes, side by side on a then active farm. This setting was especially lovely, surrounded by pine trees in the hilly portions, giving way to cottonwood trees and willows near the river which ran through its very center. The location was uniquely pastoral in tone, and served as a place for raising great varieties of animals; from cows to horses, and pigs to chickens. Over the years that passed, we were to harvest annual crops of hay, slaughter cows for meat, and preserve many fresh fruit and vegetable crops for food. I have a brother and a sister in my immediate family, as well as six cousins in my uncle and aunt's home nearby. We formed our own small community, all of us related by blood.

It was in this wholesome environment that we grew up in a family setting that was distinctly loving, and very close. Our earliest years were exciting ones with lots of activities that can only be enjoyed on a farm. There were calves, kittens, and baby chicks being born regularly, and the marvel of life, new in the Spring, and nurtured by careful hands through the year enriched our lives and gave us an appreciation for nature's gifts. Our family abounded in love. Our every need was addressed with concern and an eager desire to do the very best for us, the children. We are all very grateful for our parents and the loving attention given us as we grew up.

Although there was no presence of organized religion in the home as a child, there was a growing awareness on the part of my parents, especially my mother, that it would be an improvement if religion could be included. Since my mother had been raised a Catholic and my father had been reared a Seventh Day Adventist, there was more than a slight chasm between them—religiously speaking. Because of a technicality, my parents were unable to be married in the Catholic Church, and they agreed to be married by a justice of the peace in a civil ceremony. From that day well on into our early childhoods, they agreed to leave the matter of religion neatly buried in the depths of those things "we do not discuss." While the environment was loving and assuring, there was no religion taught or demonstrated even during the most important Christian times of the year, until our later childhood. The first signs of religious activity occurred when a Reverend Thomas McQueen was heard on radio giving a sermon from his church, The Plymouth Congregational Church in Spokane. The warmth of the message and the style of delivery were stirring indeed, and so my parents elected to visit the church and take us along. In the manner of churches of that type, we children were syphoned directly into a Sunday school program and the adults were shown into the church proper to hear the Reverend McQueen. We continued to attend Plymouth Congregational Church for less than a year. The occasion for our departure was the fact that Reverend McQueen was asked to leave, and his replacement was a very distant second to his delivery style. In fact, the subsequent experience was markedly inferior, and my parents, like so many others, decided that there was no compelling reason for attending church! At the time, I was about ten years old and my brother and sister were slightly younger. We didn't miss Sunday school...religion had no permanent meaning for us!

I recall an occasion that stirred the feelings of emptiness in my mother.

During one of his more moving sermons, the Reverend McQueen had offered an "altar call," an opportunity for people to come forward to profess Christ as their personal savior and, in effect, to join the Congregational Church community. As much as she wanted to respond to some sort of call from her God, she was aware that she knew very little about what this church truly represented. She felt reluctant to march forward, and my father expressed no inclination at all. But the event itself served to awaken her to inner needs; she realized that a life without her religion, Catholicism, was neither possible nor desirable. She began to attend Mass as a "back pew Catholic." Her first Mass schedule was for evening Mass at the Cathedral of Our Lady of Lourdes in Spokane. But as time went on, she found it better to attend the 10:00 Sunday morning Mass. She always offered to take any or all of us, including my father. The chorus was always the same, "No thanks!"

In the meantime, an interesting thing happened to me. Some enthusiastic parents had banded together, and bolstered by a substantial investor, began what was then known as St. George's Episcopal School, located along the Little Spokane River north of the city and not far from the farm where I lived. In an evening presentation of the values and goals of the new school, my parents listened and agreed that such an experience would be both constructive and essential to our development. I was enrolled in the first year of the school's operation in 1955 and my brother followed the next year. The founding headmaster was the Reverend H. Douglas Smith, Canon of the Episcopal Cathedral of Spokane, St. John's. He was my first direct exposure to any clergyman, and a major influence in my growing sense of men of God having some sort of legitimate role in society.

My father's comments always implied that men of the cloth were calculating refugees from an honest day's work! This blanket condemnation had been reinforced by the charge that only the socially maladjusted could find fulfillment in such a way of life. And Catholic clergy were all thought to have some sort of sexual maladjustment as well. So, in my first encounter with the clergy I was expecting to find more than religiosity. Instead, I found kind, thoughtful, extraordinarily polite behavior. The shock, while considerable, was quite comforting!

At St. George's Episcopal School, religion was a part of the curriculum and was mandatory for all students. While the headmaster presided at chapel, which was also mandatory, he taught several classes as well. His presence to the student body was certainly broad and universal. The men who succeeded Canon Smith as chaplains were all men of extraordinary character. For me, they were all distinguished examples of "men of God," whose lives of service to the school singled them out as admirable. While I grew in understanding of the Bible and basic Christian values through the school, I also grew in my appreciation of the whole idea that people could commit themselves to the religious service of others as a profession, and I admired them greatly for it.

A couple of years passed, and with the advice of a physician, my mother entered Sacred Heart Hospital in Spokane for what was thought to be an ordinary, routine hysterectomy. Following the surgical procedure, she developed complications which included a considerable amount of hemorrhaging. In the beginning, this dreadful danger was not detected. She knew she was growing weaker and the fear of dying began to fill her every waking moment. Stationed at the hospital was a truly perceptive, very gentle and comforting man, a Jesuit priest named Father Dempsey. He visited mother daily, and although she was separated from the Church and could not receive Holy Communion, she was considerably relieved by his presence and his prayers for her. She explained that she had not done anything for her children in terms of teaching them religion. She had not even written a will! She so wanted him to meet her children, to let them know that Catholic priests can be warm, direct, pastoral servants of the people. She felt he possessed these traits and would demonstrate them just by a few words with her children. One afternoon, about 4 o'clock, after school, we appeared on the wing of the hospital floor. And mysteriously, walking the hall was Father Dempsey, who took the opportunity to drop in for a chat. He was a huge man in my recollection, dressed in a black cassock, and wearing a warm smile, and with an intense interest in getting to know us. At this writing I cannot recall exactly what he said. I remember that we wanted to know what to call him. When we heard the name of "Father," we were somewhat overcome with shock, but then relieved when he did, in fact, respond to us. Whatever the small talk of that day, the feeling was most important. He left us with a feeling that he was a marvelous example of humanity, that he was profoundly interested in our mother's happiness and her recovery, and that for some reason, he felt a warmth toward us. This quiet, noble man, with no children of his own, was able to radiate a warmth distinctly his own, and unlike anything that a parent could give. He earned a place in our hearts.

After Mother had recovered from surgery, the days turned into months, and then into years of student life at St. George's Episcopal School. Among the courses offered was one in comparative religions. I recall that it was in the sophomore year of high school. One of the topics covered was the early foundations of religion reaching as far back as the Eastern and South American primitive religions. Then the focus shifted to early Judaism, and finally to Christianity. With the early church being described—for the most part—as Catholic in character, as time passed, the subject turned to a study of the Reformation. The class was being taught by a man who had become the chaplain for the school and was the teacher of the religion classes, Canon John Moulton of the Episcopal Cathedral of Spokane. He is indeed a man of God, a kind and considerate man, whose behavior is unmistakably influenced by the Gospel message. He veiled the importance of the subject matter as we moved into the area of those difficulties with the Catholic Church which prompted the formation of different and new churches around the world. There were some facts, some innuendo, and a great deal of justification for the founding of the Church of England.

Canon Moulton knew that I was the son of a former Catholic and was kind to me. But the discussion in the book left me wondering how sensible Catholics could continue to support a church which supposedly had become corrupt in its many years of operation—as was implied in the class. I was developing questions faster than I was getting answers! I began to wonder: "Who are these people called Catholics? What do they believe? Why is their church quietly pursuing union with Christ through its sacraments, never speaking up very clearly in its own defense? Protestants allege that Catholics think they are the only ones going to Heaven, but what is the truth?" I had to begin looking for answers.

I decided to contact a friend named Peter, who was a student at Gonzaga Prep School in Spokane and a "cradle Catholic." He was approximately my age and was a willing helper in my search for information. He knew the

head of the religion department at the school and arranged a meeting for me with what turned out to be a
master apologist! I couldn't see going into a meeting like
this without first gathering every abusive, negative charge
I ever heard about the Catholic Church. I brought all the
documentation from Ellen Gould White's account of the
Vicar of Christ, the Pope, being the anti-Christ described
in the Bible. John F. Kennedy at that time was warming
up as a candidate for the presidency and eager Protestants
everywhere were commenting that with a Catholic in the
White House, there would be direct control of the future
of American history by the Pope. Communism had
spread to some predominantly Catholic countries and
charges were being made that this was only possible
because of the combined ineptitude of the Church in
leading the people, and because, in some contorted way,
it was the will of the Catholic Church that these countries
become Communist. So, I took it all with me, every last
bit of dirt, and laid it all in front of this Jesuit priest. His
patience, his calm, his knowledge, and his love for his
Church were remarkable indeed! He answered every ob-
jection with clarity, with fact, and without any vindictive
bitterness toward those who had made the charges.
Frankly, I found this response so unexpected that I was
forced to admire it!

Some Protestant writers and speakers had been
wholesale in their condemnation of Catholicism, and here
was a man who had not one negative thing to say about
any other church, its people, or its comments. He just
loved the Catholic Church, knew what it believed and
taught, and wanted to explain it all to me. He was a major
factor in my growing respect for the Church.

While I insisted that I "was not sold yet," I did feel
that I wanted to know more, more about what Catholics
believe. I had taken care of some of the dirty laundry,
examined the negative aspects—both factual and fictional
charges, but I still did not know the positive aspects of

what Catholics profess as their faith. And until I heard their side of the story, I felt I was just going to get everyone else's worst impression of Catholicism! So I asked my mother what to do to get more information. At that time, she wasn't sure which parish we were supposed to belong to. After a couple of phone calls she found herself talking to Father Ralph Schwemin, pastor of the newly-formed Assumption Parish on the north side of Spokane.

Father Schwemin proved to be just what I needed. I had asked to receive instruction, and my brother decided to join in, and eventually my sister joined, followed by three of my cousins. We formed our own class of inquirers, and Father Schwemin presided at our classes, using the text *Father Smith Instructs Jackson*, accompanied by his own in-depth understanding of Catholic theology. Father Schwemin was an active, hardworking pastor, who could be found on most days we reported for class doing some chore around the parish—riding the tractor and mowing the large lawn, or framing a picture for a classroom in the school. He was an accomplished unicyclist and would amuse us with his skills on that unusual means of transportation. His golf game was very good, and he was even a "recreational" welder. Using this skill, he made many decorative items for the parish. In short, he was an OK guy, the best type to teach the inquiring Canwell children what the Catholic Church believes, and is.

Father Schwemin kept assuring us that the Church is never unreasonable. The Church never asks anything of people that they cannot give or do. At that time, we had meatless Fridays, the long fast before Communion, and other aspects that have since become history and forgotten memories. He explained them with skill, kindness, and conviction. Somehow, it all made so much sense to us when we heard it from Father Schwemin! He was a master instructor and we all profited from his deep and abiding love for his Church. He was a remarkable man, unusual for his humility and perseverance in founding and launching this infant parish in a growing section of Spokane. He takes his place in our experience as unforgettable; one who helped to shape our lives!

With the completion of classes at Assumption Parish, we were faced with a decision of whether to become Catholics through the sacrament of Baptism. My father, although always loving and supportive of us children, was concerned that we were buying into something that we did not fully understand. He brought some books home for us to read that were supposed to give us a fuller understanding of the Catholic Church. Unfortunately, most of the material was just more of the negative, half-truths I had read earlier. These were the very charges and allegations that had spurred me on to further inquiry! And so they did little more than to confirm my commitment to be baptized. All of us were baptized on June 8, 1960, at Assumption Parish.

After graduation from high school in 1961, I went to Georgetown University in Washington, D.C., for two years. This was a growth experience indeed, because I was able to study college level theology and philosophy. I began to discover that Catholicism is fortified by a whole system of philosophy and theology that goes far beyond anything I had known before. It addresses issues and concerns that have been on the minds of mankind from the beginning of time. With two more years at Gonzaga University in Spokane, I finished my college education with an ample compliment of philosophy and theology, and was rightly impressed by the depth of its understanding of humanity and the human condition.

In 1963, I met Joleen Peterson, who would become my wife. Joleen was raised an Episcopalian and regularly attended church services, church camp, and was a part of the young Episcopalian community of Spokane. She had a number of experiences in college that led her to ask, "Who are these people called Catholics?"

One of her earlier experiences with the Church was in response to a term paper assignment in college at the University of Washington. The subject of the paper, now lost in fading recollections, dealt in part with original sin. She called the Episcopal Church near the university and was greeted on the phone by a busy and somewhat disinterested pastor of the church who was preparing for a parish dinner that evening. He was neither informative, nor cordial, and failed to understand that one of his own was calling for help, help that was needed in order to meet the deadline of the assignment. In frustration, she hung up the phone without the answer, but with some disillusionment over the experience. She then called the Catholic Church of the Blessed Sacrament in the university district.

Joleen talked with a priest, who readily gave her the information about original sin and the role of baptism in its remission. He was interested in her problem, her life as a student at the university, and most of all, he had time for her! He gave her every reason to believe that for him the most important task of the moment was to answer her inquiry and show concern for her urgent need to get information and prepare the paper. He never saw her before or after, but he had time to explain the answers he gave. This was a powerful, though brief, encounter for Joleen.

And so she always wondered about these folks called Catholics. After meeting me, her inquiring mind was whetted, and a year later she decided to take part in an inquiry class with Father Schwemin at Assumption Parish in Spokane. With all the depth and kindness I explained earlier, Father Schwemin began to bring Catholicism to life for Joleen.

I met with a professor of mine at Gonzaga University to express my concern about what I should do if Joleen, after receiving instructions, should decide against becoming a Catholic. He explained that St. Thomas Aquinas taught that the human conscience is the highest order of choice, and that, once enlightened, if the conscience rejects something, the person must follow the dictates of the conscience. So I was forced to leave the matter to Joleen and the Holy Spirit. On July 3, 1966, Joleen was baptized a Catholic at Assumption Parish.

We continued to date and on December 27, 1966, we were married. Father Ralph Schwemin officiated at the ceremony. He also baptized our first child. Although now retired, Father remains one of our most treasured benefactors, because it was he who brought to life the faith which we now embrace as Catholics. Our conversion began when we decided to adopt a body of truths and it will continue until we are joined with our Creator at the end of time. We see conversion as a dynamic process that carries one through life and into eternity.

We never received any encouragement from our Protestant friends in our pursuit of the truth about Catholicism. Most of them felt somewhat threatened by our choices, as though we had abandoned something near and dear to their hearts, though many of them were only lukewarm in their own faith. The Catholics we have met and grown to love in our community offer ample consolation and warmth to us, and together we journey in our faith, struggling to follow the path our Savior plotted for us. We are sustained by others and hope that we help to sustain those around us.

We harken back to the words of Bishop Nicholas Walsh, spoken at a retreat, to the effect that Catholics must be of good cheer, kind heart, and pleasant demeanor, for it is through their behavior as followers of Christ that others are encouraged and enriched. As one Catholic family in the community of the faithful, we rejoice in the message of redemption and work for the gift of salvation, because our lives are truly a journey in faith! Praise God for all the outstanding Catholics who helped us discover who these people called Catholics really are. We're delighted to be part of you!

Christopher Canwell *was baptized in 1961, while still in high school. He received a degree in business administration from Gonzaga University in Spokane, Washington. A sales representative for a nationwide company, he has served as a member of his parish council, as chairman of the parish school commission, and as a retreat captain. He resides in Tacoma, Washington, with his wife, Joleen, and their two children.*

In Search of the Savior

Ronda Chervin

On January fourth, 1959, at the age of twenty-one, I was baptized a Catholic, at the Church of the Holy Name in New York City.

I often describe myself as a Jewish convert, because I am proud to come from a Jewish ancestry, but really it was a very non-Jewish Jewish background I came from, for my mother's family had been enlightened non-practicing Jews for several generations; and my father's father, a Sephardic Jew, had rejected that heritage without passing any of it down to his son.

My twin sister and I were brought up to think that all religion was a form of superstition. We never celebrated any holidays, and we were taught to be militantly proud to be atheists.

The only believing person in the whole family was my grandmother on my father's side—a devout Protestant who daily wept over the atheism of her son and even more over her grandchildren. She read the Bible every day and wrote into it those passages wherein she especially found comfort, adding the words "for my dear grandchildren, that some day they may know the love of Jesus." I love to think of her as a Protestant St. Monica, and to think of her joy from heaven knowing that both grandchildren love the Lord and spend their days in ministry in the Church. An anecdote of this grandmother's last days will give you an idea of how fervent was her faith. Apparently she instructed her son to arrange that her coffin be placed into the ground in a vertical position. Asked why, she replied that when the trumpet blows on the Day of Judgment she wanted to be sure to be first in line!

And yet, in spite of all the atheism, my childhood years were permeated with Jewish cultural elements. Since my conversion, I have come to see that all the usual psychological traits of Jews which may seem to have no spiritual significance, took on a new coloration in the light of their fulfillment in Christ.

For example, I always think of our home atmosphere as passionate, yearning, romantic. Some of this may have come from the mingling of ancestral German welt-schmerz, Spanish flair and Russian wildness. Yet all this intensity might be even more an expression of our histori-cal Jewishness: a people shut in on themselves by perse-cution, burning with longing for the Messiah!

After all, we are "the chosen people"—chosen as the magnet to lure Jahweh down to the world from heaven. Never are we allowed to become complacent. Our anguish forces us to search, though often on wrong paths, for some way to reach "the promised land." This takes the form for some of endless seeking for truth, for others of trying to remake the world at any cost, for others of bringing down the kingdom by steadfast mournful and ecstatic prayer.

And so, even in an atheistic setting, where we were taught that there was no all-encompassing meaning to life, there was still, paradoxically, a passion for truth expressed in continual reading and discussion. There was also continual tense excitement caused by my father's great love for playing music on the phonograph at top volume. Instead of a background of radio, T.V., or neighborhood gossip, we had the blasting crescendos and tremendous climaxes of Berlioz, Beethoven, and Rachmaninoff.

If there was no conscious seeking for the Jewish Mes-siah there was, nevertheless, a search for some sort of "redemption." We were to be redeemed from the mediocrity of the petty, the vulgar, the stupid, through the intensity of our immersion in what really mattered: *truth and beauty*. However ungratefully, we were really sharing in the attributes of the God we scorned as a nonentity.

As I write this I have the feeling that God wants me to realize that He is present obliquely not only to Jews but to every person and people. The Word is also "made flesh" in the delicacy of a Japanese flower arrangement or in the vivacity of an African drum beat.

To return to the theme of Jewish cultural traits present even in non-religious homes such as ours, I have been thinking recently that the virtual idol-worship by Jewish parents of their children may have its roots in the prophetic tradition of the Old Testament. Every Jewish girl might become the mother of the Messiah. Every Jewish boy might be the Savior of his people.

On the negative side, this adoring attitude toward the child can have deleterious effects on psychological development. Many offspring of Jewish parents can never seem to match up to expectations. In school it must be straight A's; in business one must become a millionaire; in the arts a world-renowned personality; in politics at least a senator. Needless to say, such high hopes may result in a dismal sense of failure even for the high achiever.

On the positive side, however, Jewish children get the benefit of lavish attention. Generally every talent is fostered even at great sacrifice on the part of the parents. Every small and large proof of success is appreciatively affirmed. The belief that many Jews have that their children may reach achievement heights may be in part responsible for the high percentage of Jews in education and related fields always trying to provide ideal conditions for individual growth.

The quasi-idol-worship of the child in Jewish families is so prevalent that it even affects children whose parents struggle to avoid the pitfalls. I cannot recall either of my parents ever making a big fuss about grades in school, insisting on achievements, or projecting specific dreams of glory on myself or my sister. Yet both of us somehow always knew that the only thing that could make our parents proud was if we became famous. Ideals such as being a good person, a loving wife and mother, or a useful citizen, were considered to be the height of dull conformity. To be intense, romantic, heroic, and finally great—that was what it was to really live! Perhaps I exaggerate. I know that in later life both my parents have re-evaluated these goals and are much more inclined to affirm the humble virtues, partly as a result of being the victim in different ways of people lacking those virtues.

Reviewing these strands of the past, I hear my Lord telling me that He can use all of this to make me into an instrument of His love.

It is hard for me to accept the need for the less spectacular virtues, at the same time my background has given me a zealous St. Paul-like drive which God needs as well for His kingdom.

Another characteristic common to most Jewish families is our closeness. I wonder how much this has to do with being cooped up together in ghettos by our enemies, the results of closeness surviving culturally even when there is no such need.

In my case the closeness was increased by the fact of being a twin without other siblings. From earliest childhood, and even in the womb, I was, so to speak, a "we"!

Like all twins we were very close yet very different and often at war with each other. Mostly I remember the coziness. In the night if I was afraid, and I was always more afraid than my "older" sister, I would wake her up and beg to hide in her bed. We would giggle endlessly. Our bedtime follies ended always with both of us chanting in unison "Go to sleep and don't make a bit of noise: one! two! three!..." Almost always one or the other would start up a fresh conversation until finally a question would remain unanswered and we knew this game was up until the next night.

I always greatly admired my "older" sister. A dancer, her gracefulness enchanted me. I was the talker and she was the bird in flight. Also, she was more the introvert and I was totally the extrovert. She seemed strong, for she could take or leave my company whereas I would do her any favor just to win the right to her company.

It is said that twins often spend their whole lives trying to reduplicate the unique unity of that original relationship. After years of loneliness before my conversion, I found in Christ the one in whom grace and truth are one. The one who is sheer beauty but also is willing to dialogue with me in prayer to my heart's content.

The ability as a Christian eagerly to witness holding back nothing that might help someone in his or her journey, no matter how intimate the sharing entailed, I owe to the typically Jewish love of the Word I found in my relationship to my mother.

From the age of one year until fourteen there was never a thought in my head which I didn't tell my mother, not only to express myself but also for analysis. The Jews are the people of the Word. I have heard theologians point out that in no other religion is God understood primarily as the Word. In the Old Testament Jahweh speaks to His people through their leaders and they speak back to Him. In the mystical writings of the Kabala a picture is drawn of the world being created through sacred syllables. If, in prayer and chant, the believer sung the right word he could unlock the secrets of the universe. During the long history of Judaism religion was communicated not so much by reading as by word of mouth—from rabbi to pupil. The great deeds of Jahweh were told in story and song. In the later rabbinic tradition all the males spent the day in a type of study involving constant discussion of holy texts, while the women not only brought up the younger children but also ran the store or worked in the fields.

Among most enlightened families of the nineteenth century, such as my mother's, all these customs were abandoned. They left the ghettos and adopted a non-religious way of life, but there was no abandonment of the ideal of intellectual analysis—the only thing that changed was the subject matter.

Since my mother and father had both been professional editors, and had always been great readers, our home was filled with books. The usual pattern of the evening included rushing to finish all chores so that everyone could go to their favorite couches and chairs to read. All through the evening we would interrupt each other to read out amusing or thought-provoking passages.

So, it was only natural that when I was away from home at camp or college, I would continue the great dialogue by writing voluminous letters. Transfigured now in Christ, this practice makes it very easy for me to share my religious insights with others, for I am unhampered by the stiff conventionality which comes from the usual way composition is taught in school.

From my father came a fierce zeal to exemplify truth in action. When I meet people who acknowledge the truths of the Catholic faith but waste years dilly-dallying about making the commitment, I thank God for the influence of my father.

In his twenties, my father had joined the Communist Party hoping to save the world from injustice. A common adage of the time was "If by thirty you aren't a Communist you have no heart—if by forty you haven't left the party you have no head." By thirty my father had become disgusted with the many contradictions in Communist practice, international and at home. He developed a great hatred for the party and a conviction that with all its faults the American system alone could save the world from the Communist menace. In his new found patriotism, he risked his life and his career in trying to expose Communist infiltration. I was lastingly impressed by his willingness to go to any extent in defense of his ideals.

As I relate these aspects of my non-Jewish Jewish background, I realize that I am partly motivated by the thought that Jewish atheists are much hated by many Catholics. Yes, they have terrible faults, but, transformed in Christ, the virtues are of high value indeed, for they enable Jewish converts to be more fearless, outspoken, and ardent than some born-Catholics with lesser flaws.

How, then, did this atheist little girl come to the Church? Certainly by a miracle, actually many miracles of God's grace.

At college and graduate school I chose to major in philosophy, hoping to find a meaning in life to justify the intensity of the search. Alas, in the atmosphere of skepticism and relativism characteristic of the universities I attended, there was no solid truth to find. The search for genuine love was equally futile. Brought up to think that sin was glamorous I indulged in one love affair after another. Frightened and lost, by the age of twenty, I was on the verge of suicide.

At Thanksgiving holiday in 1957, I came home from Johns Hopkins, from Maryland to New York City.

Totally by chance, my mother flipped on a program called *The Catholic Hour*. When she saw that there was an interview being conducted with two Catholic philosophers she called me over to watch. To my surprise these two professors, Dietrich Von Hildebrand and Alice Jourdain were using words such as truth, love, beauty. Instead of debunking these concepts they were employing them with reverent conviction. On the spur of the moment I wrote a long letter to them in care of the station telling them of my search for meaning and my frustrations with philosophy. This led to a meeting with Alice Jourdain who lived but two blocks from our New York apartment. That encounter was to change my whole life.

On the appointed day I walked over and rang the bell of her apartment. The door was opened by her roommate, Madeleine Froelicher, now Madeleine Stebbins, president of Catholics United for the Faith, later to become a close friend. She likes to boast that she was the very first among their large circle of Catholic friends to make my acquaintance. I was impressed by her warmth and cordiality. She introduced me to Alice Jourdain, later to become Lily Von Hildebrand. She was also much warmer than anyone I had met before among university people. She took both my hands, smiled, and ushered me into her room, extraordinary in the number of exquisite religious paintings and statues it contained.

The most impressive thing about Lily then and now are her large translucent eyes from which she stares out at people directly, never shifting her gaze in the slightest. This established an immediate bond. Her glance reaches right into the heart and soul of another. In three minutes' time I felt that she wanted to share my anguish and would do anything in her power to relieve it. After some ten minutes of dialogue, she suggested that I might want to sit in on a few classes at Fordham University in the Bronx where Von Hildebrand and other excellent professors taught philosophy, and then I might consider transferring there to continue my studies. I grabbed at the idea. I think I would have tried anything she mentioned for I had the sensation that I was talking to a holy person—a long awaited "guru"—my Zossima?

I shall never forget sitting in on those classes for the first time. Accompanied by Stephen Schwarz, a philosophy student who was the son of Professor Balduin Schwarz, one of the same circle of Europeans who had come over during the War in flight from Nazi persecution, I rode up to the Bronx and was introduced to Catholic philosophy. Right way I was amazed at the difference from my previous college experience. The professors at Fordham were interesting, vibrant human beings. They laughed boisterously in the halls. They lectured with fiery intensity as if the truth were a matter of life and death, as indeed it is.

The period that followed my admission to Fordham was a short honeymoon. I would study during the morning, happily lapping up concepts that could liberate. Then I took the long subway ride in the snow up to Fordham Road. I would spend a little time in the medieval stained-glass enclosed Gothic style library building, pass the enigmatic graceful statues of Mary—arms outstretched open to wisdom—such a different symbol from Atlas with the world on his shoulder. Then on to the classes! There was the great Von Hildebrand, a larger than life person. Besides being a man with a terrific vibrant personality, he had the genius to be able to refute the errors of skepticism and relativism within a single lecture.

That summer after my first semester at Fordham found me in a new state of mind. I could see that there was a truth worth seeking; and I knew that moral values were real and objective, not merely conditioned and subjective. I vaguely thought that materialism could not be correct if there were such non-physical things as truth and moral norms which were higher than society. But I could not see at all that these concepts had anything to do with the existence of God. Still it was clear to me that my professors had qualities which I had never seen among humanists. There was a loving quality in them which I had never found elsewhere in such purity and intensity; and they claimed that all this goodness emanated not from themselves but from God.

Then I had the good fortune to go on a Catholic Art Tour of Europe run by Dr. Schwarz. I had never appreciated architecture or painting before, but under the tutelage of Professor Schwarz I came to be overwhelmed by the greatness of Church art. When our tour group entered the Cathedral of Notre Dame in Paris, I burst into tears, overwhelmed by the beauty and spiritual intensity of that wonderful church.

It was not long before I wanted to know what the people believed who had built these magnificent churches. I must express my gratitude to Professor Schwarz who spent almost all his time on the bus rides between sights patiently answering the hundreds of questions I fashioned. He gave me a small New Testament to read. I had never read the Bible. In many public schools there is almost no mention of God or Christ, and Christianity is treated often as a blight on the history of man. I read the story of Christ with fresh eyes and became thrilled by His personality.

More converts from atheism first come to believe in God and then to decide whether or not the Person Jesus was God. For me the process was reversed. In the Person of Christ depicted in the Bible, I sensed for the first time what the divine is. I came to see what Professor Schwarz meant in marveling at the *uninventibility* of Christ. To claim that later Christians just made up the figure of Christ as a ruse to start a new religion, as some skeptics claim, was unthinkable! They would have had to be holy themselves "to invent" such a personality, and if they were holy they would not have lied.

The sense of the divinity of Christ which came through reading the Gospels was heightened by a religious experience. When our tour came to Rome, we went to the Vatican Museum. For only a few seconds we stopped in front of a tapestry by Raphael depicting the miracle in which Christ tells Peter and the other apostles to let down their nets after they failed all night to catch any fish. There is a luminous smile on the face of Christ as He lovingly watches the apostles bending over their overflowing nets. As I looked at the tapestry, I felt the divinity of Christ flowing through His humanity as if He had been standing in person before me. So intensely did this picture strike me that an inner conviction of the divinity of Christ overcame any doubts which lingered after reading the Gospels.

During the same few days that our tour spent in Rome, I had another great experience. Our group was to have an audience with Pope Pius XII. I had thought before the trip that this part of the itinerary I could easily skip, but Professor Schwarz insisted I go. He was so anxious that I should see the face of the Pope that he brought a little footstool for me to stand on so that I would not miss anything. The sight of the Pope's face was one of the most unforgettable moments of my life. I was touched by the total and luminous humility of this man whom I had pictured as a haughty, pompous relic from former times. I saw his overflowing love as he beheld a poor stricken child who had been brought to be blessed. The humble love in his demeanor as he looked at the suffering child made such an impression on me that I felt that truly such a man could not be nourished by any falsehood or hypocrisy, and that the Catholic Church might be holy after all.

Still another moving experience took place in an artistic setting. We were in Florence visiting a museum which housed the unfinished sepia painting of Da Vinci. There is a charming sketch of the Nativity with a very simple, pure Madonna. Looking at the face of Mary which conveyed virtues I had so thoroughly rejected, broke my heart. Returning to the hotel I fell into the arms of Leni Schwarz, who later became my godmother, and weepingly confessed my sins against purity. I was sure that these wonderful people would reject me once they knew, for I had never told them any of the evils of my life. Of course they surrounded me with still greater love, happy to see me emerging toward the light from so deep a darkness. Their acceptance of me as I truly was certainly speeded me along much more swiftly toward the embrace of Christ.

When I came back to the university after our tour I continued to study Catholic philosophy, but my greatest interest was in reading books of apologetics. Writers such as C. S. Lewis, Chesterton and Newman were able to show in an intellectual manner why it was rational to accept what is beyond reason: the mysteries of Christianity. For example, C. S. Lewis in *Mere Christianity* shows that it is impossible to conceive of Jesus as a mere man, or even the best of men, because a man who claims to be divine is either mad or really authentic. The books of Newman, especially his *Apologia* and his *Development of Christian Doctrine,* show why the need for unity of religious truth depends upon one Church guided in matters of doctrine by the Holy Spirit. My own way of explaining this comes out of years of studying philosophy. Christ comes with a message of love. In order to spend our time loving, we cannot be expending all our energies in theological debate. Faith in dogma gives us a source of truths we can be certain of so that we can go ahead and worship and love instead of bickering or setting up rival sects.

During all this time you may wonder if I never asked myself how this wonderful Church could be reconciled with the Church known through history as the persecutor of my own people? How could a Jew even conceive of going over to "the enemy"? There are several factors which prevented this annoyance from becoming overwhelming.

First of all, I always thought of Jesus as a Jew. He was one of us, not a strange God. My visual image of the Lord was based on Rembrandt's heads of Christ. These in turn were drawn from the faces of Jewish folk in Amsterdam. El Greco's Christs also look Jewish to me.

Once I raised the question of the Inquisition with a fellow graduate student. He researched the affair and came up with the standard Catholic approach which is to emphasize the political reasons for the horrors which were masked by religious rhetoric.

Many years later I read a biography of Isabella of Spain describing these factors even more vividly. More effective still was the dramatic account of Italian Jewry in the renaissance period in Gertrude Von Le Fort's incredible novel *The Pope from the Ghetto*. The story, written in successive chapters from the Jewish and Christian standpoint, shows the interwoven threads of prejudice, hysterical rage, courage, tragedy, admiration, and yearning, on both sides.

I was also given a copy of the B'nai Brith White Paper on the activities of Pope Pius XII and other Catholics during the Nazi era. It gives statistics about the thousands of Jews who were saved by Papal help. It was written to refute a popular play at the time which depicted the Pope as a coward in his response to the Nazis. The B'nai Brith paper was an expression of Jewish gratitude for Catholic aid.

Several other books influenced me as well in terms of the seeming impossibility of a Jew becoming a Christian. One was by a Jewish-convert priest, John Oesterreicher. The book was about Jewish philosophers who had become Christians such as Simone Weil, Henri Bergson, Raissa Maritain, etc. It answered many questions in a way appealing to a philosophy student.

Later I was to read Sholem Asch's wonderful series of historical novels: *The Nazarene, The Apostles, Mary* depicting the lives of Jesus, Paul, and Mary from a Jewish standpoint. Although Asch never became a Christian, he was ridiculed by Jews for daring to write accounts which seemed to be confessions of faith.

I would also like to refer to the accessible popular books by Fr. Arthur Klyber, a Jewish convert Redemptorist priest, *He Was a Jew, Once a Jew*, and *Queen of the Jews*. These books may be obtained for free by Jews and for a low price to others. (Write to Catholics United for Life, St. Martin de Porres Dominican Community, Star Route, Box 42, New Hope, KY 40052.) I think these are the very best short accounts in existence today of the reasons why Jews should become Catholics.

A rather different angle of Jewish Christian relations can be found in the book *The Last of the Just* by Andre Schwarz-Bart. It is an account of a Jew in the Nazi times who becomes acquainted with the legend of the Just Men. These are men selected by God to bear the sins of a whole generation. They are good and pure but suffer unspeakably. Toward the close of the book, the hero goes to Mass as part of a plan to escape persecution by passing as a Christian. Suddenly he realizes that Jesus is one of these Just Men.

I am sure, however, that the main reason why I felt at home becoming a Jewish Catholic was a personal experience. Once during the time that I was reading the Gospels I took a short nap. I had a powerful dream. I entered a large room with a long banquet table in it. I was down at one end, but I could see at the head of it the figures of Jesus and Mary. They beckoned to me and asked in Hebrew if I would sit down between them. I awoke with a euphoric sense of belonging. (Presently I am a member of the International Hebrew-Catholic Association. For information contact Mr. David Moss, P.O. Box 798, Highland, NY 12528.)

In spite of all my intellectual and spiritual breakthroughs something was still lacking.

I longed to be a Catholic, but I did not think I had enough faith to take the step. The moment of total conviction was a strange one. I had been praying that I might have the grace to believe in such a way that I could fully commit myself to Christ. I was told that I must leap into the arms of Christ and that this would require a moment of courage. I feared desperately that I would not be able to make this leap and everything would be lost. Then it seemed that Christ Himself took my hand and led me across the gulf between doubt and total faith. After a session with a priest for formal instructions in the Catholic Faith, I was walking down the street and suddenly I believed totally and simply and happily.

Then, I lived in anticipation of Baptism, which took place on January 4 of 1959. My godparents were Professor Schwarz and his wife Leni, whose love and kindness and patience with me then and still today are indescribable. After the ceremony I burst into a flood of tears in gratitude for my salvation.

I have now been a Catholic for 25 years. There have been many difficult times for me during that period, but always the Church has been my consolation. I love the sacraments. Daily liturgy and communion is the mainstay and joy of my life. I teach Catholic philosophy, write books about spirituality and ethics, give lectures, retreats, and try to bring Jesus into the family.

Ronda Chervin *is a professor of philosophy at St. John's Seminary, Camarillo, California. Wife of the playwright Martin Chervin and mother of Carla, Diana and Charles, she is also a writer and speaker and foundress of Marian Women in Ministry. She is one of the five women consultants to the U.S. bishops writing a pastoral on the concerns for women. Dr. Chervin and her husband live in Los Angeles, California.*

A Letter to Charlotte

A Woman of Charismatic-Protestant
Persuasion Discovers the Church

Nancy M. Cross

Dear Charlotte:

Many of the children are off at activities this Saturday and the few who are home are busy about their own projects—a free morning!

You have asked about our journey into the Catholic Church. I've hesitated to answer because our guidance has been fitted so neatly by the Holy Spirit to suit our needs. However, we have such strong feelings of love for her, such a longing to share with people who might understand, that I'm going to try to replay our discoveries for you—just remember these are only personal reflections gained along the way.

As a Protestant attending theological school, Bob was taught that the course of the "true" Church has always been Protestant, that the real tradition of the Church was broken and then Catholicism took over sometime in the early centuries. The true tradition was not restored until the Protestant reformation. This was taught with a complete body of knowledge to go along with it—factual and logical.

When we became involved in the Holy Spirit renewal of Protestantism we came under Pentecostal teaching which holds that the true Church must be patterned after the First Century Church. For that reason their churches claim to adhere only to those things present in the earliest church as they understand it, that is, information they gain only from the Bible. As far as I know they are ignorant of those giants of Christian thought, Ignatius and Irenaeus, who made such a point of Church hierarchy; obedience to Bishops being equated with obedience to Jesus, and this just twenty to fifty years after the close of that all-important century. Their "first century" understanding is uninformed even in light of the letters of Paul and John bemoaning neglect of apostolic authority. Nevertheless they call themselves by names they garner from this identification, Pentecostal, Apostolic, First Century, etc.

Supposedly based wholly on Scripture, their interpretation of Church is strongly believed and on the basis of this belief other church groups are judged. The group most often critically condemned is the Roman Catholic. In fact, these churches seem to form their own religious organization more in contrast to the Roman Church, and opposed to her, than in any positive scriptural direction. I base this on acts such as their willingness to ordain women pastors, regardless of strict scriptural prohibitions, and their own systems of governance which must not smack of clericalism (though the roots of clericalism— Bishop, deacon, and elder are Pauline), but more often end up more authoritarian than as they describe Catholic priests or Bishops. In other words, anything Catholic is repellent and guarded against. The Holy Spirit Himself could hardly lead such a group toward a truth if the Catholic Church happened to espouse that truth. It's been interesting that there has been a growing contradiction to that observation in the abortion alignments. Abortion is such a horror it has brought about a unique cooperation.

Bob and I at different points in our spiritual search have been completely committed to these schools of thought—both the Protestant, and then for a time, the Pentecostal-Protestant.

What is the truth about the tradition of the Church? Was the Roman Church guided into being by the Holy Spirit who was grieved and eventually left that Church to its own devices? Has the Roman Catholic Church been guided by the Holy Spirit, or is it mostly a human fabrication? Was it a deviation from the truth of Christ that took place at some critical time in history? How has the Roman Church had the audacity to proclaim itself the One True Church? How can it claim such a thing in the light of its sinful hierarchy and priests and inquisitors? Hadn't Christendom suffered enough under this evil to justify a Luther even centuries before he had the courage to stand against it?

These were some of the questions that pressed upon us when we began to feel drawn, despite ourselves, toward the Roman Church. That peculiar drawing began in 1966. It began with an inner sensation—a longing. It was not through the contact with people at first. After the renewal in the Holy Spirit that Bob and I experienced together one December night in the Episcopal Cathedral of St. Paul in Detroit all spiritual things became new. Over the next few years to a small secret list tucked in my Bible were added aspects of faith that were previously distrusted suspiciously but which now felt like personal needs: the need of sacramental confession and absolution, the need for communion, the Body and Blood of Christ often (as Presbyterians we had communion four times a year and then only symbolically), even the need for purgation before a heavenly life.

Gracious! Where did these things come from? My Baptist minister grandfather, George, must have been stirring anxiously in his grave. This was really very curious because before this renewal in the Holy Spirit these things had made no sense to me at all. I was offended by them and opposed them just as my Protestant heritage told me to. "No need to make anything 'magical' out of communion—don't we have the Lord always with us?" "When we are 'in Christ' what could this purgatory thing possibly be but a medieval concoction?"

These stirrings, then, were disturbing, but also intriguing. The little tantalizing tastes of insight made me exceedingly hungry for a bigger bite.

From that time on I began meeting Catholics. There was Sr. Teresa Smyth who was managing a home for the aged in Flint called Marion Hall; then, a priest, Fr. Charles Conroy, S.J., whom we met through Sr. Smyth. I was enchanted. I sensed in them something so beautiful it intensified the hunger—something I had never sensed in the Protestants I knew. That was very strange, for I knew many good and devout ones. I have wondered about this a lot through the years, and I think that quality has to do with humility. Catholic faith requires submission and the result is a beauty that has its roots in "It is not I who live (in Him), but Christ who lives in me."

Just previous to this, I had been in a Catholic bookstore and randomly picked up a book on a rack—*This Tremendous Lover* by Fr. Eugene Boylan. I couldn't get enough of that book. I read it and groaned over it. I still have its tattered remains on the shelf with "Ohhh," "Ahhh" marked all over the margins. Nothing other than the experience of the Holy Spirit itself affected me so deeply as that book.

It seemed at this point everything got suddenly clearer. The Roman Catholic Church! Could it possibly be what it claimed? *The* Church?

Even then I heard a great "Yes" inside. I still had not talked about Catholicism to any Catholics at all—not to Sr. Smyth or Fr. Conroy. There was one exception. A few years before I had tried to convert a former Catholic neighbor who, though she was very poor in understanding her Church, never was diverted by my not-so-subtle questions.

I should add here that when I was young, maybe about twelve, I had summered in a cottage where there had been a copy of *In The Imitation of Christ*. My understanding of what was said in that book was very limited, but I had the same taste for it that I describe here. It was a mystical thing for me then, a kind of calling from far away that made me feel homesick. I would take the little book up into the sand dunes and cry. Especially haunting was À Kempis' descriptions of the Eucharist. Now, when I think back on that experience I experience wonder because in the Church I do feel I've found the solution to that poignant homesickness. This is odd considering a background which had been evangelical Protestant—a line of devoted preachers, teachers and missionaries for generations.

For years this isolated experience was not connected to anything else tangible, not until the Baptism in the Holy Spirit. After this I began to visit the chapel on the top floor of a large Catholic Hospital near where we were living—not too frequently, just when I had the occasion to or when I felt more than usually troubled about things. This chapel, as lovely as it was, was just a room from a Protestant point of view. But it was different from any other "room" I had ever been in. Someone was there. I knew nothing at the time about the belief of the Church in the Presence of Jesus Christ in the tabernacle—the Presence of the Host. But in this room my attachment to the Church grew.

I had not to this point grappled with my intellectual hang-ups about Catholicism. These didn't seem important. I knew someday I would have to come to grips with them and think them through, but the reality of what (Who) was in the Church was more important to me already than the reasons why it shouldn't be so.

Now, Charlotte, you and I have talked over this matter of the scriptural woman's role *ad infinitum* (I almost want to say *ad nauseum* and you'd understand that, too). You know that it has been a saving factor in my marriage, so you won't be surprised that the message of wive's submission to their husbands, rightly understood, played an integral role in this whole process. It was my experience of a flood of grace after finally submitting to God's ordering of my home that brought much of the truth of the Roman Church to light in my mind. This miracle made my heart ready, even achingly ready, to submit to God's will in the whole of my life.

To experience Christian submission (which you and I know is nothing like what people think—not groveling servitude at all, but freedom) required that I lay down the intellectual theories I had built about the marriage relationship—all the reasoning about what should or shouldn't be, all the rationales about how children should be raised, what the ingredients were of successful parenting, all the psychology, all the ideas about what equality meant in marriage. I put these down with great difficulty. I was a wholly independent woman and one with very little trust in anything but my own active mind and work. To think that God would work it out through His authority in my life—dear Robert, was an overpowering idea, but it was scripturally and spiritually sound and assuring.

When the "letting go" occurred, thanks to God's help, I found a deep river of peace flowing right underneath the hard intellectual rocks of my reason that I had thought was "it." So many rights and wrongs were turned around. Ways opened up in family affairs that seemed contrary to what I had always thought. Bob's ways of doing things, or often of not doing things, worked kinks out of children problems, house problems, time problems, that made me realize I had often been deceived in expectations and demands. It had all seemed so right, so rational and so thoroughly uncontestable.... What was this thing called "submission"? What was "truth"? My "truths" now appeared like mist before the sun—absolutely nothing—vapor.

If all the careful thinking out I had been through in terms of marriage, relationship, child rearing, was a vapor, what about the whole rationale about the lack of submission of the Protestant tradition to authority? My grandfather was proud of the same kind of thinking in regard to his being a Baptist. His father had been proud of the same kind of thinking in regard to his being a Methodist. And his father in regard to being an Anglican. Conclusions had been reached all along the line by individual preference and individual interpretation of Scripture wedded to an absolute denial that anyone or anything should claim authority in truth.

Again there loomed the seemingly impossible view of the Catholic Church about herself—the true authority of God on earth, the real successor of that authority of Jesus given to Peter deliberately. It was, I felt, a presumptuous claim—presumptuous in the same order as Jesus calling Himself the Son of God. If despite all my apparently careful reasoning about these other things which I had thought were supported by social, psychological and historical truth in some way, I had been espousing mere empty opinion, or worse, things opposed to the will of God, what then about the mental processes that established the Protestant tradition? It became suspect to me. I began to be disenchanted with the constant apologetics of the rightness of the Protestant and Pentecostal position. I began to think that if we proud *Protest*-ants would give up and submit to an authority appointed, after all, by God, we might see the shadowy argument evaporate before the light, in the same way truth had finally burned through the spurious defense of autonomy in my marriage relationship.

Learning my role as a woman in at least partial willingness to become obedient was basic to the total process of moving from Protestant to Catholic for both Bob and me. He was very impressed with the change my conversion of heart had brought to our marriage. It was no longer two teams meeting on the fifty yard line. "Fight! Fight! Fight!" It was astonishing to him to find himself "the quarterback" with a person out there ready at least to listen to the plays and to fumblingly try to help him execute them. Two people on the same team. Wow!

Woman herself began to make sense in the great fabric God had woven that is humankind. And with woman, Mary began to grow in my consciousness—her meaning and incalculable worth in the whole scheme of things. If she were then the key to human and divine life in a way only the Catholic Church recognized, another full facet of Catholic faith and life was slipping into place uncontested.

Bob's position on my Catholicism through these years was one of tolerant amusement. He was not drawn in the same way to think about these things. That plainly was God's safeguard for me. I really believed at this point that God's will for us could only be finally discerned through His leading of Robert. I was free to give input, but God would sort out and lead Bob to decisions. I was, therefore, not persuaded when a nun told me I should unilaterally convert. I couldn't conceive of breaking my marital unity to achieve my heart's desire in the Church. No, Bob would have to make such a decision for his family. He never would, I was sadly sure. He was very content as a Protestant minister.

Yet, he gave me freedom to grow spiritually in whatever way I was led—not of course to the point of converting to another religion. He treated it lightly, as a whim, and during the process I was never able to accurately tell him what it was I felt or was drawn to. I didn't really know myself. He would say to friends, "If I die, Nancy will run across the street and join St. Mike's." This drew a big laugh from friends. But he was unconcerned about it, though in time he began to become more and more involved himself, without design. Never consciously was he at all interested in Catholicism. He maintained this attitude up to the day Our Lord spoke to him about the course He wanted him to take. He did not read, or study about Catholicism, and did not consider it as a possible path for himself.

Through Fr. Conroy, Bob was invited to help on the first inter-faith retreat held in the Convent of Mary Reparatrix in Detroit. The youth (despite age) and vital Christian love of these cloistered sisters impressed him deeply. He also loved Fr. Conroy and still cherishes that love. Later he went to a silent retreat for men at Manresa Jesuit Retreat House in Detroit under the leadership of this same good priest. Despite these acts, his consciousness about Catholicism did not appear changed on the surface. He was a happy Presbyterian minister who was thoroughly content to follow his day to day guidance (you'll remember, Char, it had not always been so—the Baptism in the Holy Spirit had changed Bob profoundly, giving him a love for his ministry where there had been little before). By this time in our pilgrimage Bob's ministry was in a hospital rehabilitation program working with alcoholics.

At the opening of a new alcoholism unit in the Minneapolis General Hospital in 1969, Robert accepted a position as Chief Therapist and we moved from Flint to Minneapolis. We immediately began a church search. In Flint we had learned from Scripture to stay put in our Presbyterian, non-charismatic church fellowship. We had seen many blessings, large and small, poured out in the church body who did not even know the charismatic fellowship that existed in their midst. The critical spirit occasionally tempted us to leave that church to join our Pentecostal friends in some separate non-affiliated existence, but we resisted. To think that the Holy Spirit, in bringing us into a new spiritual experience as yeast, would now lead us out of the dough to ferment uselessly with other so-called yeast in some isolated spot seemed incongruous to what the Spirit's work really is—the work of unity.

The demands of love were now more exacting than ever. If it was true, that the Spirit had more control of us than previously, then the burden of proof was on us to love our Christian brothers and sisters in humility and to serve them. If we succumbed to the Temptor in arrogance, spiritual pride, or attention-getting, we would be failing in the love expected and described in 1 Corinthians 13.

So in Minneapolis, we looked for a church fellowship, not necessarily a charismatic congregation. We attended a Presbyterian church for several months. We looked other places. Finally one night we ended up at the last meeting of Emily Gardner Neale's mission in an Episcopal church not far from our home. We liked the humble open attitude of the two priests in that church. Much to my great happiness at the time, Bob decided that we would make it our church home. For a year and a half we were diligent in attendance, in learning new liturgical forms—genuflecting, kneeling, and making the sign of the cross, and in taking communion. (We were granted this privilege though we were not Episcopalians.) We tried to become a part of that church.

I think of it now with some wonder that we did not become imbedded. When we finally moved on it was as though we had never attended that church. Though thirteen of us had taken up a pew every Sunday morning, we knew hardly one soul and never felt as though there was any attachment there at all—very strange. If we had been phantoms in their midst, they couldn't have missed us less when we left. It was indeed, not a home, but a bridge.

In the peculiar restlessness that gripped us, we tried to reason. Perhaps it was the church music we missed, or we needed more Christ-centered sermons. We didn't know. But eventually we went with friends to a Lutheran church. There we had those things we thought we were looking for—well done Biblical sermons, beautiful music and congregational singing, the possibility of frequent communion which had become important in our Episcopal days. Bob obtained permission for our admission to the communion table, but we continued on our journey before we ever took communion in that church. We were miserable. What was it? We had no fault to find.

The feeling of unrest wouldn't leave us. To overcome our inconstancy Bob recommitted himself to obedience to the Presbyterian organization by faithful attendance at Presbytery meetings. Looking for God's will in this dark uncertain night, he decided we would attend the Ignatian Retreat in October of 1971 offered by the Cenacle Retreat House.

The first night of the retreat, while reading the 55th chapter of Isaiah, the words of the prophet came alive in new light: "Come buy wine and milk without money and without price. Why do you spend your money for that which is not bread?" Bob heard in these words the message of Our Lord that he was to take his family and join the Roman Catholic Church. It was a silent retreat, but Bob indicated our need to talk. We went out for a walk on the grounds of the Cenacle and he told me about his decision. Afterward confiding in the retreat leader, Fr. Leo Huber, he went forward with never a regret or backward glance.

On the Monday following he sought out his superior in the Presbyterian church and asked that his name be stricken from the rolls. Gone with that stroke was the standing of a long theological education, his professional associations, uncounted friends, and every clerical position he was entitled to. There was never any upset. He spent not one sleepless night.

All our children, many of whom were in their late teens, seemed immediately prepared. They all joined the Church even though their wills in the matter were crucial. Every detail was tailored to our needs including the man of God, Fr. Rinaldo Custodio, the parish priest, who came to prepare us and who is still a spiritual guide. After all these years I still marvel that God made his care for us so evident. When the Exodus deliverance of God's People is read during Lent each year it seems like our personal story.

That was the way it happened—but light was added to our understanding along the way. The summer before I had tried reading, looking for some answers to those questions I stated near the beginning of this letter. Thomas Merton, also a convert, had become a favorite, and I read *Seven Storey Mountain*. I sought more insight by reading *Here I Stand*, a biography of Martin Luther, and some history of the Church. I kept asking the Holy Spirit to help me discern.

I gained these ideas—make of them what you will, Charlotte. Luther did follow the will of God concerning what he saw as a grave error in the Church, but his own disobedience in spirit led to the break in the Body of Christ. He hated the Pope. In despising his sin, Luther could not distinguish that the Pope was still God's appointed authority and so Luther justified his own rebelling against him. Instead of saying, as many of the martyrs and saints of the Church have, "I cannot recant, God is my Judge, but you are His authority in my life. Do to me what you must," he ran away. He saved his own life, but broke the Body through. That disobedient spirit bred more and more disobedience until the whole Church had been rent a thousand times over. It seems clear to me that had Luther died for his stand, the Church would have again been purified by the grace that God might have poured into the situation through his self-giving obedience. Disobedience and rebelliousness brought evil into the Church and broke the unity of the Body. No one would submit.

Luther saw the same phenomenon break out in his lifetime as those under his leadership disagreed with him and split from his communion. If a man had a private revelation that was contrary to the group to which he was attached, he felt free to break away from that group again, and then again, for the sake of preserving a tiny personal insight that, it turned out, could be deception. I had seen this spirit crop up in our Holy Spirit prayer groups. It has lead me to believe that as long as we put personal revelation ahead of submission and love, Satan will have an important opening to our future course. Submission to God's authority is the purifier of revelation. God alone maintains the Truth—a person cannot do it. He can only ruin everything by putting forward the small sliver of truth which he has the insight to glimpse as though it were the whole picture.

This process of division of the Body of Christ is, for me, killing Jesus again and again. It breaks my heart, and I now believe that the intense desire that the Holy Spirit gradually put into our lives for unity and love for the whole Body is another great motivating force to our becoming Catholics.

No small error, or small truth, should get into the way of Love—let God take care of the big picture while we submit to one another and to the human authority God has established over us. That's love. God will then have the Truth and be the Truth and we needn't struggle over it. He will also use that authority to whom we submit to protect and cherish and promote the Truth. And it will be the Real Truth, not just that little piece that you and I might fall upon and then be absorbed by. Isn't the breadth of the riches of the Church in its depository of truth amazing?

In my reading, I was impressed again and again that despite the sins and errors of Church people, God has never taken His Holy Spirit from her. In all her ways she has been guarded and guided. If you read something to the contrary on a certain subject you can be sure that you have a lopsided account that doesn't encompass the whole story. What I learned about the inquisition and the Gallileo affair! The centuries have been for her benefit, that she should become the bride without soil or wrinkle that God is preparing for Himself. If He had wanted the First Century Church as His bride, history would have ended then, the consummation accomplished. The process of growth, painful indeed, is all part of her growing perfection. That humans have muddied her and disgraced her is not to be wondered at—the wonder is that she is what she is despite all these obstacles.

Jesus is at the center of everything in the Church. His Body and Blood are for Catholics the Reality around which all worship revolves, around which, from that altar, all life revolves. With each dissenting group, with each break in the Body of Christ, the shame grows, and He is placed a little more to one side—communion becomes less frequent til on the fringes it is non-existent: ask a Jehovah's Witness. Scripture cannot fill His place, as good as Scripture is. Good sermons are not in the class of spiritual food that His own Body and Blood is in.

That the great foundation stones of faith are intact, that the Roman Catholic doctrines, though dry bones to some, are still the very bones of the Body, essential and necessary, and that all this abides despite evil men and Satan's constant attack is truly a great miracle. That through all these centuries, despite the errors, and the misled, there have been uncounted legions of faithful: priests, sisters, lay people, finding the fulfillment of all the promises that the Church has made—this is the miracle.

If anyone doubts that the Church is what she says she is, the True Church, think a moment about Satan's attacks. What other denominational group must suffer profanation of worship because of demonic parodies? The Mass is so completely of Jesus that Satan must drag it down by obscenity with Black Mass imitations. Wherever paganism of other lands has made fertile soil for it, and where Catholic missions have worked to displace diabolical influence, he confuses the world by labeling the sor-

cery and witchcraft, the superstition, as products of
Catholic countries. Where the same influences of superstition and idolatry abound, but Protestant missions are
established, there is seldom such correlation. Catholicism
is discredited everywhere with special vengeance. Rarely,
if ever, does Protestantism withstand such slanderous
attacks. "It's where the Body is that the vultures are
gathered together."

You asked about those in other Christian commu-
nions. Of course, I believe as the Church does, that there
are many non-Catholics who know Christ and are growing in salvation. But I also believe that this is all the more
available, in the right order, and with complete protection, and abundant grace within the true Church. I feel
that this process for those outside the Church is possible,
but much more difficult and not as joyous. I also feel that
ecumenism can only mean, not that we shed differences
and somehow grow together, but that all submit to one
leader. Love will never come into a marriage through
making fragmented agreements about this and that. Love
comes into a marriage as the woman submits to God's
order and lets love reign (there is a sense in which the
husband also submits, but he never gives up his familial
leadership).

Bob and I did not understand and assent intellectually
to every facet of Church doctrine when we submitted to
her dominion over us. We were trusting God to lead us in
these ways. They are His business—if the day ever comes
that something we see as an error is forced upon us by
those in authority in the Church, then, for the great love
of the Church we shall hopefully say with the help of
God, "We love you, we think you are in an error we
cannot accept, but do to us whatever you must, we are
still a part of you." And then we would trust the outcome
to God. We have learned this from people like St. Thomas
More and his response to his liege Lord, Henry VIII,
whom he accepted as God's own authority, and St. Mar-

garet Mary Alacoque who behaved similarly with a difficult superior in regard to her special revelations.

In the course of our early prayer group experience we
saw the errors of each person's inspiration and leading.
There was truth in much of it. There was error in more of
it. Those members of the early groups who followed their
own lights were led into peculiar, fanatical twists. The Evil
One became well known to them, disguised as the Angel
of Light. All prayer groups seem to be tested eventually in
this way—will they or will they not accept institutional
authority for discernment and learn to submit their inspi-
rations. This is what I see as one of the foundation stones
of Catholicism, learned the same way we learned it in the
prayer groups.

Remember the Corinth church to which Paul addressed the first Corinthian letter. It was a charismatic
fellowship for all the world like our prayer groups. Paul
was correcting them about possible youthful excesses
wrongly attributed to the action of the Holy Spirit. It was
this church and others like it that was the First Century
Church, the baby Church. The growth to maturity has
spanned the centuries and is not over yet. Why should we
be tempted to go back to recapture an infantile stage
when it necessarily means reliving all the growth pains,
all the errors that were so grievous to the growing Body
and so time consuming? If the protection offered by the
Magisterium and Pope is accepted, no prayer fellowship
ever need relive Montanism or Gnosticism, devastating
errors of the First and Second Centuries. Yet, many
groups are doing that right now. We have the most perfect administrative authority which gives us complete protection when we allow it for the discernment and rout of
Satan. It is truly the great ark that keeps us above the
floods, holding us until God's time is up.

I have never known such joy and peace as I know
being in her care. I do hope others who might see her as
she is will be guided to pray more and more earnestly that

the spirit of submission, which is the Holy Spirit, will more and more open hearts and minds to where the unity of the Body of Christ lies. We should fast for the unity of that Body. A friend had a dream the other night that seemed to speak of this need—the other Christians outside the ark, away from the shadow of the hull of Peter's bark, will be terrified and shaken in the evil and dark days which are coming. We need to pray that they get into the ark in time. Perhaps the Supreme Court ruling on abortion is an early forerunner of this time of approaching darkness. Perhaps the growing attack of the secular order on woman, on feminine virtues and strengths, on authority and order, on Biblical morality, are preludes to a gathering storm. The ark is equipped to make safe passage. Sadly, there are those within her who unwittingly work, as do her enemies, to make her less seaworthy.

An influence that moved Bob toward his decision must be mentioned again—it is so important. We had both been in churches since babes—Baptist, Congregational, Presbyterian, Episcopalian, with contact in many others. We had known many Christians in these denominations, but we could not say that even in the most devout of them were the fruits of the Spirit so evident as in the devout Catholics we met. The lives of the sisters of the Cenacle and the priests to whom we were exposed were great witnesses to us. We remembered Jesus' words, "You will know them by their fruits." We remembered that He hadn't said, "by their Biblical belief" but "by their fruits."

Late in John's Gospel he quotes the Lord that there was much that He wanted to tell the disciples but which they could not bear. And that He would lead them by the Holy Spirit into all truth. This gave us much to think about. As Protestants we had believed the Catholic Church was on shaky ground to place "Tradition" in the same revealed category as Scripture. After all, you can't find...this and that...in Sacred Scripture," we would say.

Yet, here Jesus seems to be clearly stating that a period of growth beyond the lives of the Apostles would be necessary before much was understood. He says that the writers of the Gospels themselves have not been initiated into all that He will teach in time to come.

I believe now that Tradition in the Church—(actually I understand that the Bible itself came out of that Tradition) the creeds, the Eucharistic liturgy, the priesthood, the papal primacy, the place of the Blessed Mother, the intercession of the saints, purgatory have come to be through the leading of the Holy Spirit. Everything here has undergone thorough testing and trying, and all has been submitted to discerning authority.

This work doesn't have to be done over by every new generation of Christians. As one of our sons explained to another son who was questioning all this, we don't have to have each generation of math students rediscover on their own the laws of Pythagorus in order to proceed in mathematics—they glady accept the fundamentals going back centuries in order to build further on the foundation and structure already in place. It would be preposterous to do otherwise.

One more thing comes to mind, Char. A day lately when I was rereading the end of the Gospel of John, I seemed to see Peter, so lovable, common, and human, attesting his love to Jesus three times over and each time Jesus begging him, "feed my sheep," "feed my lambs." Then I saw Peter, valiant in the Spirit, feeding the lambs, tending the sheep from Peter's chair over the centuries. And such food! The Body and Blood of Our Lord! With my years of goatishness still fresh in mind, years when independent of the Church I ate many things not good for me, I cried out in thanksgiving, "Peter, make me one of your lambs! Feed me, Peter, til our Lord comes again!"

So, Charlotte, there it is, and God bless you in the very same way.

Much love,
Nancy M. Cross

Nancy Cross *is the wife of Robert Cross—now a permanent deacon and formerly a Presbyterian and Baptist minister. Mrs. Cross has developed and taught a Catholic overview of the Scriptures. She has authored many articles, chiefly on the scriptural view of woman and her meaning, and a booklet:* Christian Feminism. *Deacon and Mrs. Cross live in Taylors Falls, Minnesota. They have eleven children and numerous grandchildren.*

"Books and the Beautiful"

Franklin B. Freeman

I wondered exactly what they were doing up there, way in front under the arched ceiling. They all knelt and a man in robes put something white into their mouths. I heard a language I did not understand. Statues stared at me from left and right. Fear, and my Aunt Lena, pinned me to my pew.

I was three or four years old when I had my first taste of Catholicism. And although it frightened me, it also left in its wake a sense of awe. I feared the Catholic Church for a long while, but now I realize this fear meant I faced something formidable, something I would always remember. My Aunt Lena died not long ago, in full communion with the Church, and I wonder sometimes if, when she knelt before the Blessed Mother's statue and said her Rosary, she was praying for me.

My mother, though, was Methodist and for a few years we went to the Methodist Church every Sunday. The towering, arched ceiling with its clusters of carved images, the stained glass and the burnished gold organ pipes fascinated me. Instead of listening to the sermon, I gazed at the beauty all around us. Then, back home, before I went to sleep, my mother would make me say my prayers.

The only other exposure I had to Christianity as a child was in Vacation Bible School. One summer I had a teacher and fellow students who were not greatly impressed when I failed to name the leader of the children of Israel out of Egypt. Another summer, however, I had one teacher, Mrs. MacDonald, who befriended me and gave me a book called *Little Pilgrim's Progress*, an abridgement of Bunyan's *Pilgrim's Progress* for children. This book helped me to see life as a journey to a Heavenly City.

Soon after this summer, my family moved from Texas to Connecticut, then, a year later, to California. During these next three years, I never went to church, but two books stirred my inner life. The first was *A Wrinkle in Time* by Madeline L'Engle. She introduced me to the world of fantasy where angels and the conflict between good and evil were terribly real and the power of love won. The second book was entitled *The Cross and the Switchblade* by David Wilkerson. It was about a minister who went to New York City to tell gang members about Christ. Wilkerson deeply impressed me with his description of a living God who really changed lives. Books were not the only important things to me, though. When I lived in Connecticut, I took long rambles through the woods, fished in ponds, and, in the autumn dusk, wondered why I felt such longing for somewhere I could neither name nor imagine.

Back in Texas at age 14, after a traumatic divorce of my mother and step-father, I felt the need for an anchor, something to which I could moor my heart. The Bill Lewis family brought me to a local Baptist Church and in a few weeks I took what my grandfather once called "the long walk" down the aisle and was baptized. I became very devout and began reading the works of C. S. Lewis. Lewis, especially in *Mere Christianity*, provided an intellectual foundation for my emotional conversion. Looking back, I also realize he introduced me to sacramental Christianity.

Besides reading about the faith, what could a new Christian do? Well, I went to church, Bible studies and prayer meetings. At the latter, when prayer was over, the subject of Catholicism sometimes came up, and the consensus was that it was terribly hard to be "saved" if you were a Catholic. Some even said that perhaps the Anti-Christ might be a future pope. I swallowed this line of thought, for the most part, but I wondered why the reaction was so virulent. I didn't actually know any Catholics, except my aunt, whom we did not visit much anymore. Could they be that bad? My interest had been piqued. High school life and summer jobs, however, submerged it, and I did not think deeply about Catholicism until my college years.

Meanwhile, in high school, I joined Young Life, a Christian student group. At one of its weekend beach retreats, I heard a speaker, Herb Agar, whose message was a challenge. He talked about following Christ all the way. Some swimmers, he said, first stick a toe in, then a whole foot, then get in up to the waist, then finally glide into the water. Others just plunge right in. He challenged us to plunge right into Christianity. He encouraged us to tell Christ we wanted to know Him, no matter what the cost. I told Christ exactly that as sincerely as I knew how. I will always be grateful to Mr. Agar for encouraging me to do so.

With that background, I went to college at Texas A & M University. There I joined Inter-Varsity Christian Fellowship. Here I met other serious Christian students and my faith deepened. Although I continued to attend a Baptist Church, my spiritual life centered around "IV" as we called it.

At some point, I grew dissatisfied with my church and began visiting other churches. I was most strongly drawn to a small red brick Episcopal Church, St. Thomas. The appeal was mostly aesthetic, for the teaching of the faith was watered down, at least by the clergy. Among the parishioners, however, I found many strong Christians who desired a richer life with Christ and who believed in what the Church has always taught. I also found the beauty of Anglican liturgy. I liked how it involved my body in worship through genuflection and kneeling. And here one walked up the aisle every Sunday!

But then I started thinking about the liturgy. I soon realized that the liturgy was centered not around a preacher or minister. Rather, God was its center. We Baptists depended on having a great preacher, someone who could really pack them in. I decided that this was misguided. I also noticed that Anglicans observed a greater reverence in church than I was used to. The church was not just a place for a social gathering; something else took place here more important than friendly chatter, singing and preaching. Something happened in this small chapel: the divine life was shared. And again, the beauty of my surroundings was important. The stained glass, the wooden pews shining in the sunlight, the gold crucifix with the Lamb of God carved in its intersection and perhaps above all the sweet solemnity of plainsong chants were for me a call from that place I longed for so often in autumn, so often at dusk, when "worlds of wanwood leafmeal lie."

As I continued attending St. Thomas, I read the booklets at the back of the church. I learned how the liturgical calendar provided a unique union of the spiritual life with the changing seasons. I discovered Advent, Lent and Holy Week. Whereas the Baptist way of worship as I experienced it tended to separate the spiritual and earthly, the Anglican liturgy unified the two. The most important manifestation of this unity was Holy Communion. I was very much drawn to Christ in the sacrament. Jesus had said He was the Bread of Life and, as He handed His disciples the Passover bread, added, "Take it and eat; this is my body." In short, I was beginning to see the beauty and truth of the sacramental life.

The Anglican way of worship was reinforced in me by my reading of Lewis and Charles Williams. I respected these two authors tremendously and found out they were Anglicans, that the literature they produced, which I found nourishing and wonder-giving, was rooted in Anglican soil. Also, at about this time, I read *A Severe Mercy* by Sheldon Vanauken, a book which left a profound impression on me of the awe-inspired love of God and the beauty and truth in the Anglican Church.

In my last semester in college it suddenly dawned on me that the Anglican tradition had its roots in the Catholic Church. I remember sitting on a hillside with a dear friend and exclaiming, "You know, the Catholic Church was *the* Church for the first 1500 years of her history." Boom! I don't think she understood, but something clicked inside me and I realized how ignorant I was of those 1500 years. All I knew of Church history, other than the life of St. Francis of Assisi, began with Martin Luther and the "canonized" missionaries of the 19th century.

I began reading Catholic literature. I read spiritual books about conversions like *Road to Damascus;* I also read *Orthodoxy* by G. K. Chesterton. The authors, Flannery O'Connor, Graham Greene and Walker Percy, all Catholics, opened up for me a realm of modern literature, respected by both Christians and non-Christians, that I had not heard of before. This was intriguing. The most respected Christian authors of the 20th century were Catholics. Instrumental in my appreciation of Catholic authors was one of my English professors, Dr. Clark, a humorous yet exacting teacher who was not afraid to discuss his Catholic Faith in the classroom.

What was it, I wondered, in Catholicism that encouraged artistic creativity? The answer was a sacramental view of life that recognized the importance of the Incarnation. Protestantism tends to focus only on the death and resurrection of our Lord and does not delve into His taking up of manhood. I saw in the Protestant view of things a strained spirituality, an aversion for the body and earth, that often discourages artistic production. Why be creative with the things of this world when these things are to be shunned? This is not to say that there are no fine

Protestant authors or painters—Calvin Miller, Frederick Buechner, Robert Drake, and the Flemish painters of the 16th and 17th centuries come to mind as examples of such—but I speak of the tone and overriding purpose of the two religions. I realized at this time that Catholicism provided a life that recognized the goodness of created things and showed how they could be enjoyed and used to the glory of God. To write a science fiction story, to paint a landscape, to play the piano because music is delightful, were not things to feel guilty about, to consider a waste of time. They could be, instead, a part of an integrated life dedicated to God. Roman Catholicism brings things together in Christ:

"Now the Church is his body,
he is its head.
As he is the Beginning,
he was first to be born from the dead,
so that he should be first in every way;
because God wanted all perfection
to be found in him
and all things to be reconciled through him
    and for him,
everything in heaven and everything on earth,
when he made peace
by his death on the cross."

(Col. 1:18-20, *Jerusalem Bible*)

I graduated in December of 1982, not sure of what I wanted to do next. Partly because of this aimlessness and partly because of a wayward heart I let myself drift into what Bunyan calls the "Slough of Despond." I continued to read about Catholicism, but I stopped going to church and a time of doubting assailed me. I realize now that doubting can be a part of a life of faith, but then I thought it was the end of faith, my faith at least. My friends, Wade and Chryse Bradshaw, helped me and kept me in the faith through their love and prayers, but I was becoming more skeptical about Christianity as I fell deeper into despair about my own life.

I felt I had not changed enough. Every Christian I knew, especially in my case, remained mired in the same old sins and frustrations we had always and would always be mired in. My experience in Protestantism taught me that the Christian life was a series of big events which produced change in the heart. You receive Christ as your Savior and you are a new creature. Perhaps later you fall away. Then you walk up the aisle again to rededicate your life. At a retreat, you feel suddenly closer to God. Now the Christian life does have highlights, but I had no sense of the slow, daily growth Catholicism teaches and no experience of the power of the Sacrament of Reconciliation. Thus, my interest in Catholicism, which was an outgrowth of my search for Christ and the Source of beauty, waned.

I then came to Boston for graduate school at Northeastern University. I attended an Anglican Church and in December of 1983 was officially received into that church. My renewed fervor, though, was short-lived. I stopped going to church, stopped praying, and decided I would forget about God. My doubts were a mixture of sincere reservations about the truth of Christianity, a tendency toward depression, and an attraction toward sensuality. Deep down I knew Christianity was true and that God loved me, but I didn't want to be a Christian; I willed to be someone who enjoyed life without God and the guilt He brought. I began thinking of God as a Being who oppressed man, rather than liberated him.

Dostoyevsky, in his novel, *The Brothers Karamozov*, has Ivan Karamozov say to his brother, Alyosha, "One can hardly live in rebellion, and I want to live." Even though in the novel this character says he is not rebelling against God—I probably would have said the same thing, for if you rebel against someone, that means that person exists—eventually he does return to a belief in God because he wants to live. I found myself in the same situation, wanting to live, but not being able to in rebellion against God. Above all by His grace, but also by my free will, I decided to return to God, to follow Christ again. Because of my previous reading, thinking and prayer, I knew the Roman Catholic Church was the Body of Christ and that I should return to Him through her. In December of 1984, I was received into the Church and soon God led me to the Oblates of the Virgin Mary, whose religious, especially Fr. David Kosmoski, have encouraged me to grow in Christ.

This desire to know Jesus is partly what guided me throughout my pilgrimage. This desire was planted in me by Protestants and grew under their care. I am grateful for this and their love for God. I ask them to consider where the source of their life in Christ originated and to ponder the fact that only an infallibly guided Church could have chosen the infallible Scriptures we both believe in.

Through the Bible and lesser books I sought to know Christ more fully. Books by Anglican and Catholic authors engaged my intellect and helped me into the Church. And Beauty, or perhaps I should say the Beautiful, in those same books as well as in paintings, architecture, music and nature; the Beautiful, that saturated me with a sweet longing for someone or place I could never quite find or envision (C. S. Lewis writes about this desire better than anyone else in the 20th century); the Beautiful captured my heart.

In the end, I found the two were one. I found the meeting place of mind and heart, of Truth and Beauty, in the life of Christ Himself in the Roman Catholic Church. Augustine wrote of this way to God in his *Confessions:* "Late have I loved Thee, O Beauty so ancient and new; late have I loved Thee! For behold Thou wert within me, and I outside; and I sought Thee outside and in my unloveliness fell upon those lovely things Thou hast made." And the psalmist's prayer is mine: "One thing I have asked of the Lord, that I will seek after; that I may dwell in the house of the Lord all the days of my life, to behold the beauty of the Lord, and to inquire in his temple" (Ps. 27:4).

The two years I have been a Catholic have not been "happily ever after" years unassailed by doubts and temptations. Parts of them have been tremendously rocky and I have often been, like the camels in Eliot's *The Journey of the Magi*, "Galled, sore-footed, refractory." However, I have never regretted becoming a member of Holy Church, nor would I ever go back. In the Church I have the truth, and its beauty, of the Magisterium, the Eucharist, a fountain of Life, and brothers and sisters. I have found my home and begun to live.

Franklin Freeman *is a seminarian at Our Lady of Grace Seminary, operated in Boston, Massachusetts, by the Oblates of the Virgin Mary. He grew up in Texas for the most part, but has lived in Boston since 1983. He received his M.A. in English from Northeastern University.*

Gypsy—Home Again!

Jeanine M. Graf

I can still remember the sounds of determined steps, shiny black shoes clacking down the corridors. The brisk pace was measured and accompanied by the rustling of coarse, black habits. Like an awesome metronome, the tempo was only softened by the percussion of jangling wooden beads to which large crucifixes were affixed (at eye level, for a small child). Ladies' bespectacled faces peered out of what seemed to be white cardboard frames, draped in long black veils.

These were not ordinary people and this was no ordinary place. I clutched at my mother's hand: partly because my new "Mary Jane" shoes kept slipping on the highly waxed linoleum floors, and partly because of fear. This was a kind of death for me: the end of the "cookies and milk" kind of freedom I was accustomed to.

When my mother left, I wanted to cry, but knowing full well (instinctively) that this wasn't the sort of place that allowed that sort of behavior. I opted instead to put forth my "I'm a brave, good girl" face instead, and waited for my name to be called in line. This was my very abrupt introduction to "things Catholic" and I think that it was also my first impression of a Catholic God, too. I had somehow arrived at the conclusion that He was very shiny, stern and orderly; and even something more fearsome: He could read minds and be everywhere at the same time. I thought that if I ever had the opportunity of a chance meeting with Him one day that He would automatically give me a hard, eternal type of disapproving look. This notion enabled me to construct a new chamber in my six-year-old subconscious mind...and furnish it almost exclusively with parochial guilt.

School wasn't all that bad, though. There were some Holy Days and Feast Days on the calendar that I delighted in. On these days, all the school children would walk in a processional past the convent, to the churchyard. Our eyes would take a little while to adjust to a dark, candle-lit sanctuary from the bright sunlit morning. There was always a strange hush when we entered the Cathedral. Even the class bullies were subdued because they knew that any noise that they initiated would be vaulted up the Gothic arches, echoing across the connecting spires, finally becoming trapped somewhere over the altar in the muraled dome. No one in our class...even the eighth graders... wanted his muffled pranks to be carried that far: in front of Moses, the Apostles, and St. Michael the Archangel!

Our class sat toward the front of the church on the left-hand side near the statue of Mary and Baby Jesus. There was a tray of votive candles beneath them whose flickerings helped me to imagine a semblance of movement in the alcove. I so desperately wanted them all to come to life. Mary's voice would be like music, I thought, and if she would touch me something like very holy magic would happen. Baby Jesus had special powers too ...after all, he managed to grow up in a few months... from Christmas to Easter. That was a mystery to me.

During chapel, there was even some mention of a Holy-Ghost there-abouts. I would very much like to have seen him. This "other world" with its host of heavenly characters filled me with expectation. Sometimes I felt that I could die for the wanting to enter that unseen world, or to have that world enter this one. The only specific longing I could identify during that time was to be like Mary...the kind of little girl an angel would be sent to.

The next two years were filled with Catechism lessons (boring) but excitement grew as the time to receive first Holy Communion drew nigh. The Sacraments in my thinking were special meeting places between two worlds, filled with holy magic. I thought that it would be comparable to looking at your own reflection in a pane of window glass at dusk: Although you could see the world outside, you were standing inside, but your reflection hovered in a world in between. Since the Sacraments were performed in this world, I believed some other action took place in the other world and therefore caused some change in the spiritual person juxtaposed between two places. This may sound awfully complicated, but I am merely trying to explain my childhood thoughts and beliefs.

The next change to chronicle was a move to the suburbs, a new house, a new school, a new church. In a general sense, this was a good move, but in a spiritual sense, it was a disaster. The rector of that parish appeared to be psychologically troubled. This was probably all right for the adult community who could understand the priest's illness and even feel holier for over-looking it; but it is very important for a child to feel that the person who is chosen to speak for God should resemble Christ in some way.

Our family pulled out of that parish after two years when the priest in question wouldn't sign a document allowing my oldest brother...after years of work...to become officially certified to become an Eagle Scout. He gave as his reason that since the Boy Scout Troop held their meetings in the basement of a Methodist church, my brother had sinned and wasn't deserving of such an honor.

We were immediately whisked off to another parish, and enrolled in public school. Although my parents tried their utmost to pursue the faith, something was missing. The feelings of mystery and special believing began to evaporate while philosophies of "me-ism" and materialism took their place. The place of special longing for God became the storage bin for other strange spiritual experimentation.

At first, the transition into the secular world didn't seem so devastating. In the early sixties political idealism was at its peak as John F. Kennedy fanned the embers of the American Dream. The Rev. Martin Luther King, Jr., was living proof that one man's dream could awaken the conscience of a nation. Injustice was an enemy that could be conquered!

Then "the Dream" died in the barrel of the assassin's gun. Fear moved in like the Grim Reaper and the youth of America were inconsolable. Like Camelot, the disenfranchised mourned the loss of their future. They roamed like refugees in their own land waiting for the claws of an undeclared war to cannibalize them. They abandoned traditional mores and religious values and began to look toward the East for the answer, some mystical brand of peace. Anything other than "traditionalism" was in: zen, existentialism, spiritualism, even witchcraft. So many "did their own thing"; everything was "like psychedelic, man" and "transcendental" and "a trip."

I doubt very seriously if I ran into any die-hard Calvinists back then. I don't even know if I would have recognized one if I saw one. Established religions were anti-intellectual. This was a period of rebellion, revolution, fraught with voguish religions. Each person was a chameleon of new convictions. New cults would crop up every day and the hipsters would catch a new religious notion like being contaminated by some air-born virus or from drinking out of the wrong cup.

I was always on the prowl for some new mystical answer. But the effort was in the contrivance. None of these temporal convictions worked any transformation at all. It was a lot like playing "dress up"; and I was most happy with the Hindu garb. Interestingly, this phase led to two "well-placed co-incidences": my landing a job with an Indian company that eventually sent me off to Bombay, and meeting my husband-to-be at a bus stop at JFK International Airport.

There is no better tonic for someone who claims to believe something than to be immersed in it. Hinduism is an ancient belief and has certainly had its impact on the Indian culture for centuries, every part of everyday life is fraught with it. One cannot simply land in Bombay as I did, clutching my Americanized version of Hinduism without experiencing a rude awakening.

The idea of reincarnation seemed to me to be the most charitable of all religious ideas of an after-life. Since I am a bit of a procrastinator, I preferred the option of an eternity of lives to work toward a righteous goal. So it only stands to good reason, following that line of thought, that the upper caste Brahmins would be the holiest people in India.

One day as I was walking with a Brahmin friend, we passed an "Untouchable" (low caste) whose child obviously was starving to death. I was visibly outraged that this was so commonplace in India. Starving babies! Why wasn't someone helping? "It is the poor soul's Karma," my friend explained, "perhaps this child in a past life has committed a terrible crime...and deserves to suffer in this life?"

Did I detect a note of pride in the inference that if that poor soul deserved such a terrible life in the here and now...that my friend equally deserved to enjoy his estate and servants? What good was a series of past lives no one could remember? Wouldn't it give far more credibility to say... "Well, this nagging back pain that I have seems to be left over from the year 1264, when I was a rascal and caused someone's horse to shy, and he ended up falling on the courtyard on his back..."?

I gleaned what I could from my Hindu phase (I particularly liked the idea of impersonal gods rather than personal ones, and "god the force" sounded much more lenient than God the Father) and was on my way. The spiritual gypsy in me was migrating toward psychic phenomena: "Man only uses a small part of his brain," the vendors of spiritualism said, "organized religions are afraid of letting people reach their potential for fear of having them leave in droves...along with their donations." Quite frankly, this appealed to me because it was anti-establishment and mysterious and gave some promise of personal power (in that order).

If I could imagine that I was riding aboard a double-decker tour bus, I would have predicted its next stop to be Tibet; or logically, even Virginia Beach, VA. (the Edgar Cayce Institute is there). The next stop on my itinerary was scheduled by anyone but me.

As fate would have it, or whatever force I gave credit to back then, the man I fell in love with turned out to be a Jew. When we first met, I told him that I didn't belong to any organized religion as such, but had been raised a Catholic. I considered myself to be a "nothing." As our relationship deepened and turned toward the home-stretch of matrimony, I was happy to trade in my "nothing" status to become one with God's Ancient People. I never realized that all those conversations with the Rabbi would re-introduce me to the cast of all the same holy men and women whose names I knew so well as a child! Adam and Eve, Noah, Joseph, Daniel, King David. Judaism became a cultural and historical theater in the round. The one great difference was Jesus. Why?

Perhaps this is the place where this story should end with some great spiritual revelation, leading to a path of new discovery of old truths, but I fell for another mystical distraction.

My mother worked in a museum where the postmistress was reputed to be incredibly psychic. Some said she was the object of study by a large university in the south. One day she came to my mother and started to describe our living room in great detail. She said, "Call home, I see fire!" My mother, naturally, called. It seems my father had fallen asleep on the sofa and his cigarette had started to burn. One can only come to the conclusion that a gift that saves lives is from God. We asked what religion it was and she said: "Witchcraft...WHITE Witchcraft." (I wish I knew then that God doesn't discriminate when it comes to the occult: be it white, black, or baby blue, witchcraft is forbidden.)

When the door is opened to the Spirit Dimension, it becomes a veritable Pandora's Box. I wish I could delete the years that came after the involvement with the unseen. One weird tragedy would follow another. Even my older brother, who was studying across the Atlantic in Sussex, England, was not out of reach. He returned from university before completing his doctorate, terribly ill and psychologically shattered. It seems some of his acquaintances there divulged their utter devotion to Lucifer. When my brother made light of their faith, well, the rest sounds like some part of the movie, "Rosemary's Baby."

When I think of the irony of it all, I would be the last one to read an account like this and give it much credence; but as a result, I have been sensitized and would be the last one to joke about someone else's experience.

The final stroke occurred in March 1971, when the hospital staff wheeled me into the operating room for the delivery of my second child. I knew there was some sort of complication when they applied the anesthesia mask. At first, I held my breath; then in moments I could hear the Chief of Obstetrics being paged and a rush of activity around the bed. The room grew farther and farther away and it seemed that I was traveling...through a tunnel and on toward a light. The light was in the distance and to the right. Suddenly, my course radically changed. I was heading down...and to the left. A thought immediately occurred to me: Have I died? Then a rapid succession of thoughts: "But I haven't seen my baby. I haven't said good-bye to my husband...." I wanted desperately to hold my oldest daughter just one more time. "This can't be happening to me."

There were voices in that darkness in which I dwelt. They jeered. I was the brunt of their joke. I kept thinking, "If I could find someone in charge around here, he'd see that they have the wrong person." I was utterly devastated by the fact that what I had *believed* to be truth about life after death didn't alter one iota the reality of what really existed. The desperation of the situation was as black as the darkness that I was immersed in. I prayed, "Oh Lord, if you let me back into life, I will seek to serve you." At once I began to surface (like coming to the surface after diving in deep, deep black water). When I broke through, I was in the O. R. still. It was seven-thirty p.m. I had gone in for a simple delivery at two o'clock.

Within the year, I learned the true meaning of Messiah. When my best friend, who was a Protestant, introduced me to her Jesus, I felt like an old friendship had been re-awakened. Since this reconversion went through a Protestant conduit, I assumed, as time went on, a very Protestant, Fundamentalist point of view, including the anti-Catholic sentiments (I held the Church responsible for my falling away). This point would be driven home years later after the Lord paraded many credible Catholics through my life: Dan O'Neill, Peter Kreeft, Fr. Henri Nouwen, Fr. Thomas DiLorenzo. But the crushing blow came during an interview with Cardinal Bernard Law when I glibly stated, "If there were more devout persons at the helm of the church when I was growing up, perhaps people like myself never would have strayed." He answered simply and lovingly, "Perhaps you would not have known."

That comment sent me reeling back through a time tunnel, and the truth drove straight to its mark. Throughout my life I had fed the festering notion (a lie) that the Church was responsible for keeping me godly. With that remark, I looked inward to see a Prodigal coming over the fields on Christmas Day, with a final step on the porch, as the door swings open releasing the rich aromas of a feast prepared for a Celebration...realizing that the same chair at the table had been left vacant all these years, while loved ones waited patiently, prayerfully...for the wandering to be over.... Finally coming home.

Jeanine Graf *is a broadcast journalist, currently residing in an old farmhouse in Massachusetts with her husband, two (teenaged) daughters, assorted pets and an organic garden. For the past several years she has been the host of an issues-oriented talk show in Boston and is currently president of an advertising agency, Aeriel Communications, Ltd.*

Reflections on the Act of Conversion

S. Thomas Greenburg

I. In my early years, extending through the teenage sequence, I was exposed to a daily conversation with my Jewish father, the substance of which was always centered on the figure of Christ. This was not yet the Christ who was the Redeemer. It was the Christ who was deeply and passionately respected as the Exemplar of human life itself—a life that gave meaning and significance to my father's honesty and devotion to value: an honesty and devotion that did not always bring with them the positive results that he sought and expected from others, personally, socially, and politically!

At the time, I was completely unaware of a Greater Power that was at work—an unknown power that was already "building the foundations" in these formative stages of my life, for what was to come years later. It is only now, on reflection, that I can appreciate the unique experience of being exposed to a constant dialogue on the Christ, by one whose own need to be replenished for the difficulties encountered during his attempts to "live the good life," was being enlightened by a grace which supplied an insight into the Source of Salvation Itself—a special grace which my father recognized only as an example of the "saintly life itself"!

I am convinced, now, that my father was being used as an instrument of the Lord, not only to bring the Christian message to bear; but also, and most significantly, to prepare me for my own future—a future which was to be dominated by the difficulties that would follow upon a life devoted to a public defense of the Christian Message itself. That I will, if it so pleases God, have the opportunity to thank my father, serves even more to enhance this remarkable experience and its even more remarkable purpose! And no doubt, in his own honest and forceful way, my father will admit that only now does he realize the "baptism of desire" that was present in him at the time!

Though my mother never actually participated in these early conversations, her constant nurturing of my ambitions (imitating, in this way, the servant who lovingly and obediently "captures" the message) served as the necessary correlative instrument for an Unseen Hand that was ever present. It was as if she knew that this son of hers, at some future time, was to climax the role that my father played. Her own stalwart acquiescence was born of trust and sincerity. It was not born from any newly acquired religious knowledge, but was a true witness to a growing intuition "that something good," though beyond her own recognition at the time, "was taking place."

I am certain that she also knows, now, the vital part that she played in the ceaseless and necessary "tutoring" that was to bring one of the sidetracked descendants of Israel back to its original roots: those "Christian-Jewish roots" that were eternally chosen by the Lord God Himself to carry on the work of Redemption and Salvation!

At the age of sixteen, when my youthfully oriented purpose in life was only to gain some prominence in the field of athletics, I was stricken with infantile paralysis and bedridden for many months.

Now, unless one has the misfortune to himself experience the feeling of being taken from a position of personal strength to a position of complete, and immediate physical dependence on others, there is no adequate way to describe or communicate to others this awesome and frightening state of being—a state of being that can bring with it a threatening feeling of discouragement which if it is not challenged, confronted and overcome, can be more difficult to bear than the physical sickness itself.

I could not fully comprehend at the time that this confrontation with discouragement was yet another "preparation" for the future: a future which could only be fulfilled if the discouragement was overcome and turned into an "opportunity" to "grow in knowledge" and in appreciation of the values that alone give meaning and significance to life. Too, it could not be fully grasped, that my immediate and obsessively driven desire, in spite of my physical condition, to read, to study, and to master the writings of the great philosophers, was itself part of the "means" whereby I would be permitted to prepare for what was yet to come. And, indeed, it could not possibly be grasped, at the time, that the Unknown Hand was at work, offering me an unmerited grace—in the midst of a physical deterioration—to overcome and transcend my "state of being" and to be raised to another "state of being," wherein, if successful, my total person was being given the "capability" to shape and determine my own future—a future for which I would have to be prepared to face even greater obstacles and greater frustrations; namely, those that accompany the "opportunity" and the "privileged honor" to actively participate in the ongoing work of Redemption!

And, finally, it could not possibly be known, at the time, that a physical "sickness unto death" (it was predicted that I had only eight months to live) was being turned into a spiritual "sickness unto health"!

My recovery brought with it a relief only from physical pain; and from a life of difficult confinement.

It did not bring relief from my ever-increasing desire to learn. In fact, the "obsession to know more" that began during my illness, raged unabated!

I chose to enter a Catholic university. The "why" was answered during my years at St. John's University.

Though I had read and studied the history of philosophy, I had not yet unified that study; nor had I discovered a true philosophical "tree" that I could attach myself to, while extending my continuing search for knowledge.

That "tree" was supplied by my in-depth exposure to the philosophy-theology of St. Thomas Aquinas. Where I had been truly enlightened by my previous studies, I was now both enlightened and simultaneously convinced that to reject Aquinas was to reject reason itself!

Because my record at St. John's was exceptional and because my desire continued unabated, I was counselled by my teachers to enroll for the doctorate at Columbia University where, they advised, I would not only be acutely tested by those who still envisioned the Medieval period as "dark"; but, where I would also gain the proper status to continue my work and to meet the further challenges of the future (a future which my teachers and counsellors foresaw better than I)—challenges which would inevitably place me in the awesomely difficult position of defending the philosophy of St. Thomas and its relationship to the Church itself! What they had foreseen, and what I had now to accept, was: Could I, in effect, defend the philosophy of Aquinas—the Church's true representative—without defending the Church itself?

The answer to this was implied in the question.

I became a member of the Church by a decision that climaxed all of the influences of my early years; all of the understanding and help from my parents; all of the insights gained during my bedridden months; all of the prodding and all of the extraordinary help of my teachers; and, *most importantly*, all of the graces that had led me to *where I had to go!*

From here, there no longer could be a question of "why was this happening?" There could only be the question "how do I proceed to carry out the responsibility that had been given to me?"

Indeed, I had arrived at the stage where there could be no turning back! There could only be a turning to!

The decision had been made.

The fires that sparked my conversion entered into my teaching, even though that teaching was to begin at a secular university.

I remember being called to task by my department chairman for "teaching philosophy according to St. Thomas." Though my position was at stake, I answered the "interrogation" with: "Is there any other way than the 'right way to teach philosophy?'" My confidence, and my turning the question around, closed the matter. No further interrogations were ever forthcoming.

During these teaching years, the "grace" that had worked its inevitability on me, brought many students to consider conversion—though not without the inevitable difficulties that attended my own turn to the Lord. At one time, I was threatened with my life for having "influenced" a young student to convert. Though a police escort became necessary for me to safely attend to my responsibilities at the university, neither I nor the student flinched from our purpose; the strength that was needed by both came from the same Source that impelled both!

That I was being led to "where I had to go," became evident with my appointment as a professor of philosophy at a small, but committed Catholic college in Texas—an appointment which was to lead to the presidency of that same institution. How could I question the unalterable "fact" that I was being directed from another Source? What other explanation could give meaning and significance to the appointment of a young convert Jew to the presidency of a Catholic college that had never, in all of its long history, even considered the eventuality of a "lay president"? What other explanation can be given to these events—events which take on an even more mysterious tone when one considers that the name of the college was "Incarnate Word College"; and, when one includes the fact that this "convert Jew" was responsible for a faculty that included more than one hundred religiously committed Sisters?

The "Unseen Hand" had to be there!

With each passing day, doubt was challenged and overcome by the certainty that this sequence of events was not one of my own making. This conviction did not allay, but, in fact, brought with it even more "test" and "challenges"...almost, as it were, bringing to the fore, the greater tests that would continue, in their turn, to bring forth greater confidence and conviction that my responsibilities were not mine alone.

During my first years of teaching, and simultaneous with my completion of the doctorate in philosophy at Columbia University, I met, fell in love with, and married the woman who was to help me throughout the remainder of my life.

The marriage was a climactic one for both of us: Susan's own "turn to God," as a convert to Catholicism, was culminated, but not initiated, by my own ongoing activities in the Catholic world. My own influence merely brought to complete fulfillment much longer and much deeper influences, from Raissa Maritain and Edith Stein, both of whom Susan admired and respected for their tremendous contributions to the life of the Church; and, for their grace-given ability to bring to bear on others, those graces that won for them their own personal victories in a difficult, in a challenging, and in a constantly tested public life.

Through the years, Susan has served me lovingly as an understanding "listener"; as a respected "consultant" in difficult times, where her judgments have often redirected some of my own decisions; and as a necessary "disciplinarian": all these, in addition to bestowing upon me an unlimited love—a gift for which I shall ever be thankful to the same Lord God who has selected both of us to participate together with others in His Redemptive and Salvational Mission.

A true evaluation of my marriage and its fruits can only be made against the background of the activities conducted by both, as instruments of the Lord God whose graces brought us together. That evaluation must also include, in a very important way, our two children, son and daughter Robert and Joyce, both of whom, I am certain, will continue to carry on with the work of the Church, always cognizant of the difficulties but also always cognizant of the benefits that accrue to a life devoted to the Church and its message.

In 1970, after twenty years as administrator and as president of Incarnate Word College; and, after establishing the Institute of Catholic Higher Education and the Institute for the Advanced Study of Catholic Doctrine at St. John's University in New York, both of which were founded to re-establish and confirm the proper Catholic identity of all the Catholic higher educational institutions (an identity which included the authoritative relationship of Rome to all of these institutions), it became necessary to actively work with Rome and the Church in these matters.

As a consequence, I was privileged to work with the Congregation for Catholic Education—a relationship that has endured for more than sixteen years, during which time I was honored to participate in, and to serve as a consultant for, two international Congresses (1972 and 1976); and during which time I was privileged to be involved in the ongoing work of the congregation, in its attempt to re-establish and to examine its own authority with regard to all of the Catholic universities throughout the world.

This brief historical review is important, not only for its involvement of a convert from Judaism who was placed in this position of defending the Church and its proper authority; but also, and even more importantly, for the "lessons" that I learned during these many years—especially those lessons that dealt with the long-suffering patience that identified the Church's exercise of its authority, and those that dealt with the awesome responsibility that is placed on those of us who have been chosen, both to defend the Church and await its patient acquiescence to our defense, at one and the same time: during these years of liaison with Rome—and consistent with my open and public defense of the faith, I consistently advocated an open and immediate confrontation with the Catholic colleges and universities that had separated themselves from the teaching authority of the Church.

In effect, my own position—one that was stated openly, strongly, and repetitively—was to challenge and forthrightly deal with these aberrant institutions in a manner that identified both the Church's authority and the institutions' irresponsibility, even if it brought with it the necessity to identify for the Catholic citizenry, those who were the "leaders" in this separation from Rome!

The disciplinary action that was recommended, some sixteen years ago, has now been taken!

This speaks "eloquently," both for the wisdom and patience of the Church; and, eloquently also, for the strength of the recommendation itself.

II. No one converts himself!

All reflections on the act of conversion must begin with an acknowledgment of, and an appreciation for, the unmerited privilege that has been offered by the Lord Himself, to actively participate in His ongoing work of Redemption. In effect, it is in fear and trembling that one finds himself amongst those whom the Lord *has chosen* to participate in His Redemptive Acts, especially when one realizes that this participation includes a responsibility not only for one's own salvation, but also, for that of countless others!

Thus, to be chosen for conversion, includes the awesome responsibility to cooperate, actively and continuously, with the selective grace that has been proferred; the challenge, together with the responsibility, to "put on the armor of God" in the battle for eternal salvation; the opportunity and the honored privilege to effectively experience the *Person to person* relationship that defines the friendship that exists between the Lord God and His adopted children; the feeling of awe that accompanies the knowledge that one has been offered a place in the long line of converts that has proceeded from St. Paul, the Prime analog of all conversions: a knowledge that becomes even more awesome when the one who is converted is a Jew, and who is one who participates in the original conversions that identified the origins of Christianity itself!

Since the source of conversion is infinite, the conversions emanating from that source are also infinite. Each conversion is unique: the infinite source cannot repeat itself. Only an infinity of conversions, each unique and radically different from the other, can adequately reflect the infinity which is the Existential Source of all; just as, only an infinity of creations can adequately express the infinite beauty of the Creator Himself!

Each one of the infinity of conversions has its particular and its own singular effect on the salvational goal that is desired by all.

In effect, conversion manifests, more than any other activity, the upward movement towards the Godhead—an upward movement initiated by the Godhead—wherein the Lord God raises the person by "pulling him upwards on the ladder of faith"! In all of these infinitely numbered cases, the Lord God provides other "secondary actors" who, in their own grace-impelled way, contribute to the cooperation with grace that is being exercised by the individual convert himself: some of these cooperators help to steady the ladder when it swerves; some others, by their example, help to redirect eyes that may be temporarily diverted from the goal; and, some others, may serve to identify, time and again, the tremendous discipline that is necessary to maintain and preserve the always precarious balance that is needed by all, and by each of those who strive to attain the cherished aim of salvation.

Only the person can be converted! The grace of conversion is received by the person as a total and complete entity. The grace of conversion is not received by an "intellect," by a "will" or, by a "body"! Nor is the grace of conversion received by a combination of these, even as they are definitively conceived as the constituents of human nature (a human nature which *cannot exist or exercise any activity on its own!)* Hence, it is not "human nature," nor its conceived constituents, that receives the grace of conversion! Abundant evidence of this principle is found, in fact, where the "sacrifice of the Mass" says: "only say the word and *I* shall be healed"! In effect, neither human nature, nor an intellect, nor a will, nor a body, can be or become Catholic! These cannot, therefore, be Catholic "intellects," Catholic "wills," Catholic "bodies" and/or, Catholic "human natures." Only the person, as a total and complete entity, in himself, can be or become Catholic!

To be a Catholic person, and to be a Catholic convert, are two sides of the same truly personal existence. By fulfilling oneself as a person, one simultaneously fulfills himself as the "image of God"; and, by fulfilling himself as the "image of God," one simultaneously fulfills himself as a Catholic person, under the influence of the grace of conversion itself!

One of the most important notions in all of Christian theology is that of "person."

Theology speaks of the Trinity of persons. It identifies the angels as persons. It calls the human being a person. It even invests the "Evil One" with the name of a person.

The Fathers of the Church knew only too well that this notion was central to the communication of the Christian message. Their work emphasized the fact that the dogma of the Incarnation and its correct formulation depended on this notion of person; and, on the proper distinction between the person and human nature: the condemnation of Arianism, of Appollonarism, etc., are evidences of this knowledge and its application.

One cannot adequately treat the subjects of conversion, of Christian education, of grace, of salvation, of the Church itself, and, of the Faith, without centralizing this notion.

There is evidence in abundance that those who are responsible for the correct communication of this notion, in our own day, have not manifested the ability to meet this responsibility. This is especially true in the modern environs of theological and philosophical speculation, where the vital distinction between the person and his nature has not kept faith with the admonitions of the early Church Fathers concerning the communication of the Christian message itself.

To say that the Holy Father is the personification of the "religious life" is to say that the constituents of the nature of religious life (consecration, sacrifice, dedication, service, etc.), are existentialized, interiorized, and concretized, in the Holy Father, more than they are in any other person.

Analysis of this declaration shows that "personification" includes,

An "agent" who existentializes and integrates within himself, the potential of the nature, which in this case, is the nature of "religious life";

A nature (religious life) that is being developed, fulfilled, and actualized;

A process of person-ification wherein the agent integrates and existentializes the potential of the nature to be fulfilled.

To grasp the "person," therefore, in his totality, is to grasp the inter-relationships between the agent, the nature, and the process of person-ification; and, to grasp the transcendence of the person who includes all three relationships without being restricted to any one, or to a mere combination of the three.

In effect, to grasp the "person" is to comprehend the ongoing fact that the "who" is ceaselessly personifying the "what he is," by interiorizing the constituents of the "what," within himself.

To Be "Christian"

We have seen where the state of being-person is charged with the exercise of action and the determination of the direction and manner of that action.

When the person becomes "Christian," he exists in a "new" state of being where he receives new commitments from his faith and from the Source of that faith; and, where, because of these commitments, he exercises and determines his activity in a new way: that is, in a new state of being.

"Christian," precisely because it is an existential modifier of the existential state of being-person, cannot be included in the order of essence or nature, either as a specifier of a new essence or as an accidental modifier of an "old" one!

In effect, there is no such thing as

a Christian mind;

a Christian will;

a Christian body;

a Christian soul;

a Christian human nature!

Only the *person* can become Christian!

The Fathers of the Church knew only too well that the notion of person was central to the Christian belief.

An adequate communication of this central notion requires no less a "knowledge" from those who are charged in our day, with the teaching and communication of the Christian message.

S. Thomas Greenburg *was the founder and first director of the* Institute for Advanced Studies in Catholic Doctrine *at St. John's University— an Institute founded specifically to challenge and redirect "contemporary teaching of theology" on Catholic University campuses. He is also the founder and continuing president of the* Institute of Catholic Higher Education, *dedicated to the purpose of returning Catholic universities and colleges to a recognition and implementation of their relationship to the teaching authority of the Church…a purpose which has been implemented by means of a continuing liaison with the Congregations in Rome. Dr. Greenburg was a professor of philosophy for more than thirty years and is the past president of two Catholic colleges. His writings include:* The Concept of Infinity in Giordano Bruno; Teaching Free Enterprise as an Enterprise in Freedom; The Notion of Person in the History of Philosophy; Reflections on the History of Philosophy.

A Wife's Example

James F. Heady

I was born in April 1933—the oldest of four children, and the only boy.

My dad had been a football player in high school and had turned down offers to go to college. Instead, he had joined the Navy to see the world. By the time I was born, he was working as a timekeeper for the WPA during the height of the depression.

Around 1940 we moved to a house on 32nd Street in Portland, Oregon, where my parents still live today. Now "Pop" had a "real" job, working for the Southern Pacific Railroad as a timekeeper. It was a company he would work for in different jobs until his retirement thirty-five years later.

Because my dad was an agnostic, our religious upbringing was left to my mother. She did not belong to any particular church, but she felt it was important that we have some type of formal religious training. The new house was only one block away from a Congregational church. When we started school, we also began to attend Sunday school.

We had workbooks and regular lessons to work up for class. Mom made sure we did the lessons and attended classes, even though she and Dad never went to church themselves.

It was a very strong fundamentalist church. The Bible was the cornerstone, and Sunday school emphasized Bible study, including memorization of the names of the books.

Most of my social activities until high school centered around the church. Each summer we attended vacation Bible school, and there were many church potluck suppers and picnics. The Friends church (Quaker) had some type of cooperative tie-in with our church. During the school year, there were workshops and craft classes that we were all encouraged to attend.

Money was scarce, so these out-of-school activities were a great incentive to keep us out of "mischief." The church taught us that God was a personal God who saw and knew everything. Smoking and drinking were forbidden. (I have never smoked to this day.) Movies and dancing were discouraged, although not totally forbidden.

Because I was the oldest and the only boy in the family, practical economics was made clear to me early in life. I was expected to save any money I earned from delivering newspapers, mowing lawns, working as a box boy in a grocery store, etc.

I did well in grade school and eventually skipped a year of grammar school. When I started high school, I was told there was no money to send me to college. What could be set aside was needed to help my younger sisters. I understood the situation with no resentment, but I remember spending many anxious nights thinking about what I could do with my life.

At church, meanwhile, I had progressed from Sunday school to attendance at the regular services. These were similar to those held in other Protestant churches. They included singing by both congregation and choir, with several long prayers by the minister and, of course, a long sermon.

Every three months a communion service was held, with the passing of bread and wine to depict the Last Supper.

The church was like a meeting hall with stained-glass windows. There were no pictures or statues. In retrospect, it all seems very cold, even though the people themselves were warm and caring. The sermons seemed to go on forever and were devoted to long, confusing exhortations to "avoid sin" or "expect to go to hell and damnation."

Around the time I entered high school, I was baptized into the church with a sprinkling of water by the pastor in a meeting room at the church. I joined "Christian Endeavor"—a Bible study group for high school students—and attended church social activities.

All these years were fraught with worry and doubts about my abilities, due to a severe inferiority complex. I prayed long and hard, asking for God's help and for answers to my problems. This habit has continued into my adult life. Sometimes I haven't liked the answers, but in the long run everything always has worked out.

Eventually, with God's help and hard work, I graduated from high school in June, 1950, at the head of my class and with a scholarship from the U.S. Naval Officer Training Program.

I entered Stanford University in the fall of 1950, with the intention of becoming an engineer. After two years, however, I had developed such a great interest in economics that I changed my major. Meanwhile, since I was living away from home, the church ties had lessened. But I often went to pray in the university chapel.

In January, 1955, I graduated with a degree in economics. I entered the Navy, and five months later, at an officers' dance in San Diego, I met Helen.

She was an R.N. from back East. We began to date. After a few dates she let me know she was Catholic. I had casually known other Catholics, but she was the first one I had been close to.

The Congregational church had preached that Protestantism was the best of religions. But my gradual breaking away from the old church ties in Portland and the liberal history studies at Stanford had taught me to look at other points of view more openly.

I became intellectually interested in the Church through my growing interest in Helen. I wanted to be with her as much as possible. And she had such a devotion to the Catholic Church that I wanted to learn more about it.

Long before we were married, I started going to Mass with her. It was my own idea. She never made me feel that it was her requirement, but I was welcome if I wanted to go. Of course, it was all strange and different to me in the beginning. This was before the Latin Mass was changed to English, but with the use of a Latin-English missal I was able to follow the services.

In September, 1955, we were married in San Diego. As a non-Catholic, I was given instructions in what the Church required of a person entering a "mixed marriage."

About a year after we were married, our oldest daughter was born. I had planned on staying in the Navy, but after marriage the long six-month separations became more and more difficult. Eventually I left the Navy and soon went to work for Farmers' Insurance, where I am still working some twenty-eight years later.

Helen never pushed me to become a Catholic. But by her example, and my continuing attendance at Mass, I felt more and more drawn toward the Church. Something was missing in my life that I couldn't identify. After our marriage this uneasiness had grown stronger.

At last, Helen asked me if I would join her in saying a fifty-four day novena to the Blessed Mother. She explained that she had a great devotion to Mary and said this novena when she really needed help. Her prayers always had been answered—perhaps not always in the way she wanted at the time, but always for the best.

I agreed to begin the novena. On the second day, it was as if blinders had been lifted from my eyes. I told Helen that I wanted to take instructions and become a Catholic. I felt it was something I had to do, but even then she would not push. I called our pastor and made the arrangements that were called for.

Father was kind enough to give me individual instructions in the rectory once a week. I started instructions in October, and on my youngest daughter's birthday the following April I was baptized into the Church. It was some seven years after our marriage.

From the day I started taking instructions, I felt much more at peace. There was a feeling of security, comfort and belonging that I could never remember feeling before. All my formative years in the Congregational church, and all the Bible schools plus Sunday school had taught me about God and the Bible, but until now something was missing.

My love of history had given me serious doubts about the lace of continuity in the Protestant churches. The Catholic Church, on the other hand, came into existence at the time of Christ and has remained consistent. If members of a Protestant congregation feels that something is wrong, they will go off on their own and form a new branch. This never seemed right to me.

During the days of Martin Luther there were many problems within the Catholic Church. But after years of turmoil, the Church eventually straightened out without setting up a number of competing Catholic religions. The continuity from Christ to the present day remains unbroken. This strongly appeals to my sense of order.

Our marriage was blessed with three daughters, all of whom grew up in the Church. The oldest one is married. The other two are perpetually professed sisters.

I mention this to convey the depth of commitment that my wife and I feel to the Church. It was our daughters' love of God that led them to their choice. We did not discourage them, because we could not refuse God if He intended them to do His work. He has blessed and rewarded us all our married life.

We have had the usual trials and tribulations that beset any marriage, but through our Catholic Faith we have always been able to work them out. We remember often Christ's promise never to give us any more trials than we can cope with.

Through daily prayers and Mass attendance, I still feel peace and tranquility every day of my life. I thank God for my conversion to Catholicism. Without His help in guiding me to meet my wife, and her good example, I would still be looking in vain for the meaning of life. As I conclude this recollection, I am reminded of Christ's words in the Gospel: "So I say to you, 'Ask and you shall receive, seek and you shall find, knock and it shall be opened to you.'"

James F. Heady *is the home office claims administration manager for a major insurance company. He holds a degree in economics from Stanford University. Married in 1955, he became a Catholic seven years later. He resides in Ventura County, California, with his wife, Helen. They have three grown daughters, two of whom are religious sisters. Mr. and Mrs. Heady are both active lectors in their parish church.*

With God's Help

Helen Hull Hitchcock

When I visit my family's farm in northern Kansas each summer I frequently walk across the pasture, on cool August mornings, to the top of the hill to a tiny cemetery where members of seven generations of my family are buried. There are five cedar trees in the center of this cemetery. Their tops all point East. Their shade preserves the night coolness of the granite and marble headstones beneath them for hours after the August sun has begun to bake the surrounding countryside.

From the top of this hill where Spring Branch cemetery lies, I can look west and see the farm where I grew up, and north of it, the little Ash Rock Congregational Church where my grandfather, in his later years, was pastor. Built of hand-hewn limestone by early settlers of the region, the church is still a landmark, although no Sunday services have been held there since my grandfather died twenty-five years ago.

Looking south from the hilltop, I can see the farm where my family now lives, and the farm where my grandparents lived all their married lives and where they raised their family, my father and his brother and sisters. Across the road from their farm is the Big Barn built by my great-grandfather on land where he'd "staked his claim" as a youth, and where his son still lives and farms. To the east lies the land homesteaded by his father and grandfather, and by my great-grandmother's father and grandfather.

Beyond this land still occupied and farmed by my relatives, I can see south to the river—the South Branch of the Solomon—and to the Blue Hills beyond. I can also see the original homesteads of the two or three other pioneer families who are buried in Spring Branch cemetery. Although there are no longer any remnants in the community of these families, their graves are decorated every year along with those of our family. I now pick a little nosegay of wild verbena and place it on the grave of my great-great-great-grandmother who was born in 1803 and died in Kansas a hundred years ago.

The cemetery originally was the churchyard of the Spring Branch Methodist Church, the site of which is now part of a wheatfield. At the bottom of the hill is the Spring Branch school, a one-room frame structure of traditional schoolhouse design, which still stands though the last class was dismissed fifty years ago.

When I was a very little girl and we used to visit my grandparents in the summer, I thought that the name "Spring Branch" intended to evoke the flowering bough of the wild plum and currant bushes that abound in that part of the country in the springtime. Actually, however, Spring Branch is a sometime creek, running water only after a rainy season, which meanders for several miles through successive pastures to the Solomon. Standing on the hill I think of the water of this furtive stream flowing into the Solomon, eventually reaching the Kansas River which joins the Missouri, finally contributing the rain which fell on my family's farms to the Mississippi at St. Louis, where I now live.

In some ways I see in the unintentional pun of my forebearers who named the church, school and cemetery, a sort of double metaphor for a spiritual pilgrimage which has been formed and nourished and brought to bud by generations—deep roots of faith, as a flowering bough; and which has also been a journey-in-reverse from the headwaters—from uncertain springs and spiritual tributaries through shallows and rapids and "streams of living water"—to the "Father of Waters"—the giant river of faith which is the Catholic Church.

Sometimes I think it is difficult for "cradle Catholics" to understand the depth and power of tradition in Protestantism. The very concept of "Protestant tradition" may, in fact, seem a contradiction in terms. The "protest" part of the word "protestant" seems to imply continual *dissent* from tradition and a denial, rather than an affirmation, of religious roots. The formation of literally hundreds of denominations and sects, each of which "broke away" from the parent church, seems to give evidence of this.

If repeated schism is the bane of Protestantism, it has also been, paradoxically, the boon. Nearly every authentically Protestant denomination has been formed in response to disputes over some point of "developed" doctrine in the parent church which the dissenters believed actually weakened the True Faith embodied in the Holy Scripture and the Creeds. Unlike contemporary "Catholic dissent," the denominations thus formed were usually *more* strict, *more* conservative of the faith, rather than more "liberal" than the parent church.

Thus the "protest" was not aimed at destroying the religious heritage, but, in fact, was an attempt to *preserve* it. This, at its best, is the "Protestant tradition." This also accounts for the vast proliferation of Protestant denominations during the past century or so when most main-line Protestant churches were deformed by Modernism. The attempt (although usually unsuccessful) was to reform the parent church to conform to its original charisma.

To protest against heresy—to dissent from false teaching—is, of course, a catholic thing to do. And believing Protestant Christians meant what they said when they affirmed each Sunday in the Creed "I believe in one, holy, catholic and apostolic church..." in the sense which transcended "denominationalism" (the Roman Catholic Church was regarded as another, albeit the oldest, denomination) and included *all* who professed the Creed and believed that the Bible was the divinely inspired word of God, whatever "branch" of the Body of Christ they belonged to.

This concept of the transcendent unity of the *true* Church was never described as a "mystery," although it is this concept which allowed for the salvation of Catholics (and others) who believed the essentials of the Christian faith, even if they might be confused by "inessentials" of doctrine and practice.

Now, in my particular family there was a healthy suspicion of most Protestant churches, which, by around the turn of the century had already been deeply afflicted by Modernism. From the time I was a small child I listened to the religious discussions of the adults (usually led by my grandfather Hull). I learned many things from these conversations—even more when I was old enough to participate in them.

I learned that to be a Christian is to be a "sign of contradiction" in the world—that Christians are obligated not only to *believe* in the Bible and in the essential teachings of the Faith such as the Trinity, the Virgin Birth, the resurrection and the life eternal contained in the Creeds, but must, moreover, be prepared to *defend* the Faith whenever, wherever, and by whomever it is attacked. I learned to be wary of "wolves in shepherd's clothing" who misled the unsuspecting and the ill-prepared. I learned that "denominational loyalty" was insufficient and could, in fact, be dangerous to one's faith. I learned about the evangelical responsibility of all Christians, and that the conduct of our lives constitutes an important part of our Christian witness to the world.

I believe that it is this emphasis within orthodox protestantism on the individual responsibility for evangelism and witness (based on the common priesthood of all believers in which all Christians share) which may have led to the prohibitions of certain kinds of behavior which may not always be *directly* sinful—things such as smoking, drinking, gambling, etc.—even restrictions on dress and use of modern technological inventions in the case of some denominations. Some critics have suggested that these personal prohibitions (which varied widely from one denomination to the other) were a result of a dualism which saw the body as unimportant and the material world as evil.

While Protestants traditionally believed that the "seductions of the world" were to be resisted, I am rather inclined to view the source of these personal restrictions in the exhortation, "Be ye perfect, even as your Father in Heaven is perfect" (Mt. 5:48) and in genuine concern for Christian witness, rather than as a denial of the body. In a situation, as in conservative Protestantism, where all believers are equally "priests," equally responsible for the accomplishment of the Church's mission in the world, you have, in effect, a "one-track system" to which *all* are called.

Christians are, of course, to be "in the world, not *of* it." "Worldliness" thus was seen as a dangerous capitulation to the *Zeitgeist*—the Spirit of the Times. Mere attendance at church services and performance of religious rituals was regarded as insufficient for salvation (the notion of sacramental grace received from participation in religious ritual was largely absent from Protestantism). Only a total personal commitment to Jesus Christ could bring about salvation; and personal behavior consistent with a "perfect" Christian witness to the world was a requirement for living an authentically Christian life. For many, personal behavior was *in practice* more important than church attendance, though the latter was seen by most as a more or less necessary component of the former.

My personal "spiritual mentor," to the extent that I had one, was my grandfather, Abram Downer Hull. I still regard him as a shining example of what it means to be a

Christian. Born in 1884, he was the youngest of five children and only son of New Englanders who settled in eastern Kansas. As a youngster he was sent "back East" for grammar school and attended the Episcopal church there. After graduation from high school in Kansas, he spent several years in college, where he lost his faith and became an agnostic. He was converted at the age of twenty-six by a group of itinerant Plymouth Brethren missionaries, at about the same time that he married my grandmother and became a farmer.

The Plymouth Brethren are a sect whose militancy about the "priesthood of all believers" leads them to deny any ordination and any ordinary church structure. It was a movement, I suspect, of extreme reaction to the Modernism which was actively being promoted through the official structures of many "main-line" Protestant churches a century ago. This group apparently believed that church structures were so vulnerable to corruption that they had best be avoided altogether.

My impression is that my grandparents maintained infrequent contact with the Plymouth Brethren missionaries for several years. While their criticism of the established churches undoubtedly influenced my grandfather's thinking, he evidently did not share their rigidity about not attending organized churches. He frequently "supplied" pulpits of vacationing ministers and often conducted funeral services. I am inclined to think he felt that no earthly organizations, including churches, were without defect, being comprised of fallible and finite human beings. Additionally, one's personal witness to the Faith could, perhaps, be most helpful to others in the context of community worship. All Christians are called to be "leaven," each in his own way and in his own particular circumstances, whether in private or public life, in the church or in the world.

I was taught that Christians must constantly fortify themselves for their evangelical task by private prayer and study, especially of the Holy Scriptures, and should expect to be "called to account" for the way in which they utilized their talents for the Lord. We must prepare ourselves, moreover, must be *willing* to follow the Lord's call to bear witness of His Truth, always and everywhere.

If my spiritual upbringing was consistently "Evangelical," the institutional aspect of my religious life was rather varied. I was baptized as an infant in the Methodist Church, and through my early years, when my father's occupation as a school superintendent took him to several small Kansas towns, my family belonged to the Methodist Church. (Nearly every little town had a Methodist Church—maybe one or two others.)

My family all attended church services and Sunday school, where even little children learned Bible stories, memorized Scripture verses, and learned countless children's songs, like "Jesus loves me, this I know / For the Bible tells me so. / Little ones to Him belong / We are weak, but He is strong"; "I will make you fishers of men..."; "Zaccheus was a wee little man..."; and "Jesus wants me for a sunbeam / To shine for Him each day...." Children were usually given "Sunday school papers" to take home, which contained religious pictures and Bible stories or stories of great missionaries (the Protestant equivalent of "lives of the Saints").

After we moved to the country, during the summer that I was ten, we usually went to the Methodist Church in town. The church year was divided into "quarters" (our Sunday school books were called "quarterlies"), and a Communion service was held once each quarter.

This event was always a particular highlight for me (although I knew that some people avoided "Communion Sunday" because the service was so long). The form of the Communion service in the Methodist "Book of Worship" was, I later learned, almost identical to the Anglican service. The manner of receiving Communion was to kneel at the altar rail to receive a little cube of bread and a tiny glass cup of grape juice. Even very small children were allowed to receive "the Lord's Supper," and Methodists practiced "open Communion," that is, anyone who desired to do so could receive, regardless of "church affiliation."

For me, the act of kneeling at the Communion rail, the distinctive taste in my mouth of the mingled bread and "wine," and the words of the minister, "Take and eat, this is Christ's Body which was broken for thee.... This is Christ's Blood which was shed for thee" were powerfully symbolic of something far more profound than simply a "commemorative meal."

("Low church" Protestants did not use real wine for Communion—perhaps a result of the temperance movement in the 19th century. I remember asking about this, since the Bible clearly said "wine," and was told variously that the word "wine" really meant "grape juice" in Bible times, or that Jesus *would* have used grape juice if He could, but in a hot country like Palestine grape juice fermented quickly. I remember one Communion service where the minister could not get grape juice, so he used grape-flavored Kool-Aid.)

Once I made a little "display" in my bedroom of a piece of velvet cloth draped over a table on which I placed a "glow-in-the-dark" plastic cross my aunt had given me, a picture of the Good Shepherd which had been a Christmas present from my Sunday school teacher, a doll goblet filled with red-colored water and a doll plate with a brown clay "loaf" on it. For a time I said my prayers kneeling before this display rather than beside my bed as I usually did.

On Sundays when we did not attend the Methodist Church in town, we went to the Ash Rock Church a half-mile from our farm. This little church was being kept alive by half-a-dozen people who valiantly persisted in holding Sunday school every Sunday, although the last regular preacher to conduct Sunday church services had left in the thirties. I remember one of the members coming to our house to ask my parents if they would support a movement to get a preacher for the church, and especially, if they would become members if this happened.

Ultimately, she did get enough commitments, and my grandfather was asked to consider taking charge of the congregation, though they could not offer him a regular stipend. He consented, and petitioned the Congregational Church for ordination specifically for that purpose. At that time the Congregational Church structure was, as the name implies, decentralized; therefore, my grandfather felt that he could conduct services and choose materials which would be "sound" without interference from the "official" church. He was ordained; and he remained pastor of this church (and I remained a member, even after I no longer lived in the community) until his death in 1962. The congregation grew and flourished under his care.

My grandfather's sermons were always thoughtful and clear, revealing his scholarship and wisdom, his genuine Christian love and concern for his congregation, and his own deep devotion to his Savior. The Ash Rock congregation did not have a youth group, as the Methodist Church in town had. When I was in high school, my boy friend and I went every Sunday night to a neighboring town to attend "Training Union" at the Southern Baptist Church. Training Union was not a youth-oriented group, particularly, but a fair number of "young people" attended. It consisted, as I remember, of a long sermon, a lot of singing of lively Baptist hymns like "Are You Washed in the Blood of the Lamb" accompanied by a piano played in an energetic and florid style. At the end, inevitably, was the "altar call" during which the piano softly played "Just as I Am" while the preacher urgently pleaded with people to "come forward" to "get saved." (Since most of the audience were presumably already saved, you could also "go forward" to ask for special prayers.)

The "altar call" was, without question, deeply moving. After awhile I learned the distinctive improvisational style of piano playing, and found some emotional release in playing the piano during the preacher's impassioned plea.

One summer, when I was about fifteen or sixteen, the Baptists were preparing a group for baptism. The service was going to be conducted at the Solomon River. The idea of being baptized in a river, just as Jesus had been, appealed strongly to me.

Baptists don't believe in "infant baptism"; rather that baptism should be a conscious act of a person old enough to know exactly what it is that he or she is doing. It was a necessary sign of public declaration of one's personal commitment to Christ. This also seemed to me a compelling argument. I felt that it was, truly, necessary to make a public commitment before the Church of one's belief at an age which would give it strong personal meaning. They agreed to baptize me, since they considered my orginal baptism invalid.

I was disappointed to discover that although the Baptists consider baptism necessary for salvation they would only baptize Christians who became members of the Baptist Church. I could not do this. I discussed this with my parents and my grandfather, emphasizing how deeply I wanted to make a formal and public statement confirming my faith to the Church. I asked my grandfather if he could "re-baptize" me. (I had never heard of Confirmation, and, in any case, no such ceremony existed in the non-liturgical Protestant churches.)

The Congregationalists, apparently, had no binding doctrine about baptism; furthermore, I believe my grandfather understood the origin of my desire. So he agreed to baptize me conditionally—"If thou hast not already been baptized, I baptize thee...." It did not take place in the river, as I had hoped, and it was by "sprinkling" rather than by immersion; but I wore the white dress I had made in the expectation of my immersion and the cross my mother had given me for that occasion.

Later, my grandparents took me with them to a church camp in the Rocky Mountains which was sponsored by the Bible Presbyterians, the church to which one of my aunts and her family belonged. Not long ago I found in the back of a New Testament my aunt had given me some of the notes I took from the lectures given there by faculty from Covenant Seminary, the denomination's seminary in St. Louis. One of the things that impressed me most about this experience was that entire families, children and adults, participated in everything together—lectures, games of croquet or badminton, mountain climbing, meals and "kitchen duty," and, of course, the singing and prayers at the end of the day.

In all of my religious upbringing there had been not only strong family solidarity about the Christian faith, but also support for Christian beliefs and moral values from the community—even from the schools—as well. I knew, of course, that not everyone believed as we did, and that even within some churches were ideas which were not consistent with the most fundamental Christian teaching. Once in awhile I had actually had religious "discussions" (more like polite debates) with clergymen over matters of doctrine.

Despite this, however, I was not adequately prepared to meet the challenges I would face when I went away from home to the University when I was seventeen. I was amazed to find the Congregational minister using a sort of "double-talk" in his sermons which gave a thin veneer of Christianity to the latest fashion in secular thinking. I discovered the same ominous situation in the Methodist Church. After awhile I stopped going to church at all while I was at college.

I also encountered the usual barrage of "new ideas" in my classes, and, far away from the sustenance I got at home, I dabbled with fascinating ideas such as existentialism, the various schools of thought in "modern" psychology, and a host of other ideas and ideologies. I remained a Christian, although, as I said, I no longer went to church during the school year, and I probably concealed my belief from others pretty effectively.

In conversation I would sometimes throw out a little "feeler," hoping to find a kindred spirit. Most of my friends were even more confused than I was. The only ones who seemed to take religion seriously were the Catholics. I relished doing intellectual battle with my Catholic friends, challenging the papacy, the Marian dogmas, kidding them about Alexander VI, etc. One entire summer I carried on an intense and lengthy correspondence about religious matters with one of my Catholic friends who was working on a doctoral dissertation on the Stoics.

I was also intensely interested in Judaism, as the root of Christianity, and took courses in Old Testament, History of Judaism, and in the Hebrew language. Many of my friends were Jewish, but none of them were believers—a fact which I found incomprehensible. They seemed to find it fascinating that I was a believing Christian who was also not a Catholic.

If I encountered wrenching challenges to Christianity (and a fair amount of ridicule of Christian beliefs) at the University, I also discovered the aesthetic heritage of my faith. I majored in Art History, and my special field of interest was Late Medieval and Early Renaissance. I taught myself enough Latin to make out inscriptions on paintings and sculpture. I bought records of Gregorian Chant, Ambrosian Chant, Bach's B Minor Mass, Mozart's *Requiem*. I longed to see the windows of Chartres, the soaring vaults of Notre Dame, the austere Cistercian churches of England, Lincoln cathedral, Ely, the Isenheim

Altarpiece, Van Eyck, Giotto, Masaccio, Florence, Rome.

I felt dimly angry with the destruction by the Puritans of beautiful works of human hands dedicated to the glory of God. I understood their belief that they were destroying idols, of course, as Moses ordered the Golden Calf to be destroyed. But what they smashed were not pagan idols. They were desecrating *churches* dedicated to Christ. They were brutalizing visual images of Our Lord, His mother, the writers of the Bible—images over which nameless artists and craftsmen had labored, using their talents and energy to show their love of and reverence for God. In some sense I was scandalized by my own Puritan ancestors whose misguided zeal seemed to deny that any works of man could be good, authentic gifts, however noble or beautiful, no matter how they might inspire their fellow men to revere and honor God.

A deepened sense of history—a realization that some very important things were happening in Christendom between the close of the Apostolic Age and 1519—combined with an awakened sense of Christian aesthetics and profound dismay at the erosion of essential Christian doctrines in the main-line Protestant denominations probably prepared me to be particularly receptive when I eventually ventured into the small Episcopal church in the college town. It was a "high church" parish, and I was delighted to find all the elements of consecrated beauty and ritual missing from "low church" Protestant churches (though the rites were familiar from Methodism) coexisting with authentic Christian teaching which was also intellectually satisfying.

I discussed my attraction to Anglicanism with my family at my first opportunity. My mother told me that she had felt this same attraction and had attended the Episcopal Church when she was in college, but since Episcopal churches were rare in our part of the world she could not, practically speaking, become a member. My grandfather confirmed for me that sound teaching could be found in the Anglican communion, and gave me books from his library to read on the Early Fathers of the Church and essays written by Anglican scholars.

What I did not realize during my student years at the University (located, as it happens, near the banks of the Kansas River) was that all my experiences there had led me to the brink of a deeper and older spiritual stream, with cultural and historical undercurrents I had only begun to comprehend—but also with an intellectual and psychological undertow from which only faith and the beginnings of wisdom could save me.

Considering my strong religious upbringing, and my own personal commitment to the Christian faith, I should have been able to avoid some or most of the hazardous "undertow" of intellectual pride and self-involvement. I am ashamed to say that I did not. I wanted to know everything, and I think I naively believed that I could. I sunk my teeth deeply into the fruit of the "tree of knowledge" looking for the taste of Truth, and instead found it bitter and indigestible.

I found it as difficult to arrange the multitude of shards and bits of personal experience and intellectual information into a spiritually comprehensible pattern as to fix the ever-changing pattern of a kaleidescope. I no longer remember, if I ever really understood, what caused me such anguish, but I do recall that on more than one occasion I was brought so low by despair that only a sense of fidelity to my family who loved me prevented me from suicide. When faith and hope were eclipsed, only the dim but steady light of their love could rescue me. During such times, my prayers, to the extent that I was able to force myself to pray, were more like inarticulate, self-pitying groans to a distant and heedless God who had called me into being only to abandon me.

By the Grace of God, I somehow managed to survive what was not only a crisis of faith, but a crisis of being. Although I survived with my faith intact, for a variety of reasons I did not resume regular Sunday attendance at church. After college I worked in an office in Kansas City which was about equidistant from the Missouri River and the Cathedral. I occasionally went to the Cathedral during lunch hour by myself, and always on Holy Days with a Catholic woman co-worker. (I do not know if "cradle Catholics" really understand that their piety and fidelity is and has always been an important witness to believers and unbelievers alike.)

Naturally, when I went to the Catholic Mass then I was always an outsider. *I* knew it, but perhaps others did not. It was less conspicuous to be an outsider in the days when even Catholics did not always receive Communion. The Second Vatican Council had just begun, then, and no one could possibly have foreseen the changes that would ensue in its wake.

I was living in San Francisco when the announcement came that Mass would be said in the vernacular. I remember discussing this event with a Catholic friend, and recall expressing my concern that the symbolic change that this would effect could be devastating: "Can't Catholics see what has happened to the Protestant churches which have been almost destroyed by 'modernism'? Haven't they noticed what happens when you 'open the windows' to the world?" I was genuinely dismayed by the proposed changes in the Catholic Church. In fact, I believe that the extent to which Protestantism remained a viable system of belief was directly relevant to the continued stabilizing existence of the "monolithic" Catholic Church which had stood for nearly twenty centuries, unchanging as a rock, as a repository of Christian Truth.

The last Latin High Mass I ever saw was on Christmas Eve, just before the "change." I went to the first English Mass celebrated in San Francisco, at St. Ignatius Church on the U.S.F. campus, with a sense of grim fascination. When I heard the congregation badly singing "A Mighty Fortress Is Our God," Luther's hymn, after the awkward

English of the service, I was seized by a profound sadness. The Catholic Church, as it had always and everywhere been, would no longer be there for the rest of us.

While I was still living in San Francisco, I decided to enroll in a philosophy course in Existentialism at the University of California. The professor gave a critical analysis of existentialism which was unexpectedly astringent and enlightening. Intrigued, I enrolled in other courses taught by C. Franklin Kelly, and for the first time was introduced in some depth to the philosophy of Thomas Aquinas, and, later, to the neo-Thomists of the twentieth century.

This "discovery" of Thomistic philosophy was intensely exhiliarating, both intellectually and spiritually. For years I had struggled with the Kantian "leap of faith," in which, by an act of will one must suspend reason for belief. I was willing to do this, considering the alternative, but it produced a profound sense of disquiet. It seemed necessary to say, for example, that "this religious Truth may not make any *sense*, but I *will* believe it, because to do otherwise involves certain destruction." *Is* one ultimately required to deny the intellect in order to have and maintain faith? Need the intellect always lead to nihilism? Is it irretrievably fallen? Is its sacrifice, in fact, the "cross" Christians are required to carry?

In my "discovery" of Aquinas, I experienced an almost giddy sense of relief and release, much like I imagined Abraham must have felt when the Angel told him he did not have to kill Isaac. In Thomistic philosophy the salvability of the intellect and its reintegration as an inseparable part of human Being could be affirmed.

Not long after this I moved to New York, and as quickly as possible was confirmed in the Episcopal Church. On Sundays I worshipped at my parish, Grace Church, a beautiful "English Gothic" structure in Greenwich Village, complete with a tiny "close"; on weekdays I attended daily Mass at Trinity Church on Wall

Street. I had, I thought, found the perfect "via media" which contained everything good in the Catholic tradition—the "vertical dimension" of the liturgy, the satisfying beauty of the ritual, the music, and the familiar, yet sacred and timeless language, King James English—without any of the troublesome papal and Marian dogmas.

I was contemplating joining one of the Anglican religious orders when I met James Hitchcock, a young Catholic historian who had been teaching at St. John's University, his first job after receiving his Ph.D. from Princeton. It was, I sincerely believe, a providential meeting. A Reformation scholar, he understood and respected my religious heritage. He understood the history of Anglicanism vastly better than I did, a fact which I found both intriguing and eventually useful.

We discovered at once a spiritual and intellectual affinity so encompassing and so full of promise that we almost immediately decided to marry. Our religious differences seemed actually to be complementary rather than conflicting.

Jim had already accepted a position for the coming academic year in his native St. Louis, a city which I'd never visited. His first gifts to me were the Collected Poems of T. S. Eliot, an Anglican and a former St. Louisan, and a glass unicorn like the one in "The Glass Menagerie," a play written by another famous St. Louis-born author.

That August, after Jim returned from a research trip to England, we set out for St. Louis. I crossed the Mississippi for the first time at dusk, and saw just above the levee the austerely elegant limestone Basilica of St. Louis, King of France, where, although I did not know it at the time, we were to be married barely three months later, on the Saturday after Thanksgiving, 1966.

In the music at our wedding we truly had the "best of both worlds"—a choir sung both a Scarlatti *Exultet* and one of the best hymns ever written, *Salve Festa Dies* (Hail Thee, Festival Day) to the musical setting of Anglican Ralph Vaughn Williams. That I could not receive the elements of Communion with my husband on this day caused only momentary sadness and could not sully the joy of the genuine unity of heart and mind which the ceremony otherwise expressed.

The wedding, in fact, announced the religious *leitmotiv* for the first several years of our marriage. Each of us participated as fully as possible in the other's parish life. I joined the only "high church" parish in St. Louis, and for several years we "double-dipped" every Sunday morning, even after our children were born, attending both parishes. Our children were baptized in the Roman Catholic Church by a Roman Catholic priest with an Anglo-Catholic priest giving a blessing.

If our religious life together was in some sense a "working model" of "aggiornamento"—ecumenical in the best sense—we soon observed an alarmingly precipitous shift in both our churches. The "open windows to the world" seemed to be letting more dangerous pollutants *in* than sending illuminating light *out*. The radical changes in the Roman Catholic liturgy which were intended to make the faith more immediate and personal to believers was having the unexpected effect of destroying the idea of the sacred. The foment of widespread social unrest at the time exacerbated an already precarious situation in all Christian churches, but the confusing effect was more dramatically visible in the Catholic Church.

For a time, the changes were less noticeable, on the surface, in my Anglo-Catholic parish. The liturgy was, for several more years, unaltered. If we suffered through various "experimental liturgies" and the woeful "relevant" music in the Catholic Church, we could be assured of a traditional Solemn High Mass, with litanies, Anglican Chant and "smoke and bells" in my parish.

Although it crossed my mind several times, I did not seriously consider becoming a Roman Catholic. Besides my doctrinal reservations, I was quite intimately acquainted with the serious erosion of orthodoxy in the Catholic Church; furthermore, I found the "new liturgy" often almost unbearably ugly. I felt that I should lend whatever small effort I could to prevent further damage to Anglicanism. Jim and I often traded "atrocity stories," and found a sort of grim entertainment in noting whose Church had just committed the worst "trendy" outrage.

The Supreme Court decision of 1973, which overturned by fiat a universal moral assumption of two millennia, opened a chasm in Western culture so vast and deep and so cataclysmic in its after-shocks that it can be safely said that no individual, no human institution was unaffected by it.

The Catholic Church, by immediate and vigorous action, gave evidence of its authentic role as a "sign of contradiction" in—and witness to—the world. The Episcopal Church, at its next General Convention barely three years later, not only capitulated to the *Zeitgeist* in the matter of abortion, but, while they were at it, also scrapped the traditional book of Common Prayer which had been substantially unchanged since 1549, and unilaterally departed from Catholic (and Anglican) tradition by approving the ordination of women, including avowed lesbians, to the priesthood.

My own realization that the Episcopal Church was no longer a viable repository of orthodox Christianity came somewhat earlier than the fateful General Convention of 1976, when the consecration as bishop of a man who had written books denying the divinity of Christ, and whose views were very well known, was approved by a majority of the incumbent bishops. This made it abundantly clear that there really was no *magisterium* in the Episcopal Church.

The effect of these events was stunning. I was aston-ished to discover that at least two prominent women in my parish were pro-abortion activists. The woman who taught me traditional Catholic altar work in the most exacting detail became a "priest," and the vestry approved the candidacy for "priesthood" a woman who was openly co-habitating. Wild experimental liturgies made a mock-ery of the Mass. One All Saints' Day the celebrant was "vested" in a skeleton costume, the female sub-deacon was dressed as a "fallen angel" and the deacon wore a torn, upside-down American flag under a black Good Friday cope.

I stopped attending services there, of course. I have never been inside an Episcopal Church again.

In September of 1977, less than a year after the General Convention, a conference was held in St. Louis sponsored by an "underground group" of disenfran-chised Episcopalians called the Fellowship of Concerned Churchmen. It was attended by about eighteen-hundred clergy and laity. Many of the priests who came had been deposed for refusal to accept the General Convention's mandates.

The momentum generated at this conference led to the formation of a "continuing Anglican Church" move-ment, and to the hasty formation of parishes which quickly organized themselves into dioceses and elected four bishops, who were consecrated in a Lutheran Church in Denver the following January. Although there were problems with this new movement almost from the start, it seemed extremely promising, and was almost certainly the *only* way that those of us who were deeply involved in its formation could see to salvage the "faithful remnant" and begin the laborious process of re-establishing the broken Church.

Within a few months, however, deep fissures began to appear within the movement. What had held Anglicanism ("high," "low" and "broad church") together had been

the Book of Common Prayer, it seemed. When this fragile
shell was broken it proved impossible to put it back
together again—even when there was fundamental agree-
ment on the essentials of the Faith.

The movement was beseiged with every possible
human failing in the most exaggerated form. The new
parishes, started with such high hopes, began to split. At
the first Provincial Synod after the bishops were consecrated, two of the bishops walked out in disputes over the
proposed constitution. A desperate clergy shortage within
the movement led to hasty acceptance of some priests and
former priests who were unqualified (or worse) and who
did much damage.

For several years, I assisted the foundering national
Church (called the Anglican Catholic Church) and the
struggling local parish as best I could. Our parish was one
of the first to be formed in the movement, and it never
had a resident Rector. For this reason, largely, it dwindled
from about seventy active members to nine.

At about the same time that I became involved with
the struggle to preserve a remnant of Anglicanism, I
began to write regularly for Roman Catholic publications,
under my maiden name, Helen Hull. While I felt a deep
sense of loyalty to my embattled Anglican parish, and
drew much spiritual sustenance from the beauty and
dignity and orderliness of the Mass which retained the
"comfortable words" of the Anglican Prayer Book, even in
our catacomb situation, I gradually came to realize
through my writing about contemporary religious and
social issues, that the real battle between Christianity (and
the moral values and social structures based on Christian
principles) and an alien ideology which sought to destroy
it was located in the Roman Catholic Church. The Catholic Church is a symbol of all Christianity, and is its greatest and most potent representative.

Because of Rome's recognition of the chaos in Anglicanism which left Catholic Anglicans stranded without

the sacraments (many of us went to great lengths to maintain that we were, indeed, Catholics), the Vatican made a profound gesture of charity to these Christians *in extremis* by allowing us to receive the benefit of sacraments in the Roman Church when we were deprived of them. I thus began to attend weekday Mass at our Catholic parish as often as I could. I am convinced, now, that the grace which I received as a result was the single most powerful factor in overcoming my "invincible ignorance."

It became strikingly clear to me that the teaching authority of the Catholic Church alone could consistently affirm and maintain Christian Truth. My increasing knowledge of the effects of feminist ideology made me realize the importance of the role of Mary in salvation history. That such a pope as John Paul II could be given to Christianity in this age of chaos and cultural upheavals seemed to me a clear sign that the Holy Spirit truly was with this Church—this *Roman* Catholic Church. If this scandalized my Anglo-catholic-protestant-evangelical soul, how much greater is the "scandal of particularity" of the Incarnation of God as Jesus of Nazareth?

I, frankly, miss the Anglican liturgy—sometimes rather acutely. I sometimes long to hear Plain Chant, the wonderful hymns well-sung, the odor of incense, the "Last Gospel." Sometimes, at a sixties-style guitar Mass, I feel like a stranger in a strange land. But I am not. I came as a stranger to *God's* land.

Far from denying my own religious heritage, I have come back to that Faith which saints believed of old. I am a Catholic—because it is within the Catholic Church that I can affirm the Christian Truth which I was taught as a child, and have believed, by the Grace of God, all of my life. I am a Catholic—because it is here that the Faith of my fathers is living still. Here I stand. I can do no other.

With God's help, I hope to be useful to His Holy Church.

Helen Hull Hitchcock *is the wife of James F. Hitchcock and mother of four daughters—Alexandra, Consuelo, Hilary and Louisa. The Hitch- cocks live in St. Louis. After graduation from the University of Kansas, Mrs. Hitchcock worked for several years as an insurance underwriter in Kansas City, San Francisco and New York. Since 1978 she has been a frequent contributor to Catholic periodicals. In 1984, along with several friends, she organized* Women for Faith and Family, *a movement of Catholic women which circulated the* Affirmation for Catholic Women, *a statement of fidelity to and unity with Church teachings. The* Affirma- tion *has been signed by about 40,000 women, including Mother Teresa of Calcutta.*

From Evangelicalism to Rome

Thomas Howard

My own pilgrimage towards Rome is, in some respects, not unlike the pilgrimage of other, better-known converts, in that it began in Evangelicalism. (Both Newman and Monsignor Knox, for example, had similar forms of spirituality in their backgrounds.)

Evangelicalism is not an easy word to define, not because there is anything complicated about the word itself, but rather because the word becomes mixed up in people's minds with "evangelism," and also, because it has so many possible usages. Evangelism, of course, is nothing more than the business of spreading the Christian Gospel, whether that means St. Peter preaching at Pentecost, St. Ninian going off to the Picts in the fourth century, St. Francis Xavier to the Japanese in the sixteenth, or a man or woman nowadays trying to tell someone just what it is that Christians do believe.

The word Evangelicalism, on the other hand, is like the mythical hydra with all of its heads: as soon as you think you've taken care of one head, you find half a dozen more sprouting. For example, the word "evangelical" itself originally referred (and should always refer, really) simply to the Gospel. All Christians are evangelical in this sense: they are people of the Gospel. The Church talks about the "evangelical counsels," which means what the Church teaches about the Gospel. But then, as history went on, the word fell into disuse, at least among ordinary folk, until it surfaced in Germany after the Reformation, when it began to be used to refer to denominations that were non-Catholic. Nowadays, *evangelische* is virtually synonymous with "Protestant" in northern Europe. The word has a slightly different slant in England, where, in the eighteenth century Anglican Church, under the influence of men like John Wesley and George Whitefield, there grew up an extremely vigorous form of personal piety which de-emphasized the sacramental and "churchly" aspects of the Faith, and stressed, very fervently, such matters as inner zeal, extempore prayer, personal Bible reading, and testimony (meaning a sprightly readiness on the part of the laity to speak up about the Faith at any time of the day or night). The particular doctrines that were brought to the fore were such perfectly orthodox matters as salvation by grace through Christ's atoning death, the indwelling of the Holy Ghost in each believer, the "new life in Christ" such as St. Paul describes in all of his epistles, and an almost breathless expectation of "the imminent return of Christ"—a doctrine always held by the Church, of course, but ordinarily thought of in more sombre terms such as "The Last Trump."

In America, evangelicalism came eventually to refer to an *outlook* rather than to any single Protestant denomination, or even to any specific doctrinal position. Its history in America includes the various "revivals" in the eighteenth and nineteenth centuries, with names like John Wesley (who came from England), Charles G. Finney, D. L. Moody, Billy Sunday, and Billy Graham, looming very large in this connection. Hence, the word does ordinarily imply an especially ardent form of Christian profession. Evangelicals are to be found scattered throughout all Protestant denominations; but they also have had a lively history of starting literally hundreds of new, small denominations. In each case the reason for the split from the parent body has been some question of doctrine or church practice in which the "evangelical" faction felt that the older church was not being faithful to the Bible.

In this sense, oddly, evangelicals have much more in common with Roman Catholics than they do with liberal Protestants, since both the evangelicals and the Catholics unabashedly believe the undiluted, miraculous account of the events that brought salvation to us: the Virgin Birth, Christ's miracles, the Resurrection, the Ascension, and so forth. An evangelical can stoutly recite every syllable of the ancient creeds, and mean exactly what he is saying, whereas many Protestants (and perhaps nowadays, alas, quite a few Catholics?) have to make all sorts of mental reservations, since they aren't sure that thoroughly modern people can quite *buy* all those extraordinary New Testament stories.

I should mention something of the form which evangelical piety takes, since it is that which forms the backdrop to my own pilgrimage—indeed, which nourished me and schooled my imagination.

Evangelical worship, as most Catholics know, tends to look informal, because it is, by liturgical standards. But that informality stretches from the happy, chatty sort of thing you might find in a small country church where the minister presides in a necktie and light blue doubleknit leisure suit; to immense auditoriums holding thousands of people, where the minister is robed in an academic gown and the choir is massed across the entire front of the church in billowing tan satin robes, and where a genuine but friendly solemnity presides over the program. Most evangelicals think that the word "liturgy" refers to being *formal* in church, and so, inasmuch as they decide to have a prayer or some congregational responses printed up in the leaflet, or have the choir sing the Sevenfold Amen after the long "pastoral prayer," they might say, "Oh—our church is very liturgical." It is difficult for a Catholic to get across to them the idea that liturgy refers to nothing else than to the Eucharistic mystery, and has nothing to do with oratorical sonorities from the pulpit, satin gowns, or ushers in striped trousers and morning coats. A Catholic knows that the liturgy can be celebrated on the hood of a jeep if necessary, and that what is occurring in that instance is just as real as what occurs at a Pontifical High Mass in St. John Lateran.

The particular church in which I grew up was a friendly little place. They had no doctrinal oddities in the sense that this may be said of various *cults*. (Catholics must try to remember that evangelicals take precisely the same view of cults as the Church does: the cults are heretical, say the evangelicals, because they have either muddled, or added to, the apostolic Faith). The eleven o'clock worship service in our church followed the ordinary Protestant sequence: a hymn, a prayer, some Scripture readings, more hymns, possibly a vocal solo, the collection, then an excessively long sermon, then another hymn, and a final prayer. We remained seated for most of it. Kneeling, in our view, would have constituted a throwback to the Middle Ages, when (we felt) Christians had scarcely any notion at all as to what was going on up front. To a Catholic, our worship would have looked like a friendly meeting. There was no altar: a pulpit dominated the front of the church. A wooden table for the once-monthly Communion Service stood on the floor, below the pulpit.

By far the most important task of the church, in the evangelical view, is to instruct the people in the Bible, and to make zealous, articulate, knowledgeable and mature believers out of them. You are "saved" at the instant when you accept the Lord Jesus Christ as your personal Saviour. For evangelicals that precise phraseology is virtually canonical in its authority and indispensability, and unless a Christian is prepared to phrase his account of his salvation in exactly that vocabulary, an evangelical will feel uneasy about that person's Christian profession. So the first job is to make sure everyone is saved—that is,

that they consciously believe in the Lord Jesus Christ as
their personal Saviour, and can say so quite forthrightly.
(Once again, Catholics have to remember that the early
Church had a vigour and lay zeal very much like this: it is
not something new in Christian piety.) Baptism, for most
evangelicals, should occur at a point in your life when you
are ready, as a responsible and conscious believer, to say
to the Church and to the world, "I now take my place as
an active, confessed Christian." Nothing *occurs* at baptism,
in this view. No sacramental grace is conferred. It is
strictly a public announcement of your faith. (Calvinists
and Lutherans and Anglicans, many of whom are otherwise evangelical, do have a somewhat more "sacramental" view of baptism, and will acknowledge that the rite
does, in some sense, constitute a child's initiation into
the household of God). It would be the Baptist and
"anabaptist"—theologically speaking, the "Zwinglian,"
after the Reformer in Zurich—view that would be the
most widespread in general American evangelical circles.
Certainly the church in which I grew up took this view.

Because teaching the Bible is the principle activity of
the church, evangelical Sunday Schools (the equivalent of
C.C.D.) are powerhouses of activity. There is an enormous industry producing Sunday School materials, and,
if what we want is to get small children both familiar with
the whole Bible *and* interested in it, then one would have
to say that it is a successful industry. There is no nonsense
about tiptoeing in gingerly with timid efforts to "meet the
modern kids where they are." Like the Jews, the evangelicals assume that there is an immense body of material to
be learned, and that it is crucial because it is God's Word,
and so we had better get cracking. (The old Baltimore
Catechism idea would be a similar approach.) The creativity and resourcefulness of evangelicals in carrying forward
this enterprise is almost unimaginable to people who
haven't been through the program. Sunday School, youth
groups, daily vacation Bible schools, summer conferences

at sporty lakeside resorts, correspondence courses, one-on-one "discipling," and a hundred other techniques, are used, with one object in mind: to get the Christian laity into the Bible, and to get them advancing spiritually. It would all be analogous to what the Church has traditionally called "spiritual formation," although evangelicals have never heard that term.

One activity that was a staple in my own church, and which might amuse Catholics if they heard about it, was a game called a "sword drill." The sword was the Bible, since St. Paul calls the Bible "the sword of the Spirit" in Ephesians 6. The idea was for everyone in the youth group to sit at the ready, Bible in hand, and, when the teacher barked out a text—"Habakkuk 1:3, *Charge!*", or "Second Timothy 3:15, *Charge!*"—to leaf madly through the Bible until you found the verse, and pop up and read it out. The first one to do so was the winner. Of course, we soon came to the place where there was very little "leafing through," since we knew exactly where Habakkuk or Second Timothy were to be found, and could open the Bible almost to the very page the minute any text was announced. The whole point of this exercise was to make us adept at using the Scriptures, like the Old Testament Jews, who knew the law and the prophets better than they knew their own names. Liberal Protestants tended to harrumph at this eager approach to the Bible, looking on it all as a form of bibliolatry perhaps: but I myself have never regretted having been run through those paces. It certainly didn't hurt me, and, as an English teacher now, I have often thought that if I knew where to find quotes in Shakespeare as readily as I do quotes in the Bible, I'd be very happy.

I would have to say that the household in which I grew up was, without any doubt, the major factor in my early spiritual formation. There were six children. Things were run on clockwork order, since both my father and my mother were tidy and punctual types, and taught us these virtues. Also, it was, in effect, a "Victorian" household, if by that we mean one that held gladly to traditional canons of courtesy, manners, and morality. Any Catholic household would have shared the whole outlook, except that, as evangelicals, we added the various "taboos" which had sprung from evangelicalism's revivalist roots in the eighteenth and nineteenth centuries: no smoking, no alcohol, no dancing, no cards, and no movies. Even the words "darn" and "heck" were frowned upon, since they were "minced oaths."

And yet it was a hilarious and rollicking household. We laughed most of the time. Obedience was non-negotiable: but this turns out to be a form of freedom, not bondage, for children who learn it early, and it prepares us for one of the most profound Christian mysteries, namely, the sense in which bondage to Christ is the true and glorious liberty for which we were all made in the first place.

My father was a tall, lean, gentlemanly figure who wore a Phi Beta Kappa key on a gold chain across his waistcoat and strode to the suburban railroad station at exactly the same minute every morning to catch the train to Philadelphia, where he was the editor of a religious weekly journal that enjoyed a place of immense dignity in American Protestantism. He had a droll, dry way of telling us tales of his own misfortunes. He was a passionate fly-fisherman, happiest in the tiny brooks in the White Mountains in New Hampshire. He was also a bird-watcher, and could imitate the calls of dozens of birds. When he would take us on bird hikes, he could get the wood peewees or olive-sided flycatchers or black-capped chickadees to come a perch right over our heads on the twigs by imitating their whistles.

He arose every day at about 5:00 a.m., for an hour of Bible reading and prayer in his study. Then, after breakfast, he would lead us all in family prayers, which included the singing of a hymn (Protestantism has an immensely rich treasury of hymnody, and I am bound-lessly thankful for all the singing we did at home), the reading of a short section from the Bible, then, with all of us kneeling, an extempore prayer committing us all to the Lord's care for the day, and ending with the Lord's Prayer, recited together. After dinner at night, while we were still seated at the table, my father would again read a short bit of the Bible and lead us in a prayer. When we went to bed, either he or my mother would come in and pray with us before they kissed us good-night.

My recent conversion to Roman Catholicism has puz-zled and troubled most of the evangelicals who know me. Why (it is asked—quite understandably)—*why* would a man want to leave that lovely, warm, fervent religion, and take up Roman Catholicism, which, from the evangelical point of view, so often appears desultory ("Catholics don't speak *up* about the Lord!") and so spotty ("Look at all the millions of Catholics in foreign countries whose religion is scarcely distinguishable from their local pagan-ism!") and so smudged ("My word—look at all those terrible Borgias, and the Babylonian Captivity of the Church, and the Inquisition, and simony, and the impen-etrable politics of the Curia, and the Jesuits slipping into Elizabethan England all hugger-mugger, and so forth and so forth!").

These tend to be the sort of thing that trouble evan-gelicals about the Catholic Church, together with the weightier matters of the papacy and the Marian dogmas. Like the Donatists of the fourth century with whom St. Augustine struggled, the evangelicals want the Church to *look like* what it *is*. Since it is the Bride of Christ, it ought to be made up of people whose lives are mani-festly pure and holy. Now, very few evangelicals would suggest themselves as Exhibit A of what the Bride of Christ should look like. Nevertheless, they would feel that it is worth starting over and over and over again with the Church, no matter how much splitting and schism this may require, just to keep the thing pure. It was on this point, among others, that St. Augustine attacked the Donatists. And it is for this reason that there are so many hundreds of very small evangelical denominations and congregations. Some of the "cardinal" parishes in evangelicalism are totally independent: the minister is accountable to no bishop or synod or superior of any description.

This tendency began to trouble me, as the years went by. While I cannot pretend that the first stirrings in my inner being which eventually landed me at the threshold of Rome were any such sophisticated historical matters as Augustinianism vs. Donatism, nevertheless, one of the factors which eventually lodged itself at the center of my consciousness was the fact that, if the Church is anything at all other than a mere clutter, it is apostolic. There has got to be a Magisterium, and not just a clamor of voices. Christianity is not analogous to Islam—a religion of the Book alone. Christianity is built on the foundation of the apostles and prophets, says St. Paul in Ephesians 2:20. *Credo in...unam sanctam catholicam et apostolicam Ecclesiam,* we say in the Creed. Christianity is no mere set of beliefs or abstract ethical or theological system. Presumably God could have brought about our redemption by waving a wand and saying, "Be redeemed, all you lost souls." But he would have had to be a god other than the one we know him to be to have done things that way. He seems to do things "physically," so to speak. Creation: the calling of Abraham and Israel, with all of those stone altars, blood, burned fat, and incense; then Annunciation and Nativity, with all of the obstetrics and gynaecology entailed there; then thirty years of carpentry; then Passion and Crucifixion; then Resurrection (wouldn't it have been nicer if he had left the physical part of this religion behind in the tomb?); and then the Ascension—in some ways the worst scandal of all: human flesh raised to the midmost mysteries of the Blessed Trinity? Come, who can believe all this? And then Eucharist: his flesh and blood for our food and drink?

Language staggers. We hardly know what we are saying. But as St. Thomas points out in his great *Tantum Ergo Sacramentum,* faith comes to the rescue of our senses and our intellect.

One thing we do know: God has achieved our redemption, not by mere edict, trumpeted from afar and left for us in a book. Rather, he has become one of us, and, more than that, has called us to be his Body. He took his flesh *ex Maria Virgine;* and he conferred almost unbearably august authority and unction on other mere humans, namely the apostles. If we are to believe his words to them, and St. Paul's teaching about his own apostolic authority, and then the witness of the men who had themselves, some of them, been taught by the apostles—Ignatius and Clement and Polycarp and Irenaeus and Justin—then we find indeed one, holy, catholic, and apostolic Church, and not a clutter of privately launched enterprises, no matter how earnest or laudable those enterprises might be.

Anyone who has ever read conversion stories is on familiar ground here. They all speak of this: Newman, Knox, Chesterton. It is the old question of catholicity and apostolicity. What is the Church? Where is the Church? Also, it entails the question of teaching authority. All the heresiarchs believed in the inspiration of the Bible. But who has the warrant to *teach* the Scriptures? Anyone? Everyone? If we consult the early Church, we find that it was the bishops in council who said to the faithful, "*This* is the apostolic faith. That which you hear being taught over there is heresy." Christ never doomed his Church to a perennial, *ad hoc* caucus of the whole, with all matters of morals and dogma forever on the table, forever up for grabs. But alas, this turns out to be the case where there is no Magisterium.

I eventually found myself crowded along to the place where I either had to say, "But none of this matters: all God wants is for us to be earnest and fervent," or I had to say, "Hum. Independence won't do. That is not the apostolic pattern." Who am I to dissociate myself from this 2000-year-old train of apostles, fathers, bishops, martyrs, confessors, doctors, widows, virgins, and infants, who testify to what Christ's Church is? Of course I know, as any Catholic or evangelical knows, all the horror stories that anyone can trot out about the history of the Church. And certainly I know what troubled Luther and Calvin— matters that also troubled Cardinal Contarini, von Staupitz, Cardinal Ximenez, St. Ignatius, Erasmus, and St. Thomas More. But do I draw my skirts about me and stand fastidiously apart from the only Church we have? There is only one run-through of history, we might say. We get only one "take," as a film director might say. I must stand with this continuum that is there, and has been there from the beginning.

Some such line of thought bore itself in upon me as the years went by, until I found that I could no longer stand apart. I had moved, at the age of 27, in 1962, from free-church evangelicalism to Anglicanism, which is at least a step towards taking history and catholicity and apostolicity seriously. But eventually I found myself unable to answer my own question: "Why tarry in Canterbury forever? Rome is there. Rome has nothing to prove."

The other principal factor in my pilgrimage was the matter of sacrament. This, of course, opens out onto immense topics which eventually involve what sort of world this is we inhabit, and what sort of creature we are, and indeed, what sort of God, God is. Libraries have been written about this. Perhaps I may put things in my own words thus.

In the ancient Eucharistic liturgy, I find the place where the crushing mystery of our mortal existence, with all of its bliss and its agony, touches the Eternal Mystery.

There is no answer at all to the riddle of human existence, and especially of human suffering and human sin, if it is not to be found in the mystery of oblation—of sacrifice—of offering. All Christian believers find that mystery brought to a point at the Cross. Here we find the God who reveals himself, not as the One who will speak the formula that unlocks the riddle, but rather as the One who takes on himself the whole of our suffering and our sin. And—mystery of mysteries—he invites us into his own self-immolation there. "Ye are a royal priesthood," says St. Peter. "I am crucified with Christ," says St. Paul, and, "I fill up that which is behind of the suffering of Christ." Surely if these words mean anything at all, they mean that we are invited into the mystery of Christ's own self-offering, to make our lives and our sufferings one with his, not merely for our own comfort, but for the life of the world. Do we add something to his merits? Certainly not. But the Church shares his priesthood; the Church is his Body, which has no purpose other than to be broken, like bread, for the life of the world. This is what the Mass is about. This is what the mystery of worship brings us to. A merely verbalist, propositionalist, disembodied religion of preaching does not go to the heart of the Gospel.

I pray, as all Christians must, for the unity of the Church. I love the evangelicals, and thank God for their zeal, their pellucid fidelity to the Bible, their courage, and their energy. None of us knows just what will occur in the world and the Church between now and the Parousia. Will all Christians return to that one fellowship whose visible sign in our history is the See of Peter? Who knows? I am one of the ones who hope so. In the early Church they had eventually to warn people against being too eager for martyrdom, so none of us is permitted to *wish* for persecution (and, heaven knows, I might be the first to crumble and recant under the thumbscrews). But no doubt most of us have at least a small question that flickers across the margin of our imagination from time to time: "Will it be the flames, or the lions, or the Gulag, that drives all true Christians together eventually?"

God alone knows the answers to those questions. I wish no Christian ill. But I do hope that we might, in our history, see the visible fulfillment of the Lord's words, "And there shall be one fold, and one shepherd."

Thomas T. Howard's *field is medieval and renaissance English litera-ture. Dr. Howard also teaches courses in C.S. Lewis, J.R.R. Tolkien, and Charles Williams, and on the American Catholic novelist Flannery O'Con-nor and Walker Percy. Dr. Howard's books include:* Christ the Tiger; An Antique Drum; Once Upon a Time God; Splendor in the Ordinary; The Liturgy Explained; the Achievement of C.S. Lewis; The Novels of Charles Williams; Evangelical Is Not Enough; Christianity: The True Humanism (*with J.I. Packer*). *His articles have appeared in* The New York Times Book Review; Redbook; Catholic Digest; New Oxford Review; Christianity Today; Eternity; Studies in the Literary Imagination; Christian Scholar's Review; Modern Age; The Re-formed Journal; The Episcopal Times; *etc. Dr. Howard is married to the former Lovelace Oden. They have two children: a daughter, Gallaudet, and a son, Charles. They live in Beverly Farms, Massachusetts.*

Hauled Aboard
the Ark

Peter Kreeft

I was born into a loving, believing community, a Protestant "mother church" (the Reformed Church) which, though it had not for me the fullness of the faith, had strong and genuine piety. I believed, mainly because of the good example of my parents and my church. The faith of my parents, Sunday School teachers, ministers, and relatives made a real difference to their lives, a difference big enough to compensate for many shortcomings. "Love covers a multitude of sins."

I was taught what C. S. Lewis calls "mere Christianity," essentially the Bible. But no one reads the Bible as an extraterrestrial or an angel; our church community provides the colored glasses through which we read, and the framework, or horizon, or limits within which we understand. My "glasses," were of Dutch Reformed Calvinist construction, and my limiting framework stopped very far short of anything "Catholic." The Catholic Church was regarded with utmost suspicion. In the world of the forties and fifties in which I grew up, that suspicion may have been equally reciprocated by most Catholics. Each group believed that most of the other group were probably on the road to hell. Christian ecumenism and understanding has made astonishing strides since then.

Dutch Calvinists, like most conservative Protestants, sincerely believed that Catholicism was not only heresy but idolatry; that Catholics worshipped the Church, the Pope, Mary, saints, images, and who knows what else;

166

that the Church had added some inane "traditions of men" to the Word of God, traditions and doctrines that obviously contradicted it (how could they not see this? I wondered); and, most important of all, that Catholics believed "another gospel," another religion, that they didn't even know how to get to Heaven: they tried to pile up brownie points with God with their good works, trying to work their way in instead of trusting in Jesus as their Savior. They never read the Bible, obviously.

I was never taught to hate Catholics, but to pity them and to fear their errors. I learned a serious concern for truth that to this day I find sadly missing in many Catholic circles. The typical Calvinist anti-Catholic attitude I knew was not so much prejudice, judgment with no concern for evidence, but judgment based on apparent and false evidence: sincere mistakes rather than dishonest rationalizations.

Though I thought it pagan rather than Christian, the richness and mystery of Catholicism fascinated me—the very dimensions which avant-garde liturgists have been busy dismantling since the Silly Sixties. (When God saw that the Church in America lacked persecutions, he sent them liturgists.)

The first independent idea about religion I ever remember thinking was a question I asked my father, an elder in the church, a good and wise and holy man. I was amazed that he couldn't answer it. "Why do we Calvinists have the whole truth and no one else? We're so few. How could God leave the rest of the world in error? Especially the rest of the Christian churches?" Since no good answer seemed forthcoming, I then came to the explosive conclusion that the truth about God was more mysterious—more wonderfully and uncomfortably mysterious—than anything any of us could ever fully comprehend. (Calvinists would not deny that, but they do not usually teach it either. They are strong on God's "sovereignty," but weak on the richness of God's mystery.) That conviction, that the truth is always infinitely more than anyone can *have*, has not diminished. Not even all the infallible creeds are a container for all that is God.

I also realized at a very young age, obscurely but strongly, that the truth about God had to be far simpler than I had been taught, as well as far more complex and mysterious. I remember surprising my father with this realization (which was certainly because of God's grace rather than my intelligence, for I was only about eight, I think): "Dad, everything we learn in church and everything in the Bible comes down to just one thing, doesn't it? There's only one thing we have to worry about, isn't there?" "Why, no, I don't see that. There are many things. What do you mean?" "I mean that all God wants us to do—all the time—is to ask Him what He wants us to do, and then do it. That covers everything, doesn't it? Instead of asking ourselves, ask God." Surprised, my father replied, "You know, you're right."

After eight years of public elementary school, my parents offered me a choice between two high schools: public or Christian (Calvinist), and I chose the latter, even though it meant leaving old friends. Eastern Christian High School was run by a sister denomination, the Christian Reformed Church. Asking myself now why I made that choice, I cannot say. Providence often works in obscurity. I was not a remarkably religious kid, and loved the New York Giants baseball team with considerable more passion and less guilt than I loved God.

I won an essay contest in high school with a meditation on Dostoyevski's story "The Grand Inquisitor," interpreted as an anti-Catholic, anti-authoritarian cautionary tale. The Church, like Communism, seemed a great, dark, totalitarian threat.

I then went to Calvin College, the Christian Reformed college which has such a great influence for its small size and provincial locale (Grand Rapids, Michigan) because it takes both its faith and its scholarship very seriously. I registered as a pre-seminary student because, though I did not think I was personally "called" by God to be a clergyman, I thought I might "give it a try." I was deeply impressed by the caption under a picture of Christ on the cross: "This is what I did for thee. What will you do for Me?"

But in college I quickly fell in love with English, and then Philosophy, and thus twice changed my major. Both subjects were widening my appreciation of the history of Western civilization and therefore of things Catholic. The first serious doubt about my anti-Catholic beliefs was planted in my mind by my roommate, who was becoming an Anglican: "Why don't Protestants pray to saints? There's nothing wrong in you asking me to pray for you, is there? Why not ask the dead, then, if we believe they're alive with God in Heaven, part of the 'great cloud of witnesses' that surrounds us (Hebrews 11)?" It was the first serious question I had absolutely no answer to, and that bothered me. I attended Anglican liturgy with my roommate and was enthralled by the same things that captivated Tom Howard (see his essay in this volume) and many others: not just the aesthetic beauty but the full-ness, the solidity, the moreness of it all.

I remember a church service I went to while at Calvin, in the Wealthy Street Baptist Temple (fundamentalist). I had never heard such faith and conviction, such joy in the music, such love of Jesus. I needed to focus my aroused love of God on an object. But God is invisible, and we are not angels. There was no religious object in the church. It was a bare, Protestant church; images were "idols." I suddenly understood why Protestants were so subjectivis-tic: their love of God had no visible object to focus it. The living water welling up from within had no material river bed, no shores, to direct its flow to the far divine sea. It rushed back upon itself and became a pool of froth.

Then I caught sight of a Catholic spy in the Protestant camp: a gold cross atop the pole of the church flag.

Adoring Christ required using that symbol. The alternative was the froth. My gratitude to the Catholic Church for this one relic, this remnant, of her riches, was immense. For this good Protestant water to flow, there had to be Catholic aqueducts. To change the metaphor, I had been told that reliance on external things was a "crutch." I now realized that I was a cripple. And I thanked the Catholic "hospital" (that's what the Church is) for responding to my needs.

Perhaps, I thought, these good Protestant people could worship like angels, but I could not. Then I realized that they couldn't either. Their ears were using crutches but not their eyes. They used beautiful hymns, for which I would gladly exchange the new, flat, unmusical, wimpy "liturgical responses" no one sings in our masses—their audible imagery is their crutch. I think that in Heaven, Protestants will teach Catholics to sing and Catholics will teach Protestants to dance and sculpt.

I developed a strong intellectual and aesthetic love for things medieval: Gregorian chant, Gothic architecture, Thomistic philosophy, illuminated manuscripts, etc. I felt vaguely guilty about it, for that was the Catholic era. I thought I could separate these legitimate cultural forms from the "dangerous" Catholic essence, as the modern Church separated the essence from these discarded forms. Yet I saw a natural connection.

Then one summer, on the beach at Ocean Grove, New Jersey, I read St. John of the Cross. I did not understand much of it, but I knew, with undeniable certainty, that here was reality, something as massive and positive as a mountain range. I felt as if I had just come out of a small, comfortable cave, in which I had lived all my life, and found that there was an unsuspected world outside of incredible dimensions. Above all, the dimensions were those of holiness, goodness, purity of heart, obedience to the first and greatest commandment, willing God's will, the one absolute I had discovered, at the age of eight. I was very far from saintly, but that did not prevent me from fascinated admiration from afar; the valley dweller appreciates the height of the mountain more than the dweller on the foothills. I read other Catholic saints and mystics, and discovered the same reality there, however different the style (even St. Thérèse "The Little Flower"!) I felt sure it was the same reality I had learned to love from my parents and teachers, only a far deeper version of it. It did not seem alien and other. It was not another religion but the adult version of my own.

Then in a church history class at Calvin a professor gave me a way to investigate the claims of the Catholic Church on my own. The essential claim is historical: that Christ founded the Catholic Church, that there is historical continuity. If that were true, I would have to be a Catholic out of obedience to my one absolute, the will of my Lord. The teacher explained the Protestant belief. He said that Catholics accuse we who are Protestants of going back only to Luther and Calvin; but this is not true; we go back to Christ. Christ had never intended a Catholic-style Church, but a Protestant-style one. The Catholic additions to the simple, Protestant-style New Testament church had grown up gradually in the Middle Ages like barnacles on the hull of a ship, and the Protestant Reformers had merely scraped off the barnacles, the alien, pagan accretions. The Catholics, on the other hand, believed that Christ established the Church Catholic from the start, and that the doctrines and practices that Protestants saw as barnacles were, in fact, the very living and inseparable parts of the planks and beams of the ship.

I thought this made the Catholic claim empirically testable, and I wanted to test it because I was worried by this time about my dangerous interest in things Catholic. Half of me wanted to discover it was the true Church (that was the more adventurous half); the other half wanted to prove it false (that was the comfortable half). My adventurous half rejoiced when I discovered in the early Church such Catholic elements as the centrality of the Eucharist, the Real Presence, prayers to saints, devotion to Mary, an insistence on visible unity, and apostolic succession. Furthermore, the Church Fathers just "smelled" more Catholic than Protestant, especially St. Augustine, my personal favorite and a hero to most Protestants too. It seemed very obvious that if Augustine or Jerome or Ignatius of Antioch or Anthony of the Desert, or Justin Martyr, or Clement of Alexandria, or Athanasius were alive today they would be Catholics, not Protestants.

The issue of the Church's historical roots was crucial to me, for the thing I had found in the Catholic Church and in no Protestant church was simply this: the massive historical fact that there she is, majestic and unsinkable. It was the same old seaworthy ship, the Noah's ark, that Jesus had commissioned. It was like discovering not an accurate *picture* of the ark, or even a real relic of its wood, but the whole ark itself, still sailing unscathed on the seas of history! It was like a fairy tale come true, like a "myth become fact," to use C. S. Lewis' formula for the Incarnation.

The parallel between Christ and Church, Incarnation and Church history, goes still further. I thought, just as Jesus made a claim about His identity that forces us into one of only two camps, His enemies or His worshippers, those who call Him liar and those who call Him Lord; so the Catholic Church's claim to be the one true Church, the Church Christ founded, forces us to say either that this is the most arrogant, blasphemous and wicked claim imaginable, if it is not true, or else that she is just what she claims to be. Just as Jesus stood out as the absolute exception to all other human teachers in claiming to be more than human and more than a teacher, so the Catholic Church stood out above all other denominations in claiming to be not merely a denomination, but the Body of Christ incarnate, infallible, one, and holy, presenting the really present Christ in her Eucharist. I could never rest in a comfortable, respectable ecumenical halfway house of measured admiration from a distance. I had to shout either "Crucify her!" or "Hosanna!" If I could not love and believe her, honesty forced me to despise and fight her.

But I could not despise her. The beauty and sanctity and wisdom of her, like that of Christ, prevented me from calling her liar or lunatic, just as it prevented me from calling Christ that. But simple logic offered then one and only one other option: this must be the Church my Lord provided for me—*my* Lord, for *me.* So she had better become my Church if He is my Lord.

There were many strands in the rope that hauled me aboard the ark, though this one—the Church's claim to be the one Church historically founded by Christ—was the central and deciding one. The book that more than any other decided it for me was Ronald Knox's *The Belief of Catholics.* He and Chesterton "spoke with authority, and not as the scribes." Even C. S. Lewis, the darling of Protestant Evangelicals, "smelled" Catholic most of the time. A recent book by a Calvinist author I went to high school with, John Beversluis, mercilessly tries to tear all Lewis' arguments to shreds; but Lewis is left without a scratch and Beversluis comes out looking like an atheist. Lewis is the only author I ever have read whom I thought I could completely trust and completely understand. But he believed in Purgatory, the Real Presence in the Eucharist, and *not* Total Depravity. He was no Calvinist. In fact, he was a medieval.

William Harry Jellema, the greatest teacher I ever knew, though a Calvinist, showed me what I can only call the Catholic vision of the history of philosophy, embracing the Greek and medieval tradition and the view of reason it assumed, a thick rather than a thin one. Technically this was "realism" (Aquinas) as vs. "nominalism" (Ockham and Luther). Commonsensically, it meant wisdom rather than mere logical consistency, insight rather than mere calculation. I saw Protestant theology as infected with shallow nominalism and Descartes' narrow scientificization of reason.

A second and related difference is that Catholics, like their Greek and medieval teachers, still believed that reason was essentially reliable, not utterly untrustworthy because fallen. We make mistakes in using it, yes. There are "noetic effects of sin," yes. But the instrument is reliable. Only our misuse of it is not.

This is connected with a third difference. For Catholics, reason is not just subjective but objective; reason is not our artificial little man-made rules for our own subjective thought processes or intersubjective communications, but a window on the world. And not just the material world, but form, order, objective truth. Reason was from God. All truth was God's truth. When Plato or Socrates knew the truth, the *logos*, they knew Christ, unless John lies in chapter 1 of his gospel. I gave a chapel speech at Calvin calling Socrates a "common-grace Christian" and unwittingly scandalized the powers that be. They still remember it, 30 years later.

The only person who almost kept me Protestant was Kierkegaard. Not Calvin or Luther. Their denial of free will made human choice a sham game of predestined dice. Kierkegaard offered a brilliant, consistent alternative to Catholicism, but such a quirkily individualistic one, such a pessimistic and antirational one, that he was incompletely human. He *could* hold a candle to Augustine and Aquinas, I thought—the only Protestant thinker I ever found who could—but he was only the rebel in the ark, while they were the family, Noah's sons.

But if Catholic dogma contradicted Scripture or itself at any point, I could not believe it. I explored all the cases of claimed contradiction and found each to be a Protestant misunderstanding. No matter how morally bad the Church had gotten in the Renaissance, it never taught heresy. I was impressed with its very hypocrisy: even when it didn't raise its practice to its preaching, it never lowered its preaching to its practice. Hypocrisy, someone said, is the tribute vice pays to virtue.

I was impressed by the argument that "the Church wrote the Bible." Christianity was preached by the Church before the New Testament was written—that is simply a historical fact. It is also a fact that the apostles wrote the New Testament and the Church canonized it, deciding which books were divinely inspired. I knew, from logic and common sense, that a cause can never be less than its effect. You can't give what you don't have. If the Church has no divine inspiration and no infallibility, no divine authority, then neither can the New Testament. Protestantism logically entails Modernism. I had to be either a Catholic or a Modernist. That decided it; that was like saying I had to be either a patriot or a traitor.

One afternoon I knelt alone in my room and prayed God would decide for me, for I am good at thinking but bad at acting, like Hamlet. Unexpectedly, I seemed to sense my heroes Augustine and Aquinas and thousands of other saints and sages calling out to me from the great ark, "Come aboard! We are really here. We still live. Join us. Here is the Body of Christ." I said Yes. My intellect and feelings had long been conquered; the will is the last to surrender.

One crucial issue remained to be resolved: Justification by Faith, the central bone of contention of the Reformation. Luther was obviously right here: the doctrine is clearly taught in *Romans* and *Galatians*. If the Catholic Church teaches "another gospel" of salvation by works, then it teaches fundamental heresy. I found here however another case of misunderstanding. I read in Aquinas' *Summa* on grace, and the decrees of the Council of Trent, and found them just as strong on grace as Luther or Calvin. I was overjoyed to find that the Catholic Church had read the Bible too!

At Heaven's gate our entrance ticket, according to Scripture and Church dogma, is *not* our good works *or* our sincerity, but our faith, which glues us to Jesus. *He* saves us; we do not save ourselves. But I find, incredibly, that 9 out of 10 Catholics do not know this, the absolutely central, core, essential dogma of Christianity. Protestants are right: most Catholics do in fact believe a whole other religion. Well over 90% of students I have polled who have had 12 years of catechism classes, even Catholic high schools, say they expect to go to Heaven because they tried, or did their best, or had compassionate feelings to everyone, or were sincere. They hardly ever mention Jesus. Asked why they hope to be saved, they mention almost anything except the Savior. Who taught them? Who wrote their textbooks? These teachers have stolen from our precious children the most valuable thing in the world, the "pearl of great price," their faith. Jesus had some rather terrifying warnings about such things— something about millstones.

Catholicism taught that we are saved by faith, by grace, by Christ, however few Catholics understood this. And Protestants taught that true faith necessarily produces good works. The fundamental issue of the Reformation is an argument between the roots and the blossoms on the same flower.

But though Luther did not neglect good works, he connected them to faith by only a thin and unreliable thread: human gratitude. In response to God's great gift of salvation, which we accept by faith, we do good works out of gratitude, he taught. But gratitude is only a feeling, and dependent on the self. The Catholic connection between faith and works is a far stronger and more reliable one. I found it in C. S. Lewis' *Mere Christianity,* the best introduction to Christianity I have ever read. It is the ontological reality of *zoë*, supernatural life, sanctifying grace, God's own life in the soul, which is received by faith and then itself produces good works. God comes in one end and out the other: the very same thing that comes in by faith (the life of God) goes out as works, through our free cooperation.

I was also dissatisfied with Luther's teaching that justification was a legal fiction on God's part rather than a real event in us; that God looks on the Christian in Christ, sees only Christ's righteousness, and legally counts or *imputes* Christ's righteousness as ours. I thought it had to be as Catholicism says, that God actually *imparts* Christ to us, in baptism and through faith (these two are usually together in the New Testament). Here I found the fundamentalists, especially the Baptists, more philosophically sound than the Calvinists and Lutherans. For me, their language, however sloganish and satirizable, is more accurate when they speak of *"receiving* Christ as your personal Savior."

Though my doubts were all resolved and the choice was made in 1959, my senior year at Calvin, actual membership came a year later, at Yale. My parents were horrified, and only gradually came to realize I had not lost my head or my soul, that Catholics were Chistians, not pagans. It was very difficult, for I am a shy and soft-hearted sort, and almost nothing is worse for me than to hurt people I love. I think that I hurt almost as much as they did. But God marvellously binds up wounds.

I have been happy as a Catholic for 26 years now. The honeymoon faded, of course, but the marriage has deepened. Like all converts I ever have heard of, I was hailed aboard not by those Catholics who try to "sell" the Church by conforming it to the spirit of the times by saying Catholics are just like everyone else, but by those who joyfully held out the ancient and orthodox faith in all its fullness and prophetic challenge to the world. The minimalists, who reduce miracles to myths, dogmas to opinions, laws to values, and the Body of Christ to a psycho-social club, have always elicited wrath, pity, or boredom from me. So has political partisanship masquerading as religion. I am happy as a child to follow Christ's vicar on earth everywhere he leads. What he loves, I love; what he leaves, I leave; where he leads, I follow. For the Lord we both adore said to Peter his predecessor, "Who hears you, hears Me." That is why I am a Catholic: because I am a Christian.

Peter Kreeft *is a professor of philosophy at Boston College and well known as both an author and a speaker. His more recent publications include:* Making Sense Out of Suffering; Socrates Meets Jesus; Nuggets: A Book of Proverbs; *and* The Reality of God's Love. *With Rev. Ron Tacelli, S.J., he is co-author of* Handbook of Christian Apologetics. *Dr. Kreeft resides in West Newton, Massachusetts.*

"Amazing Grace": Never Again Alone

William K. Larkin

Grandpa had just warned me not to sit on the swing if the green paint wasn't dry. Painting the front porch swing was a ritual of spring. After a long Iowa winter, there it was, up once again, swinging by two chains. I checked the paint, figured that it was dry enough, and began to give the swing a workout. The chains began creaking away and soon Grandpa and Grandma were quickly out the front wooden screen door. "Billy, you can't swing that high. Is that paint dry?" I assured them it was and slowed my soaring plane back into a front porch swing. One or the other of my grandparents would join me while the other sat in the rocker.

Staying over at my grandparents' was also a Saturday night ritual. That ritual also included another, which today is full of paradox. A part of the reason I would stay with my grandparents was to go to Sunday School and church the next Sunday morning. On Saturday evening, the other part of the ritual was to sit on the porch, say hello to the Catholics as they passed to go to "their" church, which was just on the corner. They would pass, say hello and my grandparents would say something like "how to do." Once a few had gone past we would begin to talk about them and the talk was always the same. "Those Catholics sure are faithful. Look how the whole family goes, and they go regular, too. Our folks should learn something from them. Too bad they are lost."

In this small county of Iowa, where the Catholic population is one of the lowest, when it came to understanding what the gospel was really about, these Catholics were truly seen as "lost." They were the people who could go on sinning, go to confession (no one could imagine making their confession to another person) and then go to church. I had heard my grandparents say many times, that they (Catholics) even drank, and usually on the Saturday night before they went to church. I can also remember my grandfather saying that if he ever saw anyone bending over to kiss the Pope's ring he would kick them in the pants.

If it is true, as scripture says, that God's ways are not our ways, it was surely the case in the making of this Roman Catholic. From my earliest memories, I can remember a kind of low-level prejudice against Catholics. None of it was vicious, but present in such a way to powerfully form the consciousness of at least this little boy.

But little boys become big boys and big boys become men and some men stop long enough and think deeply enough to make up their own minds about what they believe. Although, as a pyschotherapist, I am increasingly amazed at the number of adults who have never taken the opportunity of the freedom to do so.

I would have been the last to believe that I would ever have been a Roman Catholic. In fact when I left for college, I had intended to become a minister in a mainline Protestant denomination. That would quickly change when I discovered the intellectual life of Yale University. I was more than bored with classes in scripture and theology, but I was fascinated by psychology. This was during the period of the late 60's and during that time everything had to be immediately "relevant." I wanted to really help people, to make a difference that was concrete in people's lives and being a psychologist looked like the surest way of accomplishing that.

The Iowa boy who believed in the existence of God quickly became the "Eastern intellectual" questioning everything. It did not take long to find out, that at that time, religion and psychology did not mesh. Religion was viewed as the neurotic manifestation of unmet needs. It was the "stuff" of projection. The religious beliefs that I held, over a period of about two years, became so watered down, that I finally gave up any belief at all. In fact, I could not believe. In the truest sense of the word, I became an atheist. I did not and I could not believe that God existed. I could not understand or comprehend God as "other" or "outside of creation" and I could not understand why, if God was loving and so all-powerful, He couldn't come up with a better way of salvation than by having His own Son crucified. I threw the whole religious baggage out of the window.

While I have not met many atheists, I still today respect a person who is truly an atheist. They are, first of all, the surest proof that faith is a gift which only God can give. And secondly, I would rather talk with an honest atheist than many who pretend to believe but really do not, and who go through the motion for a variety of motivations. That I would not do, and so I left the faith of my childhood and became a man of the "life of the mind" rather than of the spirit.

The years at Yale were fascinating and full of new experiences. I was part of a rich environment of learning and culture, the likes of which I had never encountered in Iowa. Though I would quickly say that my education in Iowa was one of the finest a student could have hoped to have received, and it was fine because of the deep caring of the teachers there. But this new environment was different; everybody believed something different.

But regardless of what everybody else believed, I believed in psychology and I engulfed myself in it, absorbing the field, learning everything that I could learn. From group therapy to independent research projects, I never stopped working and received high honors in many of the endeavors.

Then one day, one small thing happened that for all time, would change everything absolutely. I was driving down to the main campus, and the song "Amazing Grace" came on the radio. It was being made popular by Judy Collins about the same time that most denominations were throwing it out of the hymn book as antiquated. I remember thinking to myself that something was happening in society, that there was a new kind of move that I was not a part of. I remember thinking that things were beginning, ever so slightly, to shift.

I parked the car and began the walk across the lawn to Sterling Library. A light snow was falling, and as I walked I simply "knew" in a way I had never known, that God existed, that there was an "other." It was no longer just me and what I could see; but I knew in some inexplicable and indescribable way, that God was real, that God existed, and that God existed beyond what I could see, touch, know intellectually. I then went into the library, reflected on the experience just a bit and went on with my work. The sensation was gone after I went on to do my work. But, it had happened and that will never change. However, much, much has happened since then.

This experience could not have been any more significant for me than if I had been knocked down and blinded. It was, it had happened, and it had happened in such a way that the rest of my days would never be the same. What began then, I did not know, because I did not really know at that time that I had been depressed. I did not realize the loneliness before that time, but I had been alone and at that moment I stopped being alone. I have never been alone since and loneliness has never more been a reality to me.

I should underline here that I was not pre-evangelized or evangelized or witnessed to by anyone. I had not been reading any spiritual literature. I had not been praying or even thinking about religion. What God did, God did. He did it in His way and in His time because He had a plan for my life that even now continues to unfold.

I made the decision, as a result of this experience, to start writing in a journal. And for about six months I did. I got up every morning at six and wrote for an hour. What started out as writing, slowly over a period of time, became prayers. Then there came another breakthrough. As I wrote on the morning of my 25th birthday, I started to write about Christ and as I wrote I began to embrace and know Christ as Saviour. With an understanding that is deeper than intellect or fact, I discovered a Saviour, claimed His sacrifice for me and for my sins and gave my life to Him. He has never stopped giving back.

During this time, I met the woman who is the love of my life. The first time I saw her I said to myself, "That is the woman I want." She had been a Catholic but had left the church, or really rather just faded away from it. A good part of the reason was a divorce and at that time, there was not room in the church for divorced or separated Catholics and she knew nothing at that time of the possibility of an annulment.

The next step in this journey was a most unlikely one. My wife-to-be and I really did not share much of my spiritual journey. It was not a large part of our conversation. One evening, both of us came to each other with the same news. Independently of each other, we had been told about a prayer meeting at Yale. A friend had told her that she should check it out and a friend of mine at the university had told me that I wouldn't believe what I would see. The both of us, that evening went to what I thought I would never see at Yale—a prayer meeting in an upper room. The prayer meeting was one of the first of what was to come to be known as the Charismatic Renewal. From the minute I walked into the room, I knew that these people had something I did not, and I wanted it. It mattered little that most of them were Catholic, I wanted to know and experience more of what they were so fervently experiencing.

From these Catholics, I learned about the Holy Spirit—what they called the baptism of the Holy Spirit, the gifts of the Holy Spirit, and prayer that was largely praise in nature. However, what I also learned from these Catholics, and did not even know I was learning, was that the conversations with my grandparents on that green swing, were wrong. Catholics were not lost. Early prejudices eroded, even without my knowing it. I even made the decision to attend Mass; however, I would have nothing to do with praying to statues, kneeling, Mary: none of this "unnecessary" business. The group that sang at the prayer group was also a folk group at St. John the Baptist Church and it was there that I began to attend Mass. I sang the responses, participated on a limited level, and slowly the "artist" in me began to know the liturgy of the Mass as a beautiful work of art, a prayer prayed over centuries. Increasingly, the Mass made sense.

However, it did not make sense because I intellectually understood it first. Understanding emerged from experiencing. Over a period of time, I simply took from Catholicism what fit and left the rest behind. After all, there were other more important struggles.

My life as a graduate student was continuing and my faith experiencing was deepening. I was still deeply immersed in psychology as my profession to be, and falling in love with God. I remember hiding my religious experiences from my classmates and colleagues because I knew that they would think that I had unresolved mother and father issues, that I must need more therapy to resolve these unmet needs, and that dependency needs such as those that religion represented must be worked through.

Inwardly, I had made a decision, though. My love affair with psychology was pretty much on the rocks. It had become very clear that this "lover" was deceptive and could not deliver all that had seemed to be promised. While there was much there, and while understanding the human person from a psychological perspective was essential, I knew that I was going to devote myself to making the two of them work together. While I didn't know how, I had decided to attempt to integrate methods in psychology and religion, particularly Christian spirituality. This was an extremely difficult struggle, because there was very little good help. All of the attempts to do that, that I had encountered, so intellectualized religion, there was little room for the Spirit. To speak of praying in therapy was unheard of and seen as coercive, influencing a person when he or she was at their weakest point. In the end, there always seemed to be little room for faith, even though there were so many unanswered questions.

I kept working and reading and thinking. At the same time I got more deeply involved with these "Catholics." When they spoke of their Catholic experience, the few times that they really would, I realized that they had something going that I did not. There is a special way in which Catholicism fosters a "devotional" life, and in my contact with Catholics I was touching this reality but not able to target just what it was.

Another very important influence in my journey was the reading I was doing about the Catholic mystics. I devoured St. John of the Cross, St. Theresa, St. Catherine, St. Julie and so many, many others. As I read, asking psychological questions all along the way, one startling observation became apparent to me. While the journey of these people was often shrouded in the language and the style of talking about religious experiences of their day, their journeys and struggles were those of my clients, their experiences were many of my own, and their goal of union with Christ had a lot to do with self-knowledge, self-esteem and the deepest discovery of the person God had created each of us to be.

I began to see that the mystical journey, or the contemplative way, as it was called, could be translated into a
kind of transparent map that could be laid across the
experience of everyday people. I saw in the lives of my
patients that their isolated struggles were not isolated at
all. From the perspective of seeing their struggles as a
journey, I began to see that it was possible to take the
stages of the mystical life of prayer and apply them to
everyday living, and I have been working on doing that
kind of research ever since. I will say more about that
later.

With all of this going on, I was still a quasi-Catholic.
There were some major stumbling blocks that I could not
understand, nor did I particularly want to. They could be
put into three words: Mary, sacraments, and papacy. I
could not and would not buy into any of them. They are
today the bedrock of how I practice professionally and
what I believe personally. I believe as well, that the renewal of Christendom depends on an embrace and understanding of the three. Just how the Holy Spirit will
carry that off, I'm not sure, but I am sure that the Spirit
will, even if it may not be in my lifetime.

Let me begin with the first block: Mary. I was not
about to pray to a saint when I could go directly to Jesus
and, chauvinist that I was, I certainly was not about to
kneel before the statue of a woman. However, I am a
seeker, and in listening to Catholics speak of Mary, I knew
there was something special there. It wasn't because they
were very articulate, because most Catholics do not really
understand what they believe. Rather, they have an experience they claim but oftentimes can't explain. It is especially difficult for them when a Bible-touting fundamentalist wants them "to find it in Scripture." I'll take
that one on later as I had to as a doctoral candidate at
Harvard University. I decided that I would try some of
this "devotional" stuff. By this time I learned that it was
oftentimes the intellect that was the last to understand

something that could be experienced first from the inside and would then work its way out to the mind.

One morning I memorized the Hail Mary. It is a beautiful prayer and now my heart prays what I first had to memorize. I went off to a nearby Catholic church, and hoping that nobody would see me, I made an act of faith. I humbled myself to kneel before the statue of a woman, asking her to pray for me, and dashed off a decade of the rosary faster than any Catholic can speed through them. It had occurred to me previously that if we can pray for each other on this side of life and God will hear, that we probably pray as much if not more on the other side. And that just as we have special gifts of prayer on this side of life, saints probably had their special gifts of prayer as well. So I came before this statue of a woman (a symbol of the reality) in pure act of faith, and the mantle of her protection has been over me ever since. But I didn't know that then.

I returned home, having said nothing of this to my wife. By that time, the love of my life and I had married. We were married at Yale, with no intention of becoming Catholic. It was a Protestant ceremony, that we would later have blessed when her previous marriage had been annulled. But we did not know what we were in for. When I returned home from my secret encounter with the "other woman in my life," my wife said to me, "Oh, by the way, I hope you won't be offended, but Margaret O'Brien (a friend) stopped by and left these for you. They were her father's and she said that she felt led to give them to you." My wife handed me a set of worn rosary beads along with a novena to "Our Lady of Victory." I took the rosary beads and the novena, or should I say, "they took me." And they have been taking me ever since. I decided that I would pray the rosary every day until I could get into the mystery of this prayer and I also decided to pray what I then considered to be a "legalistic" unnecessarily rigid novena. I decided to put this prayer to the real test.

I had five clients in counseling that I could not reach. In my prayers I had asked God to send me the people He wanted me to see. While I expected believers, He sent unbelievers. Were they ever unbelievers! Two were Jews who didn't even know the God of Abraham. Two others were a married couple who told me the "I-Ching" sticks told them to come. "I-Ching" is a practice of the occult. And the third was a flamingly angry feminist who did far more of a job on me than I was ever able to do with her. I couldn't get to first base with any of them, so I decided to pray to "Our Lady of Victory." I did so for thirty days. In that time both couples had joined a prayer group and both had converted to Catholicism. The feminist was the clincher, though. She came to her appointment telling me that things had gotten so bad, she had actually turned back to the Church. She related to me that she had been driving all over trying to find a church that was open at night so that she could pray. With the sweet assurance that only a mother can give, this young lady told me that the only church she could find open was "Our Lady of Victory."

Today I have come to know Mary in her seclusion. In my life and in my practice she often opens the doors to the gift of faith and into the heart of her Son, but often doing so remaining hidden for the glory of the Saviour. She is my "Lady of Victory" and she has protected me from evil, crushing it underfoot and enabling the work I do to proceed with a speed it would not, without her.

Even past the blockage of Mary, I was still not a Roman Catholic. There was still the block of the sacraments, particularly the Eucharist. Again, I decided to make an act of faith. I would go to Mass every day, until the Eucharist either did or did not come alive for me. I decided to go to a parish where the priest would not know that I wasn't a Catholic. Little did I know that this priest was one of the most conservative priests in the diocese—one who "hollered" from the pulpit. If there was a priest who could turn off a would-be Catholic, this had to be the one. But I decided to ignore him and just participate in the Mass and receive the Eucharist. As I look back I am embarrassed at such brashness. But I had to know and I had to find out. What I did not know and was later to find out was that this "conservative" priest who always greeted me with the friendliest and most receptive of smiles and demeanor, knew all the time that I was not a Catholic. It was one of the first things he told the priest who would replace him.

But what of the Eucharist? As I write this article, I am preparing to give a retreat on the Eucharist. Let me simply say that I know in my inner being when I have been away from the Eucharist. It is the body and blood of Christ and it is a lens through which all of creation, redeemed by Christ, is something I see through the eyes of my heart as a sacrament. But this central reality is still unfolding.

To write more fully of my encounter with the sacraments would take this entire book. I have come to know them as guarantees of the presence and activity of Christ when I get lost, when I can't feel faith, when I am unsure and when I am full of sin. They have become, for me, like an old pair of slippers that tell me I am home and that I can fall back into the arms of Christ like the arms of my favorite chair.

But still, even with the deepening appreciation and knowledge of the sacraments, I was not yet a Catholic.

The third block, you will remember was papacy. Actually, the block was more than papacy, it was magisterium, authority, the ecclesiastical structure of the Church. I just didn't get it and I didn't think that I ever would.

One startling event would happen that would put me on the road to getting past this last wall. The doctoral program in which I had become involved at Yale was dropped. It was a new program which looked as though it would allow me the freedom to pursue the integration of methodologies in psychology and religion that I continued to work on. But the program was dropped and my heart and my spirit dropped to one of the lowest points in my life. I could not see myself working on a doctorate in another field. By this time I was married with children and a family to support. I remained at Yale for another miserable three years as a Research Fellow, which meant that I was not working for any specific degree, just that I had the freedom to attend any classes I wished and to use any of the facilities. I would receive no credit.

These were three years of the deepest searching and wandering in my life. But my thinking and my practice was becoming more firm. I was also teaching and as I taught psychology, my ideas about what it could be and what pastoral psychotherapy could be, became even more fixed. The only school I could find that had a program in psychology of religion was Harvard. It was the last place that I would have expected finally to bring me fully into Catholicism, but that is where it happened. The last obstacle would be crossed here.

To my amazement I was accepted at Harvard and also given a year's credit because of the time spent at Yale as a Research Fellow.

I remember well, beginning doctoral studies. I was full-time Chairman of a Department of Psychology at another college teaching a full load. It was impossible for me to live in Cambridge. None of it could possibly work out. But I knew that I had to do what I had to do. There were so many, many ends that were not tied together.

One of these ends was the fact that my wife's annulment had still not come through. Here we were, attending Mass, she not receiving, no one knowing where I stood (at least we didn't think so) and wondering where all of this would go. My wife had no idea that I would ever become a Catholic and pursued the annulment for herself.

I commuted to Harvard from New Haven. Yes, I commuted. I arranged my classes in two days, my teaching schedule in the other three, and worked all the time—during which my wife became pregnant, again. (We had three children, this would be the fourth.)

My first trip to Harvard was filled with fear about how this scattered existence, scattered on almost every level, could ever work out. I remember getting on the subway at South Station in Boston feeling as underground as the subway. At one point the subway goes over the Charles River, and on this fall day the light broke as we emerged from the underground and I saw the sailboats on the river. It was beautiful. I thought to myself that maybe this wouldn't be so bad and that maybe, just maybe, if God had gotten me this far He would get me the rest of the way.

The rest of the way included a stop off in a class at Harvard Divinity School in a course called "The Bible in Roman Catholic Theology." And it was there that it happened—my final decision to become a Roman Catholic. A wonderful professor, Father George MacRae, taught the class which gave me in the last leg of my journey, the intellectual answers I needed. The class concerned a comparison of *Sola Scriptura*, "Scripture Alone" as compared to the Catholic belief of the source of revelation (the knowledge of God) as Scripture *and* tradition. As the class proceeded from week to week, I can remember the point at which it all crystallized for me. Without going into all of the intellectual material, I sat and knew that I was a Roman Catholic. In short I realized that while the whole of revelation is inherent in the Scriptures, that the fullness of that revelation continues to unfold and to be understood through history—"tradition." The safeguard of tradition is the teaching authority of the Church. And so when someone asks me if I can "find it in Scripture" as a support of my Catholic family, I have to help them first of all to rephrase the whole question. Somewhere I had crossed over a line and I had become what I was looking at. If you will pardon the analogy, in a sense, I married the woman with whom I had been sleeping.

As I sought to join the Church, one obstacle remained: my wife's previous marriage had not been annulled. While all of this was going on, my wife delivered our first son "Christopher," bearer of Christ's light; and as Christopher came bearing Christ's light, the day of the birth of my son, the postman came bearing the letter granting the annulment.

I became a Roman Catholic with seven priests on the altar. Each had had a part to play and I think they came to claim a part of the victory. My parish priest had asked me to make this a celebration that was more public than private. It was all a kind of a sign as I see it now.

What has followed stuns me more each day. I finished the doctorate in psychology and theology in record time and with nearly a nervous breakdown. I left teaching and went into private practice utilizing therapy as a way of helping people find God's call for their lives. I pulled no punches in letting people know that I practiced as a Christian therapist, and believers or not they would have to look at their faith life, even if they didn't buy into one. The practice became too large and I realized that individual therapy is too often a luxury for the upper middle class and that much that is done on a one-to-one basis could be done in retreats. I started doing retreats and the retreats found their way to cable television. Cable television found its way to commercial and satellite television, and today I am founder and president of The Pastoral Theological Institute. Our programs for radio and television take the Catholic Christian faith to 44 countries of the world and to a potential audience of 800 million. We have recently built a $200,000 radio and television production facility for the production of Catholic programming for evangelization and teaching. And I know that the vision is still unfolding.

However, there is something that has not changed. Early on I believed that God had a call, a vision for each human life and I found the road map in the mystics, the great men and women of faith who experienced God.

My Catholic faith is the experience through which I have journeyed to experience God. I am not in love with its structures, though I love them. I am in love with the God I find in them.

Just a final observation. We are much too fearful of being Catholics. We are much too fearful of proclaiming our faith, and I am delighted to see a book such as this one being published. Too often we see our Catholicism as the divisive factor in Christendom. That is far from true. What is divisive is everyone's interpretation of truth and more and more store fronts of individual understanding that cannot appreciate the place of authority nor the reality that it takes the human race time, much time, to receive revelation and allow it to penetrate. We need to be braver and bolder and to realize that love shares what the heart holds dearest.

This is not a popular age for proselytizing, and a most difficult age in which to be a missionary for Christ, especially as a Catholic. However, I believe that what I must do is to simply, in love, share what is in my heart. Being a Catholic is a gift—a gift that only God can give. It has been a long way from Iowa and that green swing on Grandpa's porch, but if God can get me from Iowa to where I am today, the renaissance of the Catholic faith, which I believe we are upon, is something He can all too well carry off.

William K. Larkin *is a psychotherapist, an author and a radio and television producer. He has won national and international awards in radio and television production. He is the founder and president of the Pastoral Institute, located in Hamden, Connecticut. At the Institute he directs a* *counseling center integrating methods in psychotherapy and Christian spirituality, a retreat and formation program, and the media production center, MarySong Communications. His weekly radio and television program,* Breakthrough, *airs nationally. Dr. Larkin also produces a children's television program called* Our Friends on Wooster Square *and a video devotional magazine for closed-circuit use in hospitals and prisons. He authors and produces numerous video programs integrating psychology and religion. He and his wife, Dot, have five children and reside in Hamden, Connecticut.*

"To Be Truly Orthodox Is to Be in Communion with Peter's See"

James Likoudis

*"O Lord, I have loved the beauty
of Thy House,
and the place where Thy glory dwellest."*

I was born in Lackawanna, NY, in 1928, of a struggling Greek immigrant family from the island of Cephalonia off the west coast of Greece. My father Gerasimos and my mother Katherine owned a small candy and ice cream store at various locations in the old First Ward of the city inhabited by people from many nations who worked mainly at the great Bethlehem Steel Plant (whose smoke stacks are now strangely quiet in view of hard times falling upon the steel industry). My parents were Greek Orthodox, and some of my earliest memories were of references to the "Panaghia" (the All-Holy Mother of God), the many signs of the cross made at meals (in Byzantine fashion, from right to left), and the majestic and solemn ceremonies of the magnificent Liturgy of St. John Chrysostom which transfixed my soul with a sense of the Awesomeness of God and the splendor of His heavenly court. I think it true from my earliest days that I have never really doubted the existence of God, the Divinity of Christ, or the fact that Our Divine Lord had established a visible Church—graces that I attribute to the supernatural virtue of faith received in baptism.

Attending public elementary and high school, I was a bright student, and it was in high school that I began to have a keen interest in religion. Novels such as *Ben-Hur* and *The Robe* excited my imagination, and I wanted to know more about Christ and Christianity. My father did not have a car, and so my family rarely got to church, since our Greek Orthodox church of the Annunciation was miles away in Buffalo. Some of my friends were Catholic, and I felt a sense of envy at those who attended the rather mysterious parochial schools I would often pass by in walking home after my own public school classes. The envy I felt was for their receiving a religious instruction and training denied me. I also developed a certain admiration for the imposing network of Catholic institutions (schools, hospitals, convents, churches) which took care of both the spiritual and material needs of their people. We Orthodox (whether Greeks, Serbs, Bulgarians, Russians, Ukranians) were far fewer in number than the Catholics of the Latin rite, and were badly split into conflicting jurisdictions (with accompanying ethnic rivalries). It frankly never occurred to me to try to frequent regularly another Orthodox church of another ethnic group, closer to home. We were Greek Orthodox, "pure Greeks" (Hellenes), and though we shared a common religion with Orthodox Serbs, Macedonians, and Russians, different languages and customs made it difficult to feel a sense of real solidarity with them. The numerical fewness of Orthodox vis-a-vis Catholics and Protestants as well as the distinct "foreignness" of Greek Orthodoxy in American culture (where religion meant you were either Protestant, Catholic, or Jew) had the effect of at least a partial alienation from my own spiritual and linguistic roots. The "melting pot" of American society even developed a resistance to learning the Greek language better—something I regret to this very day. In addition, the Catholic Church seemed to have accommodated itself to the American cultural milieu far more successfully, though in my high school days I was aware that in a number of ways, Catholics were at odds with the influence of secularism and Protestantism.

In my senior high school year, Catholicism was symbolized for me by the magnificence and Baroque splendor of Our Lady of Victory Basilica in Lackawanna, which was not too far from my school and which I often visited. The Catholic Church was a spiritual force that could not be ignored in my little world; it was both attractive and menacingly formidable since I was aware that Catholics claimed that theirs was the "true Church." I was deeply puzzled by this, since my Greek Orthodox Church made the same claim!

It was while a student in history and philosophy at the University of Buffalo (then a private institution) that I began literally to read myself into the Catholic Church. In the University Library (Lockwood), the Newman Club had its own special shelf of books dealing with the Catholic faith. I would often find my regular school assignments less interesting than to dip into the fascinating Catholic world of such writers as Cardinals Newman and Manning, Ronald Knox, Father Faber, Belloc and Chesterton, and that marvellous priest-author of the *Masterful Monk* stories, Fr. Owen Dudley. At a time when my secular courses in history and philosophy began to pose all sorts of difficulties regarding historic Christian beliefs, I found in such writers (including St. Thomas Aquinas) a treasure-trove of arguments, and the genius to challenge intellectually their rationalist and skeptical opponents. I delighted in the Masterful Monk's defense of Catholic faith and morals as he combatted the ideology of H. G. Wells, Julian Huxley, and other agnostic or atheist luminaries. I admired the Catholic Church for its intellectualism and its contributions to Western Civilization; I cannot say I understood St. Thomas Aquinas and Thomism well, but there was no doubt in my mind that the Catholic Church had led its believers to many of the highest achievements of reason and faith. I also was deeply impressed by the remarkable Saints it had produced. I could not reconcile the efflorescence of heroic sanctity in a Church which had succumbed to the heretical depravities and innovations of the devil. Such was the tenor of the encyclical letter issued by the Patriarch Anthimus of Constantinople in 1895 declaring that the Catholic Church "had privily brought into herself through the Papacy various and strange and heretical doctrines and innovations, and so she has been torn away and removed far from the true and orthodox Church of Christ" (Reply to Pope Leo XIII's "Letter on the Reunion of the Churches"). I was in awe at the heights of sanctity reached by St. Thomas Aquinas, St. Bonaventure, St. Francis, St. Dominic, the Jesuit Saints of the Counter-Reformation (St. Ignatius, St. Robert Bellarmine, St. Peter Canisius, St. Andrew Bobola), and such holy souls as St. Bernadette and St. Thérèse of Lisieux.

My pro-Catholic sympathies were in evidence when the university student newspaper highlighted some violent attacks—à la Paul Blanshard—on the Church regarding the themes of religious liberty, "separation of Church and State," and the Church's alleged opposition to democracy. I was further impressed with the respect (sometimes begrudging) paid the Catholic Church by some of my professors. Whether agnostic, Protestant, or Jewish, these genteel scholars from time to time in their lectures paid due tribute to the impact of the Church on Western thought and civilization (something lacking in too many of their secularist counterparts today). And then there was the slender and stately figure in white of the saintly Pope Pius XII who came to symbolize for me the Church's indomitable struggle to maintain spiritual values in a world that had gone totalitarian and quite mad. It remains my fond hope and prayer that the Angelic Shepherd will one day be declared a Doctor of the Church.

It was in my last university year that I first met my lovely wife Ruth, who worked in the university library, and who shared a similar feeling for Catholicism. Her family practiced no religion (her father had been baptized Catholic but had never really practiced the faith, and her mother was vaguely Protestant). She and her brothers and sisters had had no religious upbringing. While in high school, however, she began to attend an Episcopal church whose rector held high Anglican views which were very close to those of Catholics. From the moment I saw her, I loved her.

We often discussed Catholicism. I realized if I were indeed to become a Catholic, and to have a Catholic marriage, I had to resolve once and for all the hesitations I had at submitting to the Catholic Church as the true Church of Jesus Christ. I read everything I could find on the origins of the Schism between the Catholic and Eastern Orthodox churches, the history and doctrine of the Papacy, and on the Ecumenical Councils of the first eight centuries. One of the books I found, *The Eastern Churches and the Papacy* by the Anglican scholar S. H. Scott, was especially helpful to me, as were the remarkable books on the Primacy of Peter by that great Anglican convert and friend of Cardinal Newman, Thomas William Allies, who spent his life in scholarly defense of the Papacy. Allies confirmed for me once and for all the patristic support for the Primacy of Peter in the early Church.

I also made good use of the wonderful Catholic lending library on the second floor of the Catholic Union building at Main and Virginia in downtown Buffalo. Established many years before by German Catholics to help defend their faith, this lending library was chock-full of Catholic periodicals, newspapers, and a fine assortment of books on the lives of the Saints, spirituality, apologetics, Church history, and every aspect of Catholic faith and morals. I shall never forget the kindness to me of Mr. Cyril Ehrenreich who was the library caretaker. He was also in charge of the books sold downstairs in the

Catholic Union store. He had a remarkable knowledge of Catholic literature, and I recall the great care he exercised to assure that no doctrinally suspect or morally bad books would be included among his wares. His great love of the Church was evident. He went to his heavenly reward years ago. May his soul rest in the peace of Christ.

It was therefore, during my last year at University that my views on the Catholic Church, the Papacy, and the history of the Schism between East and West solidified. It was clear—in the words of the Greek lay theologian, Dr. Hamilcar Alivisatos—that "the accumulated indifference, ignorance, suspicions, hate, crimes, and fanaticism of many centuries" since the Crusades had contributed to the growing estrangement between Eastern and Western Christians, a process that culminated in the "cursed schism."

Curiously, such matters as the dogmatic question of the Procession of the Holy Spirit from the Father *and the Son (Filioque)*—together with the canonical question of the inclusion of the 'Filioque' in the Creed—and the use of unleavened bread (azymes) in the Latin Mass, as well as a host of other liturgical and disciplinary differences—were considered by the medieval Byzantines to be far more important reasons justifying their rupture of communion with the Apostolic See than the repeated claims of Papal Supremacy. The great Catholic Czech scholar Fr. Francis Dvornik had shown by his researches that the famous Patriarch Photius (often presented as the fervent opponent of Papal Supremacy over the entire Church) had actually died in communion with Rome. The latter had never repudiated the teaching of the Popes of his time (Nicholas I, Hadrian II, John VIII) concerning their succession to the Primacy of Peter whom Our Lord had established as head and center of the Universal Church. By the Orthodox polemicists' own fatal admission that "prior to 1054 the Roman Catholic Church was fully joined to the Orthodox Church," it was evident that the

Eastern patriarchates had been in communion with Popes who were unequivocal in declaring their universal jurisdiction over the Church in both East and West. The statement made by dissident writers to our own day that "the Bishop of Rome was *never* at any time accorded any rights or powers over the entire Church" was simply false to the history of the Byzantine Church before 1054 and even into the middle of the 12th century when the first denials of Papal Supremacy began to be made. Pro-Unionist Byzantines continued to defend the Petrine Primacy of the Popes before and after that great Reunion Council of Florence (1439) which at first appeared to have ended three centuries of rupture, discord, estrangement, and formal schism. In his classic work *Russia and the Universal Church* the "Russian Newman," Vladimir Soloviev, had written powerfully of the Papacy as "that miraculous ikon of universal Christianity" demonstrating that the Roman Primacy was of the *essence* of the Church as a visible institution in the world. Since the Orthodox agreed with Catholics in professing that "the Holy Spirit unfailingly preserves the form of government established by Christ the Lord in the Church" *(see* Vatican II's *Lumen Gentium,* No. 27), then the testimony of the early pre-Schism Popes regarding their own role in the Church could not be rejected.

Pope St. Boniface († 422) had assuredly summed up the tradition of the earliest centuries when he wrote about the heresies and schisms of his day:

> ...It is clear that this Roman Church is to all churches throughout the world as the head is to the members, and that whoever separates himself from it becomes an exile from the Christian religion, since he ceases to belong to its fellowship (Ep. 14,1).

The doctrinal teaching of the great Pope St. Leo The Great († 461) on the powers of his See was acknowledged by scholars of every religious persuasion:

Though priests have a like dignity, yet they have not an equal jurisdiction, since even among the most blessed apostles, as there was a likeness of honor, so was there a certain distinction of power, and the election of all being equal, pre-eminence over the rest was given to one, from which type the distinction between the bishops also has risen, and it was provided by an important arrangement, that all should not claim to themselves power over all, but that in every province there should be one, whose sentence should be considered the first among his brethren; and others again, seated in the greater cities, should undertake a larger care, through whom the direction of the Universal Church should converge to the one See of Peter, and nothing anywhere disagree with its head (Ep. 14).

Pope St. Gelasius († 496) wrote to the orthodox of his day:

Yet we do not hesitate to mention that which is known to the Universal Church, namely, that as the See of Blessed Peter the Apostle has the right to loose what has been bound by the judgments of any bishops, whatsoever, and since it has jurisdiction over every church, so that no one may pass judgment on its verdict, the canons providing that an appeal should be to it from any part of the world, no one is permitted to appeal against its judgment *(Thiel,* Ep. 26).

Pope St. Agatho († 681) in his famous letter to the 6th Ecumenical Council which was greeted with the acclamation "Peter hath spoken by Agatho," had written the following in full consciousness of the dignity of his See:

...Peter's true confession was revealed from heaven by the Father, and for it Peter was pronounced blessed by the Lord of all; and he received also, from the Redeemer of us all, by a threefold commendation, the spiritual sheep of the Church that he might feed them. Resting on his protection, the Apostolic Church (of Rome) has never turned aside from the way of truth to any part of error and her authority has always been faithfully followed and embraced as that of the Prince of the Apostles, by the whole Catholic Church, and by all the venerable Fathers who embraced her doctrine, by which they have shone as most approved lights of the Church of Christ, and has been venerated and followed by all orthodox doctors... *(Mansi XI, p. 233)*.

The witness of the great Eastern Saints of the "undivided Church" similarly refuted the pretension that only an empty "primacy of honor" was envisaged by the famous Petrine texts (Matt. 16:18-19; Luke 22:31-32; Jn. 21:15-17) which singled Peter out to be the Rock-foundation of the Church, the Holder of the Keys of the Kingdom, the Confirmer of his brethren, and the Chief Shepherd of the Church after Christ's Ascension into heaven. In a magnificent passage, St. Maximus the Confessor († 622), one of the greatest of the Byzantine doctors, thus defended the prerogatives of the Roman Church watered with the blood of the Chief Apostle:

For the extremities of the earth, and all in every part of it who purely and rightly confess the Lord, look directly towards the most holy Roman Church and its confession and faith, as it were to a sun of unfailing light, awaiting from it the bright radiance of our fathers, according to what the six inspired and holy Councils have purely and piously decreed, declaring most expressly the symbol of faith. For from the coming down of the Incarnate Word among us, all the churches in every part of the world have possessed that greatest church alone as their base and foundation, seeing that, according to the promise of Christ Our Savior, the gates of hell do never prevail against it, that it possesses the Keys of right confession and faith in Him, that it opens the true and only religion to such as approach with piety, and shuts up and locks every heretical mouth that speaks injustice against the Most High (P.G. 91, 137ff.).

The witness of the pre-Schism Popes, Fathers, and Councils (whatever the historical and theological difficulties encountered) was overwhelming in their cumulative impact as supporting the dogma of Papal Primacy as defined in the decrees of Vatican I. The utterly supernatural nature of the Apostolic Primacy of the "first of Bishops," the Roman Pontiff, was profoundly grasped by the great 19th-century German theologian Matthias Joseph Scheeben. His especially rich theological exposition was of particular value to me in dissipating the misconceptions of Orthodox polemicists. At a time when these same misconceptions concerning the nature and scope of Papal authority seem to have been revived among neo-Modernist theologians spreading dissent and disobedience in the Church these last two decades, Fr. Scheeben's remarkable exposition is worth repeating here:

"...The unity of the Church in its social life depends in a special way on the unity of the pastoral power. This unity of the pastoral power must be a clear sign that the Spirit operating in many organs is a single spirit, who brings all these organs together in one whole, and causes them to exercise their activity in an orderly manner conformable with the unity of the whole. The members and organs of the Church form one body of Christ and assemble around the Eucharist as the source of their common life, and *they are called to image forth the highest unity of all, that of the Trinity.* In the unfolding of their life and activity, these members and organs constitute a closely knit whole, in which the unity and harmony of external social life is the faithful reflection of its true, internal, mysterious unity. *This fact must be manifested by the unity of the pastoral power.*

"This unity of pastoral power is guaranteed by the revealed doctrine that the plenitude of such power is in one supreme pontiff....

"...Owing to the fact that the plenitude of the pastoral power resides in him; and that no such power can be envisaged in the Church as independent of his, the Church is made truly and perfectly one, not only in its summit, but in its deepest base—and from the base up; not only in its top-most branch, but in its root—and from the root up. *Any other, lesser unity in the Church is unthinkable, unless the social structure of its social organization is to be quite at odds with its inner nature.*

"The Church...is formed around an already existing supernatural center, namely Christ and His Holy Spirit, and this center must, by intrinsic necessity, manifest itself in the social organism in the person of a single representative, a single organ. The Church does not project this central point from itself, nor is the center set up by God merely for the purpose of completing the Church as an undivided whole. Rather, it is intended to be the foundation upon which the Church is constructed; by which the Church rests upon the God-man and the Holy Spirit, and by which the unity of the Church is not incidentally brought about or crowned, but is essentially procured. *The Church as a society is held together in this central point, as it is in Christ; through it the Church is in Christ, because it is only through it that Christ, as the supreme head of the Church, is in the Church with His pastoral power....*

"Why should we be reluctant to admit a mysterious foundation for the external organization of this structure (of the Church), whose entire being is a mystery? Why should not the Holy Spirit, who dwells in the priesthood with His marvellous fruitfulness in order to distribute His graces in the Church through its agency, be able so to dwell, and why should He not actually dwell, in the central point of the Church's social structure, in the bearer of His pastoral power? Why should He not bring the whole flock together in faith and love from that point, and through it impart unity and stability to the structure? Such union of the Holy Spirit with the (visible) head of the Church would be a tremendous wonder; but it ought to be precisely that. The. Church is throughout an awe-inspiring, divine edifice. What wonder that its Rock-foundation should be so remarkable? The Church is the Bride of the God-man. What wonder that it should be so closely united to Him through its visible head, and be so marvellously guided by Him through its visible head?

"Only in terms of the fullness of the pastoral office in the head of the bishops, can we form an adequate notion of the sublime maternity of the Church..." (M. J. Scheeben, *The Mysteries of Christianity,* English edition, 1946).

I did not ignore examining the other Catholic doctrines (the Procession of the Holy Spirit from the Father and the Son, Purgatory, the Immaculate Conception, the Assumption, etc.) which had been attacked or denied by Orthodox theologians. Their objections were without merit and oftentimes Orthodox theologians disagreed with each other.

The basic self-contradiction and incoherence of the Byzantine Greco-Slav schism lay in its rejection of *a visible head for the visible Church Militant.* An acephalous hierarchy was a monstrous entity. The "undivided Church of the first seven Ecumenical Councils" was an historical fiction except on the Catholic premise of an hierarchical Episcopate having a visible head and centre of unity with the supreme authority to call or confirm such Councils. The very *unity* and *infallibility* of the visible Church (professed by most Orthodox) could not logically be upheld without the admission of a visible head possessing infallible authority in faith and morals.

The great heretical and schismatical movements combatted by the first seven Ecumenical Councils had involved sometimes hundreds of Bishops engaged in rebellion against the See of Peter and the Bishops in communion with him. When Patriarchs and Bishops disagreed with one another over the most complex and intricate questions of dogma, how could a simple believer (much less scholars) possibly resolve the question as to which group of Bishops had preserved the orthodox and apostolic faith? The "Eastern Orthodox" had no answer to this burning question. Catholics, however had a *visible criterion* easily applied by *any* believer to determine where the true Church was—which group of Bishops had embraced schism and/or heresy and which group was in continuity with Catholic Tradition. St. Ambrose had put it as succinctly as possible: "Where Peter is, there is the Church." The *visible criterion of Catholicity had always been visible communion with the See of Peter.* The true Church of Jesus Christ is always identifiable by its communion with the infallible Chair of Peter. Since the "cursed schism" with Rome, the autocephalous Eastern Orthodox churches lacked that supreme authority with which Christ had endowed His Church to assure its remaining always One, Holy, Catholic, and Apostolic. In the 13th century, as Byzantine polemics against the Apostolic Primacy increased, the Angelic Doctor St. Thomas Aquinas pointed out the disastrous consequences of negating the *Petro-centric structure of the Hierarchical Church:*

> "And while they deny that there is one (visible) head of the Church, that is to say, the Holy Roman Church, they manifestly deny the unity of the Mystical Body, for there cannot be one body if there is not one head, nor one congregation of the faithful where there is not one rector. Hence, 'there shall be one flock and one shepherd'" (*Contra Errores Graecorum*, Part II).

The logical result of denials of the Catholic dogmas of Papal Primacy and Infallibility has been, sadly, the abandonment of traditional ecclesiology stressing the visibility and infallibility of the hierarchical Church. Thus the

Russian theologian Nicholas Zernov has written in Protestantizing fashion:

"There are not and there cannot be external organs or methods of testifying to the internal evidence of the Church; this must be admitted frankly and resolutely. Anyone who is troubled by this lack of external evidence for ecclesiastical truth does not believe in the Church and does not know it.... The ecclesiastical fetishism which seeks an oracle speaking in the name of the Holy Spirit and which finds it in the person of a supreme hierarch, *or in the episcopal order and its assemblies*—this fetishism is a terrible symptom of half-faith" *(The Church of the Eastern Christians,* 1942).

Similarly, the Greek theologian P. Bratsiotis revealed the utter breakdown of the traditional principle of hierarchical authority once exercised in the "undivided Church of the first seven Ecumenical Councils" when he dared to write:

"...The supreme authority in the Orthodox Church lies in the Ecumenical Councils *whose ecumenicity must be recognized and witnessed by the conscience of the whole Church.* In other words the decisive criterion of an Ecumenical Council is the recognition of its decrees *by the whole Church which is therefore in fact the sole authority in Orthodoxy"* (The Ecumenical Review, Vol. XII, p. 161).

By the above criterion none of the first seven Ecumenical Councils could be recognized as truly ecumenical since none received the adherence of the whole Church; each was rejected by large numbers of the laity and hierarchy. Clearly, without a visible head of the Church able to confirm Councils as "ecumenical" in the name of "the whole Church," the very notion of "Ecumenical Council" was rendered meaningless.

The above analysis was developed at far greater length as I sought to unravel certain difficulties encountered. Suffice it, however, to note that by my last year of University study I had become convinced that to be true to itself as well as to the simplest facts of Church history, Eastern Orthodox ecclesiology logically demanded belief in the Catholic dogmas of Papal Primacy and Infallibility. Belief in One Visible Church constituted by Christ as "a People made one with the unity of the Father, the Son, and the Holy Spirit" made historical and theological sense *only* in the context of a Primacy of supreme authority bonding in unity the entire collegial-episcopal structure of the Church. "Thou knowest that I love Thee," thrice replied the Prince of the Apostles to the Risen Lord before receiving the chief authority in the Church (Jn. 21:14-18). This Apostolic Primacy of Peter and his successors, the Roman Pontiffs, was also a Primacy of Love. This Primacy of fatherly love in the Church established by Jesus Christ, the 'Lover of Mankind,' to endure perpetually in Peter and his successors had its fitting exemplar in the effusion of love that characterized the Procession of the Holy Spirit from the Father and the Son.

Since I had reached the point by God's grace that I could no longer justify being separated from the *Catholica* (as St. Augustine described the true Church) built upon the impregnable Rock of Peter, I took the opportunity to be formally reconciled. This occurred in 1952, shortly after I was inducted into the Army and before leaving for Korean service. Ruth had entered the Church even earlier, and we were married after my basic training ended. Needless to say, both our families were upset with our becoming Catholic, and with our marriage. We have always felt, however, that the Catholic Faith is "the pearl of great price" for which no sacrifice is too great. I have always looked upon my embracing Catholicity and our marriage as among the greatest graces received in my life.

I pray daily for the reintegration of the Byzantine Greco-Slav peoples into Catholic Unity. Would that more Catholics did so, recalling that one of the major reasons for the calling of the 2nd Vatican Council was to achieve the end of that "cursed schism"—a goal desired by so many Saints across the centuries (including the recently canonized Croatian confessor St. Leopoldo of Castelnovo, OFM. Cap.). May God grant it in the reign of our Slav Pope, His Holiness Pope John Paul II, through the intercession of the Immaculate Mother of God, Help of Christians.

Glory be to Thee, O Christ Our God.

James Likoudis *is Vice-President of the international lay association Catholics United for the Faith (CUF) and is widely known as an author and lecturer on catechetics, sex education and historical theology. His latest book,* Ending the Byzantine Greek Schism, *elaborates in greater detail the doctrinal and theological issues which continue to keep Catholics and Eastern Orthodox apart. It is available from Catholics United for the Faith, 45 Union Avenue, New Rochelle, New York 10801. Married to the former Ruth Hickelton, and father of six children, he lives in Williamsville, New York.*

The Wonderful Ways of the Lord

Judith Bane Livingston

Born in Oklahoma and raised a Baptist, I was a most unlikely convert to Catholicism, for prejudice was a fact of life in our home and church. We were taught that the Catholic Church was a pagan religion in which people worshiped just about everything but God. It was especially irksome that they worshiped Mary and any number of people they called saints.

I was a faithful attendant at church when we moved to California. At about the age of eight, I received my first Bible—a prize for memorizing so many Bible verses. It was the King James Version, and I especially loved the psalms. I read through the Old Testament, stumbling over all the genealogies of the various great men, and had smooth sailing through the New Testament until I reached Revelation. When I inquired about the Anti-Christ, I was told he was the Pope. When I asked about the "Whore of Babylon," I was informed that this meant the Catholic Church. Consequently I steered clear of anything or anyone who was connected with the Church. When we had to pass the Catholic Church on our way to the library, we always crossed the street so as to avoid anyone who might be coming out or going in. My prejudice was so deep that God had to use rather extraordinary means in order to reach me.

As I entered my teens, I began to question my beliefs and sensed that something was missing. I know now it was the sacraments.

I had been baptized at the age of twelve, after having accepted Jesus as my personal savior by going before the congregation and acknowledging my sinfulness and need for Jesus to come into my life. Baptists don't believe in original sin, so for us baptism was more of an initiation into the church and a removal of actual sin we had committed than a removal of original sin and incorporation into the mystical body. We certainly didn't believe in confessing our sins to a priest (John 20:23), since we felt that one could go directly to God for forgiveness.

Just before my eighteenth birthday I married—and to complicate matters even further, I married a Mormon. Our beliefs were somewhat different, but we certainly could agree on our dislike for and distrust of the Roman Catholic Church. Fourteen months later I became a mother.

As the trials of marriage and motherhood began to get me down, I felt a need to draw closer to God. I always had been an avid reader and now I started to read books on other religions (being careful to avoid anything about Catholicism). I read books by Joseph Smith, the founder of the Mormon Church, and really tried to become interested in my husband's religion. However, I couldn't accept Joseph Smith's claims of being a prophet. Then I studied Eastern religions—Buddhism, Yoga, etc.—and with all my searching I succeeded in becoming more confused than I had been when I started.

Finally my husband moved us to North Dakota, since he had obtained a job working on the construction of the big Garrison Dam. He worked the night shift, six nights a week, ten hours a shift, and came home exhausted—unable even to talk to me. He would fall asleep at the table while eating breakfast. I had the task of keeping our baby son quiet so daddy could sleep undisturbed.

The small town in which we lived was not very friendly. The people weren't pleased to have a group of big-city construction workers and their families invade their peaceful domain, so I became isolated, very lonely and homesick for my family. I had never been away from them before. Now I see that this was all part of God's plan. I began to pray more earnestly, seeking God's help. I began to ask Him to show me His Church, since all of my searching and reading had only confused me. Every night before I went to bed, I prayed, "O Lord, show me Your Church."

Winter came on with a fierceness I had never before seen— blinding snowstorms and a temperature of 40 degrees below zero. Because the project at the dam site had come to a standstill, I begged my husband to take me home to California for those winter months. He agreed and we returned to stay with my parents until the job opened up again. How happy I was to see my family and friends!

One night after I had said my usual prayer asking God to show me His Church, I fell asleep and had a most extraordinary dream. I was living at some point back in the past and was wearing a long robe and sandals. I was in a dark cell with other women, among them my mother, my sister, and several of my friends. We were all frightened and singing hymns to encourage one another. Suddenly we heard a group of men coming. They were dressed like the Roman soldiers of old. The one in front carried a spear, which he stamped on the floor as a signal for the others to halt. The door of our cell swung open, and he called out the names of three women. To my horror, my sister was among the unfortunate ones. I understood that they were to be taken out to die by having their heads cut off.

Our cell was below ground level, but if we stood on our tiptoes we could see through slits in the wall out into the arena and the hills beyond. My sister was dragged out and marched upstairs. I called after her not to worry because I would pray and ask St. Cecilia to intercede so that God would save her. Then I fell to my knees, made the sign of the cross, and began to beg St. Cecilia to come to my sister's aid. Suddenly my friend Joan, who was also a prisoner, tapped me on the shoulder and told me to go look out the narrow opening. I looked out and standing on a hill beyond the arena was my sister Jenny. She raised her hand and waved to me. I was overjoyed and said, "I knew St. Cecilia would help her!"

I awoke with a start, shaking and in a state of shock. That dream was so vivid that I still remember it now as though it had just happened. I was confused. I couldn't imagine what had made me dream such a strange series of events. In the first place, why had I acted so differently? I mean, I had never prayed to a saint. I had never even heard of a St. Cecilia. I had never made the sign of the cross in my life. I had never read about early Christian martyrs, except in the Acts of the Apostles in which Stephen was stoned to death outside the gates of Jerusalem. To say I was troubled is putting it mildly. I was beside myself. I was afraid to go back to sleep because I might dream that dream again, and I didn't think I could survive the fear.

Morning came at last and I went into the kitchen and sat down at the table. When my mother came in to start breakfast, she looked at me and said, "Judy, what on earth is the matter? You look like you've seen a ghost." I was afraid to tell her, but since my mother was quite good at getting to the root of a problem, she pressed me until I blurted out the dream. She stared at me with an accusing look and asked, "You've been reading Catholic books, haven't you?"

I raised my hand and swore, "Mother, you know I'd never do that."

"Well, where did all that nonsense come from then?"

Just about then our next-door neighbor, Mrs. Williams, went to take her trash out. My mother ran out and stopped her. Mrs. Williams was a dear little woman from Pennsylvania. We liked her, even though the poor soul was Catholic. To my dismay my mother told her about the dream and questioned her about St. Cecilia. Mrs. Williams blessed herself and told my mother that I should go to see her priest. Yes, there was a St. Cecilia. She was the patroness of church music. Mother came in and told me everything. I retorted, "You've got to be kidding! Me go see a Catholic priest? Never!"

That night I was reluctant to say my prayers and even more reluctant to go to bed. I didn't know what the outcome of my prayer for God to show me His Church might be. And besides, I thought that perhaps the devil could be trying to knock me off balance and detour me somehow. Surely the Catholic Church couldn't be the true Church!

I went to sleep quite troubled. Around 2:00 a.m. I woke with an excruciating pain in my lower right side. It was so sharp I couldn't get out of bed. My husband and mother decided to call a doctor. He arrived and diagnosed acute appendicitis. He gave me a shot of Demerol for the pain and said I should be operated on immediately before my appendix burst. My husband called Dr. John Wood, who had delivered our son. We knew and trusted this surgeon even though he worked in a Catholic hospital. I was bundled into the car, and my husband broke all the speed limits to get me to the hospital in time.

But when we reached there, a count was taken and the doctor saw that my white count was normal. He concluded it wasn't my appendix. However he wanted to keep me overnight for observation. He gave me another injection for pain and I drifted off to sleep.

I awoke in the morning when the door to my room opened and a smiling young sister, looking like a vision in white, seemed to float in. The medication was still in effect or I wouldn't have spoken to her. "What in the world ever made you want to be a nun?" I blurted out. She smiled. Then she sat down beside my bed and told me the story of her vocation. She asked me if I were

Catholic, and I quickly assured her I wasn't. I had always thought that a person had to be born a Catholic, because no one in a mature frame of mind would join a religion like that. To me, Catholicism was like a genetic defect. She assured me that the Church was very mission-minded and asked why I was interested.

"Well, I said, I had a dream about one of your saints." She immediately became excited, but I pretended not to remember the saint's name. "Oh, was it the Little Flower?"

Well, that did it. I hastily replied "No" and became a little alarmed. Who or what was the Little Flower, anyway? These Catholics were really strange after all. Maybe they would pressure me to join, since I was sort of at their mercy, down in bed and unable to get away. But no. She just changed my bed and said that if I would like some information about her faith she could bring me something to read. I agreed and hoped she would forget about it.

The doctors ran several more tests and finally released me, saying they could find nothing wrong. I was packing my overnight case when suddenly a little old sister came into the room with some pamphlets in her hand. She put them on the foot of the bed without much comment. I hastily packed them away and went home with a sigh of relief.

Spring arrived and we drove back to North Dakota. Once again I had to spend a lot of time by myself. I unpacked our bags and came across the pamphlets. In reading them, I noticed a coupon that I could send to Kenrick Seminary in St. Louis for a course on the Catholic Faith. I was assured that no one would bother me. I sent in the coupon and received a book explaining Catholic doctrine and practices. I was surprised to see it full of Bible quotations: were Catholics allowed to read the Bible? I went through the whole book, and slowly some of my prejudice began to melt away. I read nothing that was contrary to reason. The grace of God enlightened my mind with the truth I had sought for so long. I knew that I must find out more about this much-maligned Church.

Discovering that our Lord left us seven sacraments, the sure way and means for living a truly Christian life and dying in His friendship, was such a comfort to me! Jesus has not left us orphans, floundering around helplessly. We are truly His beloved children and He cares for each of us. In fact God had cared enough that He literally put me to sleep so He could reach past my prejudice and plant the seed of conversion. He had put me in a Catholic hospital, where I obtained the means of learning about His Church.

I wish I could say that this was the end and I lived happily ever after, but the trials were just beginning. When I told my husband I wanted to join the Catholic Church, he flew into a rage and said I could just forget it because if I persisted he would leave me and I would never see him again. He said, "Over my dead body will a child of mine ever enter a Catholic Church, much less be baptized." I knew he meant it, for he never made idle threats. He said, "You are a young woman (I was twenty) and I don't know much about Catholics except that they don't believe in divorce, and you will get mighty lonesome by yourself." That seemed to be the end of it.

When the construction had been completed, we returned to California, settling in Anaheim. I kept praying that God would change my husband's attitude. He couldn't stop me from reading, so I checked out books from the library and became familiar with the saints. I looked up St. Cecilia and found out she was an early Roman martyr. She had been shut up in her bath and they had tried to steam her to death, but instead of dying she sang hymns to the Lord. As a last resort they took her out and tried to chop her head off, but the executioner botched it because she lived for three days more. I was struck by the means of her death. In my dream my sister was to have been beheaded. How strange that I should have asked St. Cecilia to help my sister!

I kept noticing the big old red brick St. Boniface Church. No longer did I cross the street to avoid it. Each time I went into town, there was a sign indicating the time of Mass. I got up my courage to ask my husband to let me see what it was like. He must have thought that once I attended and saw how different everything was that I'd regain my senses and forget the whole thing. He took me and dropped me off.

I climbed the stairs and entered the dimly-lighted church. I looked around in awe. How beautiful it was! I gazed at the stained-glass windows, the votive lights burning before the statues, the beautiful red lamp hanging from the ceiling in front of the tabernacle. I noticed a statue of a lovely young nun holding a cross and a bouquet of roses in her arms. Later I found out she was St. Theresa, the "Little Flower of Jesus," that the sister had mentioned to me in the hospital.

I went halfway down the middle aisle and sat down in the middle of the pew. The church was beginning to fill. I glanced around me and was astonished to see men kneeling in prayer. We always stood to pray. I began to feel out of place. What in the world was I doing there? I decided I'd better leave well enough alone and forget the whole thing. Just as I stood up to leave, the rest of the congregation stood with me, and I saw the priest coming out into the sanctuary. The Mass was beginning.

When the priest read the announcements, I knew why I was there. He said they were starting an inquiry class for anyone interested in learning about the Catholic Faith. It would be held Monday and Friday evenings at 7:30 in the rectory next door. I knew that message was meant for me.

When I went home after the Mass, my husband seemed to be in a benevolent mood, so I got up my courage to tell him I wanted to go to the classes and see for myself what the Catholic religion was all about. He smiled and said, "Well, if you want to go, you will have to walk, because I'm not driving you there!" I accepted his ultimatum, even though it meant I'd be walking at least a mile along a dark street past an orange grove.

I spent the next six months taking instructions and didn't miss a class. I met a very nice lady who was also taking instructions. She would pick me up and take me with her, so I only had to walk a few times. I had proved that I was sincere and God took care of the rest.

The instruction sessions were long, because I questioned everything. Later, the priest told me that he had to return to some of the books he had used in his seminary days to find the answers to some of the questions I asked. You see, I wanted to make sure that I was really joining God's true Church.

When I was ready for the big step, I told my husband. He forbade me to join the Church. I told him that he didn't own my soul, that I *had* to do what I knew was right. God hadn't brought me this far to quit now.

It was putting a real strain on our marriage. I remember buying a rosary, hiding it under my pillow and saying it every night for his conversion. If he had known I had it, he would have thrown it away. I was encouraged when I saw my friend Joan (the one in my dream) and learned to my happy surprise that she had recently become a Catholic. In fact, all but one of the women I recognized in that dream have become converts through the years, including my mother and sister.

After my baptism, life settled down more or less. At least, I thought it had. Then out of the blue my husband's parents moved out from the East, and when they discovered I had become a Catholic they became very much disturbed. My father-in-law came over every evening and preached to me. I thought I would lose my mind if he didn't stop. I told the priest that I was afraid my in-laws might convince my husband to leave me. After all, he had threatened me once before about running away with my son and never allowing me to know where they were. The priest told me not to worry—that some day my husband would be an exemplary Catholic if I would just trust God and the Virgin Mary.

The attack continued. My mother-in-law came and bothered me in the daytime and my father-in-law continued to do so at night. My husband just sat there and hardly said anything. I prayed to the Holy Spirit to give me right answers. Finally one evening my father-in-law went too far and made a statement about Catholic morals that was so absurd that even my husband had to defend me. He said, "Dad, I don't know much about the Catholic Church, but I do know my wife and she wouldn't belong to an outfit like that." He challenged his father to go down to the rectory with him and confront the priest. They ended up doing just that. The inquiry class was in session when they arrived, and the lesson was on the sixth and ninth commandments.

I was a nervous wreck the whole time they were gone. I got on my knees and prayed the Rosary. It seemed they were gone for hours.

When my husband returned he said, "You don't have to worry. Dad won't bring that up again. He couldn't find a thing wrong with what the priest said."

I dared to ask, "What did you think about what the priest said?" He said that he thought he would go back again to get some things cleared up.

When I saw the priest he said, "Don't you see, Judy? When your husband defended you, he was also defending your religion." My husband began to take instructions, spending many hours in the library double-checking what he learned. After months of intense study—by the grace of God—he joined the Church. God's plans are so different from ours. God had used the very person I was most worried about in order to convert my husband.

Ours has been a long journey and at times perilous. For example, after years of attacking my beliefs and listening to me dispel her prejudices with the help of the Holy Spirit, my mother-in-law decided to join the Church. When my father-in-law found out he became violent and threatened our lives more than once.

After attending the University of Minnesota my brother-in-law had lost his faith in God and had become an agnostic. He came to seek work in California, hoping to convince us to leave the Church. He came to visit every week, and the discussions started all over again. The difference this time was that his method of attack was more intellectual. Once again the Holy Spirit came to our aid. Just as I began to feel it was hopeless, I said one evening after a long discussion, "I don't know why you don't discuss this with a priest." He grinned at me and replied, "Oh, I've been going to instructions for six weeks now." He later joined the Church and went to Africa as a lay missionary.

Through the years family members on both sides came to attack our Faith and ended up joining the Church. Was it worth it—all the trials, troubles, unbelievable stress? I can only say "Yes," a thousand times yes. God has blessed us beyond our wildest dreams. We have five sons and three daughters, two of them Daughters of St. Paul. Would I have believed any of this before that strange and wonderful dream? Never!

Judith Bane Livingston *was baptized a Catholic on July 7, 1951, at St. Boniface Church in Anaheim, California. She has been happily married for more than forty years. The Livingstons have five sons, three daughters and several grandchildren. Active at the Byzantine Parish of the Annunciation in Anaheim, Mr. and Mrs. Livingston also enjoy traveling. In 1986, Mrs. Livingston was able to realize a long-time dream of making a pilgrimage to the Holy Land and Rome, which included a visit to the Basilica of St. Cecilia.*

"Love One Another..."

Ferdinand G. Mahfood

In December of 1975, my wife, Patricia, bought me a book entitled *Something More* by Catherine Marshall, as one of my Christmas gifts. I started to read it during the holidays and planned to finish the book while on a business trip from Florida to Chicago in January of 1976.

I was thousands of feet above the ground when I began the chapter on "The Holy Spirit." As I read about the Third Person of the Trinity, He chose to come into my life—virtually out of the pages of this book. Tears started to run out of my eyes like a river. I started praying. I was overcome by a power that was much greater than I am.

It was not until much later that I understood these tears to be not of sadness but rather of purification. I had been brought up and raised a Catholic, but had never experienced any personal relationship with God.

I was still on the plane when I heard a voice in the form of a beautiful soft whisper ask me if I would go to Mass every day for the rest of my life. I was confused; I did not know who originated the question. "Are you God?" I posed mentally. After a long silence and some deliberation on my part, I concluded that the prompting was not coming from my own imagination, and I responded in the affirmative. "Yes, Lord, I will go to Mass every day for the rest of my life."

Since then, my life has never been the same. Over the years, as I have thought about this question, I have come to see that God was asking me if I would be willing to make a sincere commitment to Him, every day, for the rest of my life.

As I entered into this new era of my life, a life in the Spirit, God revealed Himself to me in a whole new dimension. I have come to know God as my Father, my *Abba*; Jesus as my beloved friend, brother and Savior; and the Holy Spirit as my special close friend and helper. I have found that over the years I have changed mentally, emotionally, physically, psychologically and spiritually. I became involved with the Charismatic Renewal which led me to be prayed over, and subsequently resulted in my receiving the greatest gift—that of LOVE! This gift of love is a free gift without qualification, without reason, and without a desire to be loved in return. It is the love that God asks us to have for Himself and for others. I just did not want to love Him only "mentally"; I wanted to love Him with my whole heart. God Himself infused my very being with this precious gift of love for Him, and for the poor. It was not of my own doing; it was the gift of Himself to me!

When someone experiences a conversion late in life, there are many habits to change and/or acquire. Because I had not placed God in the center of my life, I had reached maturity with a lot of anxiety, and I was suffering from a severe depression, which had resulted in a nervous breakdown. As a matter of fact, before my religious conversion, I did not even know how to pray. A nun at a retreat house introduced me to prayer and to the Bible. It was she who suggested that I read Psalm 26.

I got a Bible, and the next morning I went outside to pray Psalm 26. The end of the first verse of the psalm said, "And in the Lord I will trust without wavering." Those words hit me like a bomb.

I closed my Bible and said, "My God, that is my

problem. I don't trust you. That is why I am depressed, that is why I am sick, that is why I am suffering. I believe you exist—that is not my problem. But I don't trust you."

For five weeks I prayed those words day and night. I used to think the words at night when I was going to sleep, and when I got up in the morning they would still be going through my mind over and over and over. Then one morning I found that God had given me the gift of faith.

As I continued to walk with my Father, I learned to designate a time and place to be in His Presence, to be solely with Him and for Him. Vocal prayer gradually turned into contemplative prayer, and I began to discover God as He is. Simultaneously, the healing process within me had begun. Slowly and beautifully, the Lord began to heal me in all ways. After 10 years of prayer and trust, I am now totally free of all depression and bouts of anxiety. I am filled with utter thanksgiving and joy because I realize, that truly, He is The Divine Physician.

As a result of my ongoing relationship with the Lord through prayer and the Eucharist, and from my willingness to observe and obey His Word, FOOD FOR THE POOR was born. I had already dedicated my business, Essex Exports Inc., to the Lord and had asked Jesus to be its chairman. (My staff and I gather for a prayer meeting every day before our workday begins.) I have seen my business prosper in a way that I could never have imagined.

Because I was going to daily Mass wherever I was, I always had to locate a priest and find out where he was saying Mass. My business takes me back to my native Jamaica quite often, and I began to develop a relationship with some of the missionary priests there. I went to the places where they said Mass—places I had never gone to before, orphanages and nursing homes and poor parishes.

I started to ask the priests, "What can I do to help you help these people?" It was a natural reaction because the people are so poor. Eventually I was helping about seven or eight priests in their work.

In 1981 one of the priests in Jamaica took me into a poor house called Eventide. Eventide is a government-operated home for some 700 men, women, and children who are mentally or physically sick, too sick to help themselves. The Jamaican government has no money to pay for proper care in the home, so many people are simply dumped there and abandoned. I spent three hours in Eventide on that first visit. I saw people who were so sick that I could not believe people lived like that in the world. I knew that people were poor, but I never knew that the society we live in has totally abandoned certain groups of people who cannot help themselves. It took me three days to get over that first visit. I felt that my whole system had gone numb.

I sat down in my prayer room, and I looked at the crucifix, and I said, "Jesus, what does one do in the face of this type of poverty? I do not have enough money to give away to help these people. Lord, what does one do?"

One day the thought came to me to become a beggar for the poor, a beggar for those who cannot help themselves. And that was the beginning of Food for the Poor.

FOOD FOR THE POOR, a non-profit charitable trust, exists mainly to help alleviate hunger, misery, sickness, poverty and ignorance in Jamaica, Haiti and other Third World countries. It also seeks to evangelize both the needy and the affluent. Based at 1301 Copans Road, Pompano Beach, Florida 33064, FOOD FOR THE POOR begs from God's people in the U.S. and transforms the donated funds into desperately needed goods that will not only meet the immediate requirements of the needy, but will also take the destitute poor a step closer to learning to help themselves. The Trust thus attempts to promote social justice and peace.

The Trust is a unique organization. We ask the missionaries of all denominations what their specific needs are, and the needs of their people. We then send them exactly what they need to help their people.

What gives me the greatest joy is to see the excitement in some of the priests when they meet me. Here is a man they can ask for anything. Food, vestments, Bibles, machinery—no matter what they ask me for, so long as it will build up the life of the poor and the life of the people, they get it.

In Cap-Haitien I heard that a Sister who works in the ghetto needed some help. She was afraid to bother me about it, so I went to the convent to see her. I found out that she wanted to start a sewing school for some of the poor ghetto women. She needed $400 for the materials to start her school.

I told Sister that I would send her the money the next week. Tears came to her eyes. She said, "God is good." I answered, "Yes, God is good, and because He is good He has given me the money to give to you."

As we were driving out of the convent I turned around to wave goodbye, and I saw tears running down her face.

To me that is worth more than giving a whole truckload of food. It is something you can't put a dollar sign on. That woman may stay in that slum the rest of her life, even if nobody were ever to help her again, because she knows now that someone else cares about what she is doing. I don't believe in the importance of volume—how many trucks you ship and how much food you ship. It's how many lives you affect that matters—how many people you bring hope and encouragement. That, to me, is what the Church is all about.

I keep falling in love with God every day, all over again. And that is why I have come to love the poor, because you cannot fall in love with God without falling in love with the human race.

If we are one universal Church, then the problems of the Haitian Church are the problems of the American Church. And the problems of the Americans are the problems of the Jamaicans. The problems of Father Lussier in Cap-Haitien and the problems of Father Bohnen in Port-au-Prince are our problems. We have to transcend the boundaries of a country, because the world is God's world.

Once you have faith, the rest is easy. Then one morning you wake up, and you start getting involved with the poor, and then you say to God, "Well, I will go and adopt two countries, and I will help nine million people, because you want me to do it."

Since 1982, the Lord has seen fit to allow us to always meet the requests we receive, whether in the form of food, clothing, or other goods. I could not do all this on my own strength. The energy for all that I do comes out of prayer.

I am interested in poor people because God is who He is, because the God who has shown His love to me also loves these people. I want to help the people through the medium of the Church, to give the priests and the nuns the tools with which to show their people the love of God and bring them closer to Him.

Simply helping poor people because they are poor does not help the world so very much. Helping people come to know God—that is what will truly help the human race.

I want to thank God for His grace, for my life and most of all for His only begotten Son, Jesus Christ, my Lord and Savior. I wish to thank the Holy Spirit, who guides, sustains and motivates my life daily. Also, I thank Him continuously for my wife Patti, for my family and for His prayer life within me.

Ferdinand Mahfood *grew up in Jamaica and eventually came to the United States, taking up residence in the Miami area. Although he had always been close to the Church, he began to enter into a deep, personal relationship with God in the 1970's. Then, when visiting missionaries in his native Jamaica, Mr. Mahfood came face to face with the poor for whose cause he has been "begging" ever since. The Mahfoods operate Food for the Poor at 1301 Copans Road, Pompano Beach, Florida, 33064.*

I Myself Will Shepherd Them

John M. Mallon

> *"For thus says the Lord God: I myself will look after and tend my sheep. As a shepherd tends his flock when he finds himself among his scattered sheep, I will rescue them from every place where they were scattered when it was cloudy and dark. The lost I will seek out, the strayed I will bring back, the injured I will bind up, the sick I will heal...shepherding them rightly."*
>
> Ezekiel 34:11-12, 16

When I was eighteen I fell in with a group of people who were practicing some kind of satanic activity. It is difficult to say or classify exactly what they were up to, except that they were running a large-scale, east-coast drug operation. The drugs, apart from supplying their income, appeared to be the front for what they were really doing. They seemed to be doing some sort of occult experimentation, or mind control, using the drugs to mask the effects. But it was difficult to ascertain the precise nature of their activity, because the urgent concern of the moment, once one had glimpsed it, was to get away from it.

It was the beginning of September, 1970, and I was at a party at "the farm," which was the headquarters for these activities. Our host had placed a cardboard kitty-litter box containing a mountain of his finest private stock (finely sifted marijuana) on the table and told us to dig in. I had been sitting across from the man in charge of the "chemical division" of the operation—that is, the psychedelic drugs—both chemical and organic. He was reportedly raised by Indians in New Mexico who based their religion on the use of hallucinogenic plants. I walked by and saw him working on a paper covered with mathematical looking, hieroglyphic-like symbols. I asked him what he was doing and he said, "I'm trying to figure out a way to get from the first dimension to the fifth without going through the second, third and fourth."

"That's cool," I replied, and went around to resume my seat directly across the table from him.

Off to the left, there were three men lolling about on a sofa saying things like, "Oh, this stuff is great! We could cut it with baking soda. Nobody would know the difference!" I was becoming disillusioned by the sleaziness I was starting to see around me. After all, didn't all this begin with lots of talk of "peace" and "love"? Just as I was thinking this, the man across the table looked up and said to them, "That's brotherhood!" Then he cast a strange, knowing look at me, as if to say, "I'm reading your mind."

It was a few moments later that it happened. Something hit me in the side of the head like a ton of bricks; it was invisible, like a gust of wind, and it screamed at me in a loud, taunting, silent, spiritual voice, "You're wrecked!" It had personality, and the image in my mind was of a little mischievous puff of wind as depicted in Casper the Friendly Ghost comics. At eighteen, I was quite a veteran of various states of intoxication, and prided myself on my ability to maintain self-control, stay on my feet, remain conscious, and keep my head and humor about me, in spite of the most bizarre and outrageous psychic, hallucinatory, or dangerous conditions I found myself in. I was experienced enough to know when my body was affected or my mind was affected. But I knew that this was no drug. Something different was at work here. I knew, somehow, that my *soul* was being tampered with.

All this was happening in an instant. When that voice hit me, insights started flashing on me—not in thoughts, but in flashes. Words flashed on me: "Wrecked!" "Wasted!" "Ruined!" "Stoned!" "Destroyed!" "These are all terms of destruction!" I could hear, sort of in the distance, the three men on the couch, exclaiming things like, "Oh, wow! I am so wasted! I am wrecked! This stuff is fantastic!" My flashes continued. "We are all destroying ourselves. Why is it so fantastic to be destroying ourselves?" "All I've wanted to do all summer is to get as stoned as I possibly could; now I've arrived. Am I happy? NO! I'm miserable!"

When that voice first hit me it was as if a clamp had grabbed me, and now I felt as though a steel mesh net had fallen over me. I had been fighting with all my strength to maintain control, because it felt as if someone was trying to suck my soul right out of me. I was holding onto my chair, white-knuckled for fear that I might lose myself completely. I had noticed, through this swimming mesh I was caught in, that the man seated across from me had been observing me and taking notes, and staring into my eyes. It seemed as though the force trying to rob me of myself was coming from him.

My flashes continued: "All I really wanted from all this drug stuff was some love. What am I doing in this place? Who are these people? They're not my friends! People love me, people care about me, people are praying for me. How did I get here?" As I looked about me through this mesh, all the people looked excruciatingly ugly, grotesquely cartoonish and one dimensional. I had noticed before, during, and after this experience that some of the people there looked like zombies—like walking dead—as if their souls and wills *had* been sucked out of them and were now under the control of these people.

In any case, the environment itself seemed to drip with a kind of slime, and I said to myself, "This is Hell. I'm here. This is what it looks like." And I immediately felt as though I were in the bottom of a barrel of snakes. I knew I didn't want to be there.

At this point, the swirling loss-of-control feeling was intensifying and the man across the table seemed to be stepping up his efforts. I was still gripping the arms of my chair. I was holding on, in the most absolute literal sense of the word, for my immortal soul. My will was fixed: "NO!" but my strength could not hold out much longer. I was fighting, I was sweating, and I was scared. Just when my strength was giving out, a glowing white and gold person came into me and said, "That's enough, John, you've seen enough. You don't belong here." And He spiritually grabbed me by the collar, so to speak, and snatched me out of danger.

I went limp in my chair. I was free; I knew I was safe. I looked up and saw my opponent slam down his pencil in disgust. He had lost. I crawled off to find someplace to sleep. I knew I was safe.

In the days that followed I was to ponder and seek answers to just what had happened to me. I knew I had encountered real evil and that something—Someone— had rescued me. I was standing in a bookstore in my suburban hometown looking through books on witchcraft to see if they could offer any insights about what had happened to me, or how to protect myself, or how to put a stop to such evil. I came across all sorts of symbols and talismans, garlic, pentangles, etc. However, as I was to remember from all my old Dracula movies, the number one symbol, the Last Word when it came to stopping evil, was the Crucifix. Then it hit me like joyful thunder—"So *that's* who that was!" Standing in that bookstore I reflected on the Crucifix: "If just this symbol is so powerful, *what about the man hanging on it?*" I thought. "There's more to *Him* than meets the eye."

The only place I had ever seen the Crucifix was in, or in connection with, the Roman Catholic Church. The Catholic Church somehow stood out as something very ancient and *real* through the mists of archetypical gothic horror and folk tales that made perfect sense in the context of the living folklore in which I was existing. Somehow I knew, deep down, that the ancient wisdom of Catholicism understood all I was experiencing.

I had grown up around priests all my life and never heard them discuss Jesus in any but an official context. Part of the job. Yet here He was in all His height, length, and breadth in the heart of my need—a need that certainly no priest I had ever met would understand: at least so I thought. In my experience of priests at the time, to query them about the supernatural was to get chuckled at, or at least brushed off. It was not something they would discuss. The supernatural was somehow buried in the sacraments. So, from this experience, the Church seemed to be the last place to turn for answers. Besides, they only talked *about* Jesus; I had *met* Him, and what I had heard about Him couldn't come close to His Reality.

I recall that in the weeks that followed I felt so bizarre and empty, and prayed, "Anything would be better than this, even a broken heart; at least then I would know I was alive, that I existed." Then one day I stopped in my tracks in that town square and prayed, "God, all I ever wanted from that drug scene was some love. Right now, I don't care if I live or die, so if You're so smart, *You* take over. You take over my life, because I'm worn out and I just don't care anymore." I turned, walked up the street, and met the most beautiful girl I'd ever seen, and within a few weeks fell deeply in love with her. She was sixteen, the daughter of devout Protestant parents. My influence helped to steer her somewhat away from the scene I had just escaped, but eventually her desire for excitement, parties, etc., was to clash with my need for peace, quiet (after what I'd been through) and her attentive love. In about nine months' time she left me, and I was to remember my prayer about a broken heart.

But I had met Jesus Christ—now what? I had no desire to be involved with any Church; I had met the Lord, but never any other person who could remotely relate to what I'd been through. So I said to Him, "Lord, you have led me places and shown me things not many other people have seen, and you must have done it for a reason; so if there are any of Your people who need to hear my story, feel free to send them to me. Use me in any way You want." And He did, in spite of the fact that I was going my own way—often into sin that I rationalized away. He would usually send people at a time when I most needed to be reminded of where I came from. In my rare visits to churches, I never felt at home in a Protestant church, even when I enjoyed the preaching. I abhorred being buttonholed during what they called "fellowship." But the Catholic congregations seemed dead and oblivious to what was going on. The real issue was pride. Mine. Besides, there were certain lifestyle adjustments I wasn't prepared to make. Like acknowledging I was in sin. I was to go on like this for years, knowing I had met Jesus, but getting into trouble.

Nine years later, in the summer of 1979, I reached a dead end. The young woman I had loved—whom I shall call Angie—reappeared in my life. She had turned to me as a friend because her marriage was falling apart, but I soon discovered that I still was in love with her, and in fact had never really gotten over her. For her part she was putting up a heroic struggle with her faith and emotions. It is a difficult thing when the very thing you want and need most—human warmth, affection, consolation, understanding, and love, or simply even laughter and distraction with the person it comes with most naturally—is off limits, as she was to me. The cross of my life had always been paralyzing anxiety with roots in my very early childhood that could be triggered by a rejection or a break in a relationship with a woman. The reappearance of this woman, whom I had wanted more than any other and had never really gotten over, now in a sense within reach, and yet in another quite real sense beyond my reach, was an absolute torment. It was horrific and gruesome pain, inordinate to the cause, and crippling me.

I had come to realize with the help of a psychologist, that this anxiety and depression also had to do with separation from God, the effects of sin. I had been stubbornly refusing the frightening call I was feeling to go to confession. I was rebelling because of some painful experiences I had had as a small child in parochial school; I still felt I didn't need the Church.

I confessed to Angie my need for God, and she told me that God would be gentle with me. After she said this, I hung up the phone, lay down on my bed and howled in tears and pain to God: "God, I love her! I want her! But I can't have her! You sent her to me in the first place, nine years ago! I never wanted her to break up with me, to go away, to marry someone else—now here she is! What am I supposed to do with these feelings? What am I supposed to do with this desire? With this lust? I don't want anybody else! How can I stop wanting her? Desiring her? How can I stop loving her?" That's where He stopped me—on "How can I stop loving her?" Suddenly, it was as though God the Father was gently shushing me with a big finger and saying to me, "I don't want you to. I want you to love her more."

"Oh. Yes, Lord, that would be easier." I had to smile. He had given me a way out. It was impossible for me to stop loving her, but instead of trying to love her less and going insane in the process, I could learn to love her more. His way.

Suddenly I knew what I had to do. I was called, summoned, to go down to the little Catholic church downtown. When I walked in, my knees buckled from the atmosphere of Mercy in the room. I barely made my way to a pew and collapsed in front of the Blessed Sacrament, and wept, and wept, and wept. I had met the Lord nine years earlier, and now on this hot summer day, Jesus the Bridegroom brought me home to meet His Mother. And the Family. I turned and looked around at the ceiling of the empty little church and it somehow seemed to be filled with persons. I couldn't see them with my eyes but they were *there!* I then felt myself being *loved* and embraced by these *personalities.* They were all saying, "John, we don't care about your sins! We love you! You're HOME! WELCOME HOME! WELCOME HOME!"

I knew then what I had—and by now wanted—to do. I had to humble myself and go to confession. I staggered up the walk to the rectory and rang the bell. The poor housekeeper hardly knew what to make of me—bleary-eyed, tear-stained, wobbly-voiced, and swaying on her doorstep. I choked out, "Can I see a priest?" She sent me around to the back door. The priest was a gentle, little old-fashioned kind of pastor. He didn't bat an eye at a thing I told him, and I told him *everything:* the farm with its witchcraft, satanism—whatever—and my various later exploits—everything. I was surprised by his lack of reaction to the goings-on at the farm, and when I pressed him he simply shrugged and said, "It's just idolatry, breaking the first commandment—worshipping false gods."

He gave me absolution—what a gift!—and I headed back down to the chapel where it seemed that all Heaven was still breaking loose. I realized what must be happening. Scripture says that when a sinner repents there is great jubilation in Heaven—and He was allowing me to experience the celebration!

Needless to say, this experience placed within me a deep and profound love for the Church, not to mention an enthusiastic fascination. I also realized that many of the angers and resentments that I had held towards the Church were simply from the encounters with the weak and fallible people that made it up, sinners like myself, and had little to do with what the Church actually holds to be true, teaches, and *is*. At any rate this experience marked my passionate return to the sacraments, and a faithfulness to simple prayer that God was to honor. I made a commitment to say, every night, on my knees, before bed, one Our Father, Hail Mary and Glory Be, no matter what, whether I was tired, drunk—whatever. I did plenty of other praying, but this was a point of discipline.

A confessor had told me to break off my relationship with Angie completely, because of the devastating effect it was having on me. Unexpressed love, I was to find, was like unexpressed grief: it can take its toll. I found I had only one outlet for my love for her, and that was prayer. There was a terrible void in my life that was shaped like her. So pray for her I did. This is what was meant when I was told to love her more, but still she was to haunt my thoughts and desires.

The third stage of my conversion started rumbling four years later in the early part of 1982. I believe the Lord took that time since I returned to the sacraments to prepare me for what He had in store for me. Toward the end of 1981, I met by phone a young woman who was a friend of Angie's. About two months passed and I tried to look her up. After quite a runaround I reached her at a psychiatric hospital. She had tried to take her life. It was triggered by some incident involving Angie. From the hospital she said, "Stay away from her! Stay away from that whole group! There's evil there; look what happened to me!" I came away from that phone call thinking, "People don't try to kill themselves because they're crazy; sometimes it's because they know something and can't handle what they know." I sensed there was something to what she was saying, that she wasn't just raving.

I experienced something—a call—something in the air. The only thing I can compare it to is the opening of the novel, *The Exorcist*, when the old priest excavating in the Middle East suddenly stops and senses something in the air; and he *knows* he is going to see his old nemesis again. I had been helping out in a parish, teaching CCD, and asked some devout men in the program if they knew anyone who could tell me about evil spirits. I knew I had encountered Satan before, and that I was experiencing some kind of call to spiritual warfare and intercession, and I wanted all the help and information I could get. Up to that time my experience in trying to get any answers about the devil from priests had been a waste of time. They would either change the subject or excuse themselves. Anyway, these men referred me to a deacon in the parish who told me, "I know evil spirits hate two things: holy water and the Rosary." He also gave me some literature in which I found the Prayer to St. Michael, which I was to add to my three nightly prayers.

I began to intercede intensely, convinced as I was that Angie was involved in some demonic snare. Indeed I was impelled to do so, and the more I prayed the more I began to suffer. I started to experience especially intense anxiety and panic attacks. It became so that the only place I experienced any relief at all was in front of the Blessed Sacrament. One day I went into the same church where I had had the impression of meeting the angels and saints years before. I was in a desperate state, and my prayer was basically, "*What* is going on?" I was pouring out to Jesus at great length and speed and not without a little annoyance, about the intense fear, panic and anxiety I was going through.

Suddenly, it seemed that I heard a woman's voice saying, "John, you have done well. Your prayers have been heard; your friends are safe. Now go out of here and live a normal life." "A normal life? You mean it?" Over the years, among other things, anxiety had kept me from holding a job. I was approaching thirty, living with my mother, and broke. Any kind of normal life had always been held teasingly beyond my grasp.

The dialogue continued: "A normal life, that's great, but *what about this pain?*"

"John, God has something in store for you beyond your wildest imaginings, but you must be patient."

"Patient? Yes, I believe you. God has something for me beyond my wildest imaginings, but I can't function; I can't work. *What about this panic?*"

"I know about the pain; I know about the panic, but you must be patient. I will give you something for the panic. Every time it strikes just say these words, 'Be of good courage, and wait upon the Lord,' and I personally will come and give you a boost of good cheer!" I tried it immediately and started to laugh, because it worked. "Now go out of here and live a normal life."

When I got up to leave and walked down the aisle, I said to myself, "I just had a conversation with the Blessed Mother. If I tried to tell anyone about it would they believe me? Did that really happen?" Just as I reached the back of the church after thinking this, something led me to the leaflet rack, and I placed my hand on something in there and pulled it out. It said, "Prayer to the Virgin, remedy against the spirits of darkness and the forces of hate and fear." All I could do was laugh; it was all true. I was to add that prayer to my nightly prayers as well.

The spiritual barrage against me remained intense—in the forms of profound skin-tingling anxiety, bleak depression, and violent temptations to the point that I felt quite literally like the rope in a tug of war between demons and angels.

During temptations I had the impression of being urged to sin, with the assurance that God would forgive me, while, on the other hand, an opposing impression that brought peace would warn and caution me. These urgings had a quality of personality behind them. If I fell to the temptation, I had the experience of being taunted and accused. But the peace-giving force would quickly be there, assuring me of God's great love for me and turning my thoughts to heavenly things. As these experiences intensified, I often gave in to the almost constant temptations. I believe it was the holy angels who were there with their consolation and encouragement, fending off the attacking demons before they could accuse me with their taunts. I experienced the words of Psalm 35:15-28. It may sound incredible, but right then there was no person on earth who knew, or could have known, what I was going through and the support had to come from somewhere. I wrote a poem at the time called, "Sometimes Your Only Friends Are the Angels." Years later, a Jesuit theologian told me that according to many spiritual writers, this is often the activity of angels and demons during particularly intense temptations occurring at crucial moments in our lives.

On Good Friday I went to church, hoping to go to confession before the service. I had had a difficult Lent. I hadn't kept to any of my resolutions. During the service I was in a front pew off to the side, sitting with people I didn't know. When they started to process down the aisle, I turned to look, and at the moment I caught sight of the large cross being carried, I broke down. I wept profusely—discreetly but profoundly. Only one prayer kept going through me over and over, "Oh, Jesus, I know, I know!" I was deeply and personally and intimately involved with His Passion—and knew that He was with mine.

I saw Angie on Easter Sunday night and came away happy from the meeting, feeling at peace with her. The next day, inexplicably, I woke up in agony. I knew I simply could not fight anymore. It was a complete spiritual collapse—time to *surrender everything* and completely let myself go into the Father's hands. The recurring message was that it was time to drop everything, and go out and be alone in the desert with the Lord. I kept getting this image of a vast desert completely away (and safe) from everyone and everything. I was just standing there alone with Jesus. And what peace there was in that!

God had certainly set the stage. I was mercifully fired from the part-time job I was holding. I hadn't wanted to quit, but the boss saw my suffering and felt it was best for me and the business if he let me go. He was right, and I was relieved. I had also just finished an unusually long stint of work as a musician and had more money in the bank than I had ever had in my life, which I was able to live on for the rest of the spring and summer.

I had read that when we are physically weak we need more food, and that when we are spiritually weak we need more spiritual food and should seek out the Eucharist more often. I began to seek out weekday Masses in the evenings. The only ones I could find were charismatic. The first time I walked into one particular room, I had a strange experience. I had never seen any of those people before in my life, but somehow I seemed to *recognize* them. I had been to one or two small prayer meetings before that and it hadn't fazed me much, but this time after Mass, a man got up and said, "This morning the Lord said to me...." I was stunned and thought, "There are others? You mean I'm not the only one? There are others like me who speak to God? I always believed it was real, but I didn't know there was anybody else. I'm HOME!"

I was ravenous. I got every piece of literature I could find on their book table and devoured it. I continued to go each week. I was incredibly excited. One day, sitting in my back yard going over this material, I blurted out, "Lord, I have to know more about this! I need to know more about this!" I believe I heard the answer from the Holy Spirit: "I'll lead you to a teacher...tonight!" Tonight! That night I was at the Mass, and the priest gave a homily that spoke precisely to what I was experiencing. I thought, "I'd love to talk to this man, but he's very popular. I probably won't be able to get near him." Sure enough, he was surrounded by people, but I did manage to ask him a question about his homily and its application to me. He was struck by what I said, looked directly at me and said, "We'll talk."

Moments later, when I turned, there was no one around him. He crooked his finger for me to follow him. He led me up several flights of stairs, sat down and looked at me. I felt that same prompting I had experienced in the afternoon moving me to tell this man my story. I did so. When I finished, he took my hands and said, "I want you to be my friend. I've been looking for a friend like you and I want you to be my friend." I didn't know what to say: I was amazed. Here I was walking in off the street, very broken and new to all of this and here was this very popular priest, obviously a leader to these people, telling me *he* wants to be *my* friend. He then laid hands on me, prayed, and said he wanted to make an appointment with me, because we should talk some more. We made an appointment for the following Saturday night.

It was a warm spring night, May 8, 1982, the eve of Mother's Day and a feast of St. Michael, the Archangel, no longer celebrated on the liturgical calendar. We were on the grounds of a convent retreat house, walking on a hill overlooking the sea. He said, "Tell me about yourself." I told him that I had been working with a psychologist who had been seeing me free of charge for the past seven years, and the major point we'd arrived at was that I suffered from an extreme fear of being abandoned by a woman. A breakup with a girlfriend could plunge me into a six-month nightmare. In fact, I was still suffering over the loss of my first love twelve years before.

He said, "Tell me about your mother's condition when you were in the womb." I told him that my mother had lost a child, a nine-year-old girl, in a car accident two years before I was born and that my father wouldn't allow her to talk about it. "So," the priest said, "the very environment you were formed in was all of that grief, anger, loss, anxiety and pain that she was carrying around in her body that she was forced to repress." He suggested we sit in the car, where he began to administer to me what is called "healing of memories"—a prayer for Christ, the Healer, who stands outside of time in eternity, but is present to all time, to go to the particular moment of trauma to absorb and heal the shocks.

As he was praying, he suddenly said in a firm voice, "I command you to give me your name!" The next thing I knew, a gnarled, ugly voice coming out of my mouth exclaimed, "Violence!" I was startled but intrigued. The priest continued, "Violence, I take authority over you in the Name of Jesus Christ. I bind you and cast you to the feet of Christ. I command you to leave this child of God!" He repeated the process, with the name "Hatred" coming forth. I thought, "Oh, my God, this man's doing an exorcism on me!" He then said, "John, I'm going to give you the Sacrament of the Sick, *because you're sick.*" I wept tears of relief as I realized that the humiliation, pain and terror I had been undergoing for so long were *not my fault.* They were tears of vindication, because here was the authority of the Church confirming what I had inwardly known all along—that I had been dealing with actual demonic forces—an awareness which had been discarded and unrelieved whenever I had tried to question others about it. It was all perceptible at last, complete with voices, manifestations, the sacraments of the Church, Christ tangibly present, and a priest who understood. Freedom.

He led me in a renunciation of these spirits, as he continued to call them out and expel them. This prayer is canonically called the rite of private exorcism, or, in popular language, deliverance prayer. I had heard of demonic *possession,* which calls for solemn, or public, exorcism and may only be performed by a priest with the permission of the bishop. But I was suffering from demonic *oppression,* in which certain areas of your life may be under the control of evil spirits, manifesting themselves in such things as addictions, compulsive and chronic sin, anxiety or depression. The door is opened to these spirits in various ways such as longstanding unrepented sin, innocently incurred emotional hurts and wounds, and most especially, involvement in the occult. In my case it had been all of the above.

The most difficult spirit to release was the spirit of lust, who had held me in an absolute *prison* of the sin of physical self-indulgence. Father explained that the spirit had attached itself to some deep psychological hurts and childhood fears of abandonment (which in no small way contributed to the anxiety in my relationships with women). I told Father about a massive magazine collection that I had, and that I didn't know if I had the strength to part with it. He said, "I'm not worried about the magazines. It's just that this spirit has been torturing you all your life, telling you you'll never be happy in a real relationship with a woman and that you need him and this habit to have any satisfaction whatsoever—but he's a liar." After the deliverance, the compulsion disappeared, and when after some months temptations occasionally returned, they were rooted in. simple human nature and urges, not in demonic compulsion. The magazines eventually went.

We were to continue for several hours, and far from being frightening or macabre, it was glorious. The Power of God applied to me personally, setting me free. We did not finish that night. Father said a prayer over me binding all remaining spirits, and we drove back to the church, where I requested the Eucharist. Father gave me the Eucharist, prayed over me and I was rested in the Spirit. I felt a deep trembling inside, and the names "Satan" and "Lucifer" came out of me. Exhausted by now, Father commanded him to leave. Father then took me into the rectory, blessed a gallon of holy water and instructed me to keep it with me. We made an appointment to meet the following week.

In the intervening week, I was drawn frequently and for long periods to the Blessed Sacrament and Mass. There I experienced the intimate closeness and personal love of Jesus for me in the most marvelous and moving ways. During these times further deliverance took place, and many of the deepest wounds of my heart—wounds that had resulted in insecurity, low self-esteem, horrors, guilts and fears—were ministered to by the affirming, tender, and at times even humorous love of Jesus. In Him is the fullness of Divinity, yet, with that, I also experienced Him as the most fully *human* person one could ever hope to meet.

When I met again with Father, he finished the exorcism. It was wild and exhausting, yet glorious. The name "Legion...There Are So Many of Us" came forth. My memory fixed on a single night in 1970 and I saw that on this particularly eerie night while I had been under the influence of LSD, Legion had climbed all over me and entered my life. To the best of my discernment, Legion was made up of a pack of about ten thousand spirits, all detestable. They all left at once in a kind of whirlwind, as I saw myself on Calvary clinging to the cross. I looked up at Jesus and was startled to see Him crying. The tears were falling on me. I forgot myself momentarily and began to cry at the sight of Him crying, but He said, "I'm crying for you, for all the pain, all the humiliation that these spirits have caused you, that no one could understand." I wept at His goodness and clung to His cross for my immortal soul. After the whirlwind stopped, I felt a tap on my shoulder and turned to behold my sweet Risen Lord! The storm was over; it was the first Easter morning. He said, "It's all right, it's over."

The deliverance experience was further affirmed by my psychologist, who later confided that he had been amazed when I told him actual proper names of demons that were revealed during the experience—names I had had no way of knowing, but which he had read while working at a theological library as a young adult attending Harvard Divinity School.

I was to go from Glory to Glory. I became wholeheartedly involved in the Catholic Charismatic Renewal and found tremendous healing in the Community, the Body of Christ on Earth. I went through a Life in the Spirit Seminar and was prayed over for the Baptism of the Holy Spirit, receiving gifts of tongues, healing and prophecy, among others.

I had the privilege of working as a volunteer at our Archdiocesan Office of Charismatic Renewal and becoming a ministry head in my prayer group on the intercessory prayer and healing ministry.

I continued to pray for Angie, who was having her trials. She recommitted her life to Christ. Then one day my burden, my obsession for her, absolutely lifted. I prayed, asking the Lord why, and this is what came to me: "*You* weren't the jilted bridegroom, *I was*, and I shared my pain for her with you, because I needed someone to pray for her. Now that she's come back to me, you no longer have that separation anxiety over her *because you are no longer separated from her*; you are united in the Body of Christ." From then on she was just another woman, a sister in the Lord.

I passed my high school equivalency exam with flying colors, with the gentle help of my priest friend who had prayed the deliverance with me. And at age thirty-one I entered Boston College as an undergraduate lay student in theology, with a passionate love for the orthodox teachings of the Catholic Church—a love I had learned the hard and glorious way from the Divine Master and His Paraclete. I even got a job at the University that covered my tuition. Every door was opened for me.

In the interest of "testing everything and holding fast to what is good," all the events recounted in this story, as well as my interpretations of them, have, at one time or another over the years, been presented before legitimate spiritual authority and Church officials, to the extent of laying them at the feet of my local regional bishop. He merely counseled me to seek out prudent spiritual direction, which I assured him I had already been doing.

> *You who dwell in the shelter of the Most High,*
> *   who abide in the shadow of the almighty,*
> *Say to the Lord, ''My refuge and my fortress,*
> *   my God in whom I trust.''*
>
> *For he will rescue you from the snare of the fowler,*
> *   from the destroying pestilence.*
> *With his pinions he will cover you,*
> *   and under his wings you shall take refuge,*
> *   his faithfulness is a buckler and a shield.*
>
> *You shall not fear the terror of night*
> *   nor the arrow that flies by day,*
> *Not the pestilence that roams in darkness*
> *   nor the devastating plague at noon.*
>
> *Though a thousand fall at your side,*
> *   ten thousand at your side,*
> *   near you it shall not come.*
> *Rather with your eyes shall you behold*
> *   and see the requital of the wicked.*
>
> *Because you have the Lord for your refuge,*
> *   you have made the Most High your stronghold.*
> *No evil shall befall you,*
> *   nor shall affliction come near your tent.*
>
> *For to his angels he has given command about you,*
> *   that they guard you in all your ways.*
> *Upon their hands they shall bear you up,*
> *   lest you dash your foot against a stone.*
>
> *You shall tread upon the asp and the viper,*
> *   you shall trample down the lion and the dragon.*

> *Because he clings to me, I will deliver him.*
> *I will set him on high because he acknowledges*
>   *my name.*
> *He shall call upon me, and I will answer him.*
> *I will deliver him and glorify him.*
>   *with length of days I will gratify him*
>   *and will show him my salvation (Ps. 91).*

"It is this same disciple who is witness to these things; it is he who wrote them down and his testimony we know is true. There are still many other things that Jesus did, yet if they were written about in detail, I doubt there would be room enough in the entire world to hold the books to record them" (Jn. 21:24-25).

John M. Mallon *is completing undergraduate studies in theology at Boston College and is interested in lay evangelization. He has published in* The New Oxford Review *and plans to continue writing. Mr. Mallon has worked as a professional musician and also has theater training. He grew up on the South Shore of Boston, and now resides in Brighton, Massachusetts.*

Two-Stage Journey

Onalee McGraw

The religious tradition in which I was raised could perhaps best be described as "mainline" Protestant. I had the good fortune to grow up within a stable and loving family. As a child I attended the same Presbyterian Church my mother grew up in. High school friendships drew me to the local Baptist church and friendships again determined my choice of the Methodist church while in college. During this time I never doubted the existence of God the Father or His Son, Jesus Christ. Yet, like most of the young people I knew, I tended to take God for granted and did not really consider Him to have any particular interest in, or expectations of me personally that required my consulting Him about my choices in life.

The college I attended in the late fifties was a typical small private liberal arts college that had once possessed a Protestant denominational identity which by the fifties had become non-denominational. Despite the cultural patterns that remained, such as optional chapel, dormitory rules, and prohibitions against drinking on campus, the philosophy that guided our required courses was the largely unstated view that we are autonomous human beings who historically came to full maturity in the so-called age of the Enlightenment with the triumph of science over what was classified as religious superstition. This bias was subtle, but quite pervasive, as reflected in the text of our required course in the history of Western Civilization: *The Making of the Modern Mind* by the prominent secularist historian of the thirties, John Herman Randall, Jr., a signer of the 1933 *Humanist Manifesto*.

Not surprisingly, the college's religion department was dominated by a professor with all the proper academic credentials who was solidly committed to the positivist school of Biblical criticism. Whatever vestiges of authentic Christian belief I may have retained from my Sunday School days were very soon eroded after my entry into this professor's course in 1958 called "The Life and Teachings of Jesus." We were taught that the "weight" of the "scientific findings" of Biblical scholars called into serious question the historical authenticity of the gospels. The gospel writers were portrayed as "conditioned" by sociological and psychological forces that shaped their "interpretation" of events recorded in the Bible.

Just recently, upon reading *The New Biblical Theorists* by Monsignor George Kelly, I realized that the same 19th century theories by which I had come to disbelieve in the historical truth of the gospels were now being adopted by prominent Catholic Biblical scholars and shaping the education of present and future priests in Catholic seminaries.

I still remember our brave classmate, a Baptist girl who did not realize that her orthodox Christian beliefs regarding the Divinity of Christ were decidedly at risk in our college. She challenged the thrust of our professor's lectures late in the course at the point where he outlined the list of "possible explanations" for Christ's empty tomb. Our professor wrapped himself ever more closely in his protective mantle of scholarly "objectivity" as he calmly and coldly informed her that he was only presenting what various Biblical scholars have speculated about and was not telling us which theory was the correct interpretation. Like most of the others in the class, I was too thoroughly puffed up with pride in my newly acquired "scholarly wisdom" to have much sympathy for this girl who received a very low grade in the class. Since coming to the Catholic faith, and entering a tradition quite different from her's, I still marvel at the raw Christian courage she exhibited in defending Christ and His truth against the strident voice of the cynical world's "wisdom."

In my senior year I discovered the world of philosophy in a course taught by the one Catholic faculty member on campus at the time. It was one of the most challenging courses that we had, forcing us to grapple with the thoughts of classic, medieval enlightenment and modern political philosophers. My own philosophical patterns of thought at the time were reflected in my choice of David Hume, the 18th century skeptic, as my favorite philosopher of the ages. Hume made the most sense to me because he argued that the human mind cannot know the cause of effects which our senses perceive. I was by this time deeply attracted to the notion that no absolute truth exists and that each person finds his own truth.

The professor of the political theory course in question was a mystery to me and to many of my friends. It was commonly acknowledged that he was the most brilliant professor in the humanities on campus and that his courses were the most challenging. We could not fathom how this was possible since we knew he was Catholic and we believed, simplistically, that Catholics could not think for themselves and merely followed whatever the Catholic Church told them to think.

Our difficulty in understanding the seemingly strange combination of faith and reason that obviously resided in the person of our political philosophy professor is a profound example of a fundamental strand common to some liberal Protestant thought.

This view is focused on the question: What is our essential nature as human beings and what kind of persons does God want us to be? I was convinced that God would not have created us with the ability to think and to reason if He did not want us to think for ourselves without His help and guidance. I believed that we fulfilled God's expectations of us by coming to decisions on our own, not "slavishly" following His will.

What are the implications of the New Testament teachings if God really wants us to be autonomous? The consequence is that the Commandments and Christ's gospel teachings are a general "guide" that has been handed down by custom in the Western tradition to aid us in our own autonomous decision-making. Dealing with the existence of heaven and hell is "no problem" for the kind of believer I was because it is assumed that only a few horribly wicked and evil people like Stalin, Hitler, and mass murderers are going to suffer the ultimate adverse consequences of ignoring God's admonitions.

The pronounced tendency of liberal-minded Christians to turn the historical nature of the gospels into sociological interpretations is understandable when we reflect on the words of the Lord: "Enter by the narrow gate. For wide is the gate and broad is the way that leads to destruction, and many there are who enter that way" (Matthew 7:13). St. Paul had to urge his Christian listeners: "Do not deceive yourselves: no fornicators, idolators, or adulterers, no sexual perverts, thieves, misers or drunkards, no slanderers, or robbers will inherit God's kingdom" (1 Cor. 6:9-10). Yet many people then and now deceive themselves, as I did, into thinking that a bland belief in a loving and merciful God can cheerfully coexist with the notion that He *wants* us to choose our own options without reflection or restraint.

This pattern of thought is in stark contrast to the evangelical tradition of Protestants who hold that the Bible is the inspired Word of God and not myths made up by a group of sincere but overly emotional followers of what they see as only a magnificent human being. C. S. Lewis in all his writings effectively debunks this contradictory notion of Christianity without the Cross.

When I spouted some of my newly acquired "wisdom" gained from the course in "Life and Teachings of Jesus" to my aunt, a devout believer in the Protestant evangelical tradition, I told her "not to worry" because "it really doesn't matter if Jesus was just a human being like the rest of us." She tried to persuade me to read C. S. Lewis, whom I had never heard of, and told me she would pray very hard for me. When I recall the Christian love my aunt revealed in that incident, I reflect on the beauty and mystery of the Mystical Body of Christ.

Having decided on a career in politics and government, I selected Georgetown University for graduate studies. It was Georgetown's location in the nation's capital that attracted me. I was only dimly aware that Georgetown was a Catholic university and this did not concern me since I viewed religion in general at that point to be of very little consequence. My ambition at the time was to become a lobbyist for the International Ladies' Garment Worker's Union. I had spent my senior year in college pouring over political opinion magazines like *The Nation, The Progressive,* and *The New Republic*—and dismissing most of my classmates as hopelessly middle-class and reactionary. As for my religious beliefs, I suppose I was something resembling a Deist when I entered the graduate school at Georgetown in 1961.

At Georgetown's graduate department in Government, courses in the history of political theory were required for advanced degrees. We studied the original works of all the major philosophers that have had an effect on Western thought: Plato, Aristotle, Augustine, Aquinas, Descartes, Luther, Calvin, Rousseau, Locke, Kant, Hume, Burke, Hegel, Bentham, Marx, Mill and many more. After months of reading and studying these thinkers it became clear to me that although there were many strands of diverse thought, there were really two fundamental traditions that had characterized the history of philosophy from ancient to modern times.

In the tradition, for example, of Aristotle and Aquinas, the philosopher sees truth as existing in a transcendent order beyond the human mind which man can discover through reason. In the second tradition, of which Descartes is the modern father, man searches for truth within himself and creates truth within his own mind. I began to see that the liberal arts education I had received in college was fashioned from various strands of thought within the Cartesian tradition, but that we had not even been exposed in any meaningful way to the first tradition. This was a revelation to one who had always assumed that being Catholic and "thinking for oneself" were two separate realms.

Moreover, my graduate class was one of the last in the early sixties to have the privilege of having as a professor the late Dr. Heinrich Rommen. Dr. Rommen, an internationally recognized Catholic scholar, had managed to get out of Nazi Germany to find a new home in the United States just before the outbreak of World War II. He was the author of *The Natural Law* and *The State in Catholic Thought*, which are modern classics in political philosophy. Like Maritain, Gilson, Von Hildebrand, Dawson and others of his time, he seemed to carry in his very being the philosophical Catholic response to modernity and the catastrophic events of the twentieth century. As I strained to understand the difficult thoughts he expressed in a heavy German accent and a voice that had grown tired with age, I grasped what he was trying to teach us: the connection between philosophical ideas and their actual consequences in the momentous events of our modern times. With hindsight, I guess one could say I was soaking up by mental osmosis the philosophical legacy of the Catholic Church. What I had yet to find was the faith to enter it.

In the midst of this exciting intellectual challenge, I met my future husband, Bill McGraw, a "cradle Catholic." I had gone to work for Bill, who at that time was in private law practice in Washington, D.C., as a temporary secretary so that I could earn money for a trip to Europe.

Bill and I engaged in "on the job" discussions in which he would take the conservative view and I would argue the liberal view, in both religion and politics!

Bill's parting gift to me when I left for Europe was a set of books which included C. S. Lewis' *Mere Christianity,* G. K. Chesterton's *The Everlasting Man,* and Henri Daniel-Rops' *Jesus and His Times.* C. S. Lewis convinced me of the soundness of authentic Christianity, just as he has convinced so many others. G. K. Chesterton made me laugh at my once dominant view that to be a Catholic was to be an unthinking slave to authority; and Henri Daniel-Rops, with his fantastic scholarly presentation of the case for the historicity of the gospels, dispersed all of the baseless arguments of my old college professor of religion.

On one of the last stops of my trip, I remember looking at an intricate piece of woodcarving in a Cathedral in Toledo, Spain, and thinking to myself, "A person of great faith must have carved that." I was not yet aware of it, but that summer my patterns of thinking became basically Catholic. Yet, I still did not have the gift of faith that I attributed to the woodcarver of hundreds of years ago.

Not long after Bill and I were married in December of 1963, I signed up for instruction classes in our local parish in Washington, D.C. Unfortunately, my priest instructor was already on the road out of the priesthood and his confusion concerning the content of the faith was reflected in his instruction. This was in 1964, even before Vatican II had ended.

Bill and I would have long discussions walking home from the classes on the difference between what "Father said" and the authentic teachings of the Church. It was unsettling to find that the treasure of truth I was seeking was marked by confusion and disunity. A few months later I tried again with a second course given by a different priest in the same parish.

In the final stages of instruction with him, I asked him in private conversation a question frequently on the minds of Protestants who are interested in Catholicism. How can the Catholic Church "pronounce" its "dogmas" on the Virgin Mary when there is no reference to these matters in the Bible? He responded that it is God Himself who has accorded the Virgin Mary these honors and given her the place in His Plan for salvation which the Church recognizes.

This does not mean that Catholics "worship" the Virgin Mary. His answer helped me to begin to understand a part of Church teaching that had troubled me in a new positive light. Yet somehow, I could not take the step of entering.

A few years later the same priest who had given me these revealing insights into the true role of the Blessed Mother became himself one of a number of priests who publicly dissented from Pope Paul VI's encyclical, *Humanae Vitae*. I continued to attend Sunday Mass with Bill and our children. We were blessed with a parish which, at that time, in its liturgy, school and parish life was not deeply marred with disunity and confusion. Living in the Archdiocese of Washington, however, we were very mindful of the national crisis through which the Church was suffering. In 1968, Patrick Cardinal O'Boyle had to suspend the faculties to teach, preach and administer the sacraments of more than forty priests who were in open dissent from Church teaching on *Humanae Vitae*. For this courageous action he was excoriated in the secular press.

Under these circumstances, my spiritual journey to the Church might have taken much longer, except for the providential development of a new friendship in early 1970 with a Catholic woman of wit and charm who came into my life. While visiting her home at the beginning of our acquaintance, she asked me if I was Catholic. I responded by indicating that I might like to be, but the available evidence suggested that "the barque of Peter seems to be sinking."

My new friend took up this challenge by responding that the Church was not sinking, but was suffering! She said that if I believed in the Church, I should not be content to remain outside and criticize the state of her affairs. Finally she said the words I shall never forget: "You must take your place at the foot of the cross with our Blessed Mother and John." How do you respond to a challenge like that? In the hearing of those simple and straightforward words, the doubts I had because of the disunity of the previous six years were simply swept away. I just looked at her and said, "You are right."

The next day I called our pastor and said I wanted to come into the Church right away and that I didn't need any more instruction classes. He kindly insisted that I have private instruction with him to fill in the gaps, and several weeks later, in April of 1970, I came into the Church. Upon my entry I took the saint's name of Bernadette for my middle name. I chose Bernadette because it was the incredible miracles attested to by unbelievers at Lourdes that had made such an impact on my still very skeptical mind several years before.

Then I began another journey to the spiritual treasures of the Church. To me the life of the Church is an immense mystery. The more you search, the more you are amazed to find what you had not seen before. In 1982, twelve years after becoming a Catholic, I discovered the spiritual "mother lode" of the Church. Up until that time, I was following the example of Martha instead of Mary. I was so taken up with all the things I was "doing for God" that I had really missed the essential point that we are meant to seek His will and cooperate with His Providential plan in all things.

I was busy with the many demands of family and career when a perfect stranger called and asked me to write a chapter for an anthology she was preparing on St. Catherine of Siena. Up to that time I had not studied or read deeply into the lives of any saints and was unfamiliar with St. Catherine. Very reluctantly, I took on the assignment. However, once I began to read the life and letters, and especially the *Dialogue* of St. Catherine, I was overwhelmed with the incredible way in which God revealed to her the answers to questions she dared to put to Him regarding the salvation of souls, the crisis in the Church of her time, and the meaning of His Providence.

Until my discovery of St. Catherine and the *Dialogue*, I had continued to see the responsibility for the outcome of events as resting primarily with us as God's creatures. We, in a sense, "worked for God," I thought, but in large measure the work we did was up to us. Now I see that when we turn the whole thing around the right way, the essential work we do is not primarily overcoming the evils of the world, but accepting and cooperating with God's Grace to do His will. This means struggling with our own fallen natures, and working to save our own souls and the souls of others whom we are called to love with a "special love."

In recent months, through the events surrounding the death of a friend dear to my husband and myself, I have learned again the lessons taught by St. Catherine regarding the ocean of God's Mercy and His thirst for souls. Our friend recently died a very painful and hard death. In religion and politics, my husband and I were worlds apart from our friend: an intellectual, skeptical unbeliever of Jewish heritage. Yet what endeared us and others to him were his many natural virtues of honesty, integrity, unselfishness, indifference to the trappings of position and power, and great generosity of spirit towards other people, even those who did not agree with him.

When our friend became seriously ill several months ago, my husband and I were moved to remember him constantly in our daily rosary and other prayers. It never occurred to either of us to do anything other than pray and offer masses for him since he was under heavy sedation most of the time in his hospital bed. No one outside the immediate family was encouraged to visit him for this reason. As his condition grew worse, our concern for him greatly increased, for in spite of his many natural virtues, he was an unbeliever. I told a close friend in Mass one morning of the deep anxiety we had for the soul of our friend who seemed so close to death.

That same day my friend called to tell me she had run across the famous story of Alphonse Ratisbonne, a Jewish skeptic who was deeply embittered against Christianity because of the conversion of his brother who had become a priest. In 1842, Ratisbonne found himself in Rome on his way to the East. During his visit there, a Catholic friend gave him the miraculous medal as a gift which he was very reluctant to wear. After putting on the medal, he entered a church to await his friend, who was making funeral arrangements. When the friend arrived there only minutes later, Ratisbonne was prostrated on the floor of the church in the chapel of St. Michael. He arose and said to his friend, "How good God is, what joy until now unknown! How great is my happiness! How are they to be pitied who do not believe!" Ratisbonne declared that the Blessed Mother had appeared to him as she was on the miraculous medal. He later became a priest and with his brother started two religious congregations devoted to prayer and good works for the conversion of Israel to the faith.

The story of Alphonse Ratisbonne was too dramatic to be ignored. Strangely enough, that very week a major Catholic periodical had carried a cover story on Edith Stein, "martyr of the Holocaust." Mary Arnold, the author of the story, said that if and when Edith Stein is canonized, she could possibly be "the patron saint of Jews, of non-believers, of intellectuals, of women, or of anyone preoccupied with finding the truth."

That very night our weekly parish novena to our Lady of the Miraculous Medal was taking place, and we obtained a blessed medal to offer our friend. When we arrived at the hospital the next morning we found the first "little miracle." Our friend was conscious, alert, and in good spirits. Somehow, we did not feel it was right to take advantage of him by bringing up the subject of religion or his situation. We felt that all we could do was offer the medal and our love. When we knew our brief time with him was running out as he was growing tired, I managed to get up my courage and suggest that "perhaps" he would like the medal to place on the bedside table or "perhaps" to wear. Then he said in a strong voice, "But I would like to wear it." With fingers painfully thin and weak, he started trying to undo the clasp he thought was on the chain. I put it around his neck and as we started to leave, we said, "God bless you." In a strong voice, he simply said, "Yes."

I realized later that we were in such a state that we did not say anything to him about the medal or what it meant. Another friend of mine said, "Our Lady takes care of things like that." Arriving home, I discovered that it was August 14, the Feastday of Saint Maximillian Kolbe. Our friend, who regained consciousness only a few times after our visit, died on the feast of St. Pius X, on the eve of the Feast of the Queenship of Our Lady. The mystery of Grace mingled with God's gift of free will remains. Yet I have now an even greater appreciation of my favorite verse in the *Dialogue* of Saint Catherine of Siena in which God tells Catherine of the truths regarding His Providence (Chapter 106):

> ...everything has been done and will be done by that Providence, because it is I who send or permit whatever happens, trials or consolations, whether spiritual

or temporal, in order to sanctify you and to accomplish My Truth in you. There in fact is My Truth: I created you in order to give you eternal life. This Truth is shown to you in the Blood of My only Son.

Before closing I wish to briefly state the apostolate in which I have been actively engaged most recently. Steadily rising rates of divorce, adolescent pregnancy and sexually transmitted diseases have, in a negative way, confirmed the wisdom of Church teaching in the area of human sexuality, marriage and the family where only a few years ago she appeared to the secular world as hopelessly outdated. Recognizing the great need today for positive alternative programs in this area, I recently joined with other professional women to form the Educational Guidance Institute. We are engaged in promoting educational programs in both public and private settings that provide moral guidance to young people and promote the family as the fundamental unit. Recent experience as the coordinator for a chastity formation program in my own diocese has convinced me that today's parents and their teenage children are open as never before to doctrinally sound programs that positively affirm the teachings of the Church on chastity.

Onalee McGraw is the coordinator for the "Love and Life" chastity formation program for young teens and their parents in the Diocese of Arlington, Virginia. She is also vice-president of the Educational Guidance Institute, a professional organization dedicated to abstinence-based education programs for young people in secular and Church-based settings. Formerly education consultant to the Heritage Foundation and on the professional staff of the House Committee on Children, Youth and Families, she is the author of several monographs on education and family issues, including Secular Humanism and the Schools: The Issue Whose Time Has Come; and The Family, Feminism and the Therapeutic State. Dr. McGraw lives in McLean, Virginia, with her husband William and their three children, Laura, Stephen and Thomas.

My Own Spiritual Journey

Dale O'Leary

As a child I was fascinated by the Catholic Church. Brought up in a family where there was a fair amount of anti-Catholicism, I heard stories about the strange things Catholics did and believed. I was particularly warned against dating Catholic boys.

I can remember when I was only nine sneaking into the Catholic church near my house. It was dark and I could see the candles burning in front of the painted statues. I fled in terror afraid I would be caught entering where I obviously didn't belong.

But neither did I belong in the succession of liberal Protestant churches which my parents attended. Even as a child I felt that neither the pastor nor the congregation believed the words they read and sang. I could not be a hypocrite. It was clear that Christianity demanded an absolute commitment, yet I saw no one in these churches who had made such a commitment.

I longed for faith, yet I did not believe and couldn't pretend that I did.

I did have one moment of grace. One spring day in my senior year in high school I took the train to Philadelphia to do research at the public library. Walking back from the library, I had to pass the Cathedral of Sts. Peter and Paul, and seeing it was open, I went in. Still afraid of being caught and recognized as a Protestant, I tied a ribbon I had in my pocket around the crown of my head like a hat. I knelt in the back of the church afraid to approach the altar. Even the act of kneeling was special because I had never belonged to a church with kneelers.

The church was designed in the style of Christopher Wren with a dome over the crossing. The church was empty. Light from the windows around the dome fell on the altar. As I gazed on the beauty of that place, I knew that God was there. I had never felt the presence of God before. I had never heard the teaching about the Blessed Sacrament, I did not know that the candle burning at the front of the church signified that Christ truly was present. I simply knew that God was there on the altar of that church.

I can remember thinking, "Does God want me to become a Catholic?" But at 18 such a thought was too difficult to entertain for long. It may be difficult for Catholics to understand how threatening Catholicism was for me, who saw Catholic churches as full of strange images and practices. I wondered why their pictures of Jesus showed a big red heart on His chest and I didn't know then that Our Lady of this and Our Lady of that were really all just Mary, the Mother of Jesus. I believed that Catholics were rude and wouldn't eat meat if you served it on the wrong day or desserts during Lent. They wouldn't go to your church if they were visiting, you had to take them to their's and if you were to marry one, you had to raise the children Catholic.

The next year I went to Smith College. The first book I was assigned was *Varieties of Religious Experience* by William James, and there I found quotes from St. Teresa of Avila and St. John of the Cross. Although we had been assigned only four chapters, I read the whole thing, reading again and again the quotes of those who had experienced the presence of God. I prayed for such experiences and nothing happened.

I offered God a compromise. I would become an Episcopalian. I could have the beautiful churches and the elaborate liturgy, but I would still be a Protestant and would not incur the wrath of my family by joining the Catholics. It didn't work. I couldn't find God in the Episcopal Church. I know now it was because God had other plans for me.

I decided to major in medieval history because I was fascinated by faith and because I was searching for God. I can remember going to the Cloisters in New York and being acutely aware that while the statues were there and the architecture was church-like God definitely wasn't there.

Finally, I gave up and became a pagan. I met a young man named Terry O'Leary. On our first date I asked him if he were Irish and, thinking I was kidding, he said, "No." I wasn't kidding and I believed him. I asked him if he were Catholic, and since he had been away from the practice of his faith for six years, he said, "No." So I married him.

I had a baby and settled into suburban life. Then I met Gail. Gail had entered a convent after college and had been entirely happy in religious life, when she became ill. Her illness was diagnosed as multiple sclerosis. She went home and called up the Harvard student she had been dating before she entered the convent. A year later they were married.

Gail had a little boy and a baby just the age of my little girl. Gail knew about St. Teresa of Avila and St. John of the Cross. We talked and talked. I was fascinated. Gail explained to me how Jesus was present in the Blessed Sacrament and how after communion she talked to Him. I had studied the Catholic teaching on transubstantiation in theology, but it had never occurred to me that anyone took it personally.

Gail was feeling ill one Sunday and I offered to take her to church. I wanted to get a look at all this. As I knelt in that church, at the moment of consecration, I said, "God, if it is really true as Gail says that you are present in the Blessed Sacrament, let me believe and I will become a Catholic."

It is true. The church was filled with light and I was filled with faith, the tears streaming from my eyes. Heaven knows what the other people thought, but I didn't care. In one shining moment all my doubts were wiped away.

Gail handed me the missal. The communion verse for the day was "Blessed are the eyes that see what you have seen. For I say to you, many prophets and kings have desired to see what you have seen and have not seen it."

I walked out of the church and into the rectory and told the priest that I wanted to become a Catholic. I cannot say that I was welcomed with open arms. The priest was shy and young and I don't think he had ever instructed a convert before. Everything he told me seemed very strange, but I didn't care. God was here and I had to be able to receive communion.

I was received into the Church just before Christmas. I was on a pink cloud. I could pray for hours, meditate in ecstasy before the Blessed Sacrament. I could not imagine that I would ever commit another sin or even have another temptation. On Pentecost Sunday I was confirmed at the Cathedral. I had read in the Bible that "the Father will give the Holy Spirit to those that ask." So as I went up to confirmation I had in my pocket a little card on which I had written a simple prayer asking for the Holy Spirit and for the gift to teach the Bible. I did not consider at the time that such a request might be presumptuous. After all, I had just received the wonderful miracle of faith. Anything was possible.

God did give me the gift I asked for. I studied carefully and a year later I asked my pastor if I could teach an adult Bible class. Looking back I am amazed that he said yes. The class was a success. I taught the history of the Old Testament, a subject unfamiliar to many Catholics.

Then God began to work in earnest in my life. I had always been subject to depression. I know now that the depression was rooted in bitterness and resentment over unresolved childhood experiences. It is difficult to describe the darkness and chaos of my life at that time. Christ was the light I held onto, but the rest of my life slipped into darkness. I was constantly exhausted, suffered from a string of physical complaints for which doctors could find no cause or cure. To the outside world I tried to keep up a good front but at home my life was in disorder. I slept 12 hours a day, watched T.V. the rest, and neglected my duties.

Terry too had a spiritual journey, and six years after my conversion, he returned to the Church on the feast of Our Lady of Mt. Carmel.

There were moments of joy. I found peace in working at church, but there were times when the darkness seemed overwhelming. Then one day, Sr. Julliette, a nun at the retirement home where I was doing volunteer work, told me about the Charismatic renewal. She said, "You should go." At first I protested, I had four small children. It would be too difficult. But she simply said again, "You should go." I knew that God would find a way and He did.

I thought that perhaps God would use me in a new way to teach the Bible since that was still a deep desire in my heart, but the leadership of that group saw something different. They saw the deep wounds within, which I felt I had kept hidden, and they saw the root. Through prayer and ministry I was healed of all the darkness. It was not instantaneous, nor was it easy. It took six long years and there were times when I thought I would never be free. But gradually the walls of bitterness and rejection were broken down, and I was able to function normally.

Now I was able to teach in a whole new way and to minister to other women who were in the same darkness. There were years of growth and joy and trials. Then I met

Sandy. She came to my class and instantly I liked her. She is beautiful and full of life. One day she told me that she had had an abortion before she found the Lord and that she still felt guilty. We prayed together and I helped her to forgive as others had helped me.

I saw that abortion not only kills unborn babies, but it also hurts women. I wondered why no one, not even pro-lifers, was talking about the women. From that moment on I had a new call, a call to fight against abortion.

The fight against abortion is demanding and I could see that while my faith had never wavered, my spiritual life needed renewal. Then I met Father Sal Ferigle, for God gives us precisely what we need when we need it. He made it all so simple. "Dale, does Our Lord want you to go to daily Mass? Can you go to daily Mass? Then why don't you go to daily Mass?"

I saw that I needed spiritual direction and discipline in my spiritual life; I had been a child long enough. On August 29, 1985, twenty years to the day after my conversion I joined Opus Dei and I have begun another journey.

I feel so blessed that God has called me. People often ask me how you know that it is God who calls you. It is hard to give them an answer. If I say, "The sheep know the Shepherd's voice," they ask me if I hear voices. I don't. It is more like a deep feeling within me which attracts one in a certain direction and a feeling of peace when I respond. Occasionally I have wandered off the track God set for me into projects that seemed good but weren't His will for me. They usually failed quickly, for which I thank God.

I have never had doubts, but I have had questions, particularly about the peculiarly Catholic aspects of our faith. Why do we believe in the Immaculate Conception, the Assumption of Mary, indulgences? I asked the Holy Spirit to please explain these things to me, and always I would find a book or a teacher who would supply the answers I sought. I have come to realize that the faith like the universe is wondrous and complex, with major and minor doctrines circling like planets and moons around suns, which whirl in galaxies, and the rhythms repeated in the individual atoms and molecules. We try to make theology simple, but God delights in complexity. There is no end to His wonders and we can never grasp it all. The delight is in trying.

The Church for me is like a great treasure, and I am a child discovering everything for the first time as though it were brand new. Chesterton, St. Augustine, Leo XIII speak to me as friends. The scriptures are constantly new although I have studied them for 20 years.

The Church is a firm rock on which I stand. I love the words "Holy Mother Church holds and has always held." Hand to hand from apostle to bishop to priest, for 20 centuries the faith has been passed down. Patriarchs, prophets, apostles, martyrs, and confessors, and I am one in communion with all of them.

Everything that is Christ's belongs to me. I find great fellowship with other Christians who are washed in the same blood, read the same word, and obey the same Lord. Though we cannot share the fullness of communion yet we are brothers and sisters. I have learned much from them. Indeed, it was from them that I learned a deep reverence for the Bible and came to recognize the power of the scripture.

As a student of history I am not surprised by the troubles facing the Church today. The Church has always had troubles, and always survived. In every age there have been those who tried to divert it from its path. None succeeded. I am glad to be living in times which test our faith. Pope John Paul II has seen the loss of faith in the Western world and has called us all to begin again, to bring the faith back to the places where it has been lost. I feel like one of the first apostles setting off for the first time. Following Jesus is never boring.

If I have made it all seem easy, in a way it is. After the initial yes, all one has to do is say yes, again and again. When things get difficult and trials come, I think, "Now this is Your problem. You got me into this, and You have to get me out." In the midst of the deepest darkness, I hold on to these words "For those who love God and are called to his plan all things work together for good."

Why am I a Catholic? I did not come for intellectual reasons, but my intellect has been totally satisfied. I did not come for fellowship, but I have found brothers and sisters, family and love. I did not come for healing, but I was restored to health. I came because God called me. It was His decision. All I can do is thank Him for His great mercy, for I know that I was totally unworthy of such a call.

Dale O'Leary *continues to speak and teach on pro-life issues—a theme on which she also writes articles for* The Boston Pilot. *She has also appeared on several radio and television programs, including the "Today" show, to explain the Church's teachings on women. The O'Leary family resides in Rhode Island.*

The Ways
of the Holy Spirit

Father James Parker

On the Solemnity of Saints Peter and Paul in 1982, I was ordained to the priesthood in the Roman Catholic Church at Springfield, Missouri, by Bishop (now Cardinal) Bernard F. Law of Springfield-Cape Girardeau. My wife, Mary Alma, and I had been received into full communion with the Catholic Church in Pentecost week 1981, and she, of course, was present as I was ordained the year after. I became the first married priest in the Roman Rite in the United States, a provision approved by Pope John Paul II and implemented by the Congregation for the Doctrine of the Faith.

My pilgrimage was long—indeed, in one way it was 400 years long—and the attainment of the goal was a joy. The path was not altogether without its difficulties and the goal was reached in an unexpected way. God is a God of surprizes which never cease and bring us all grace and happiness.

I had been an Episcopal priest for twenty-five years and married for twenty-nine when I became a Catholic priest.

Since that day in June of 1982 there have been many other Episcopal priests, married and celibate, who have also been ordained for service in Catholic dioceses across the United States—and the numbers continue to grow in a *Pastoral Provision* requested by the bishops of this country and granted by the Holy See as a pastoral response to a need of conscience.

This new and unique situation finds its roots deep in history. Among the several points of view within Anglicanism, I accepted and committed myself to the position which argues that during the 16th century English Reformation, unlike that on the continent, the Catholic Church in England underwent more of a political upheaval than a theological one. In the initial stages of division the English ecclesiastical provinces of Canterbury and York went into schism from the See of Peter. According to this theory the successive Books of Common Prayer were able to be interpreted as maintaining Catholic doctrine (though often this appeared obscure), while attempting to be inclusive of theological influences coming from sources across the Channel which were alien to the Church's tradition in order to facilitate political harmony.

As an Anglo-Papalist I accepted the fact of schism. I believed fervently in the need to repair the breach with Rome and to restore full communion with the See of Peter. As an Anglican, I believed and taught the whole of Catholic faith including the papal claims and the Marian dogmas. My reason for remaining an Anglican was a sincere desire for *corporate* reunion, and I felt myself part of a 400-year-old stream of Prayer and catechesis for reunion between Canterbury and Rome. This may have been a goal unrealized in any individual's lifetime; nevertheless, papal aspirations appeared to be encouraged by the ecumenical concerns of the 20th century.

However, the 1970's and 1980's brought changes within the Anglican church throughout the world unlike any in its history. No longer could it be argued that anomalous and non-Catholic beliefs were not the official teachings of the Church. No longer could the Anglo-Catholic and Anglo-Papalist reject false practice as individual opinion of the poorly instructed. The highest councils of the Anglican Communion made serious theological decisions in the name of administrative action which would reach to the very core of the commitment of those who formed themselves by Catholic Faith: in the U.S. Episcopal Church the Canon Law was amended to allow the remarriage of the divorced by a change in the principle of indissolubility; the Episcopal Church, the Anglican Church of Canada, and later other such national Anglican bodies began to ordain women into Sacred Orders; and these churches failed to maintain any sense of Catholic moral principles regarding abortion, homosexual practice, and contraception (once firmly condemned by a Lambeth Conference of all Anglican bishops).

These and other concerns brought me and other Anglo-Papalists to question our aims. We began to review with anxiety our understanding of our faith and no longer viewed corporate reunion as the possibility it had seemed for almost 400 years.

Beginning in 1976, I was instrumental in appeals to the Holy See regarding reconciliation for such Anglicans. For several years I had been North American Provincial Vicar of the Society of the Holy Cross (S.S.C.), a priestly fraternity or secular institute within Anglicanism founded in the Anglican days of John Henry Newman. Its purpose is the spiritual formation of its members, and it required a deep commitment to the cause of reunion with the Vicar of Christ. A provincial synod of the S.S.C. unanimously authorized me to present to Archbishop Jean Jadot, then Apostolic Delegate in Washington, a request that married Episcopal priests be considered for Roman Catholic priestly ministry and to lay before him the hopes of a few small groups of Episcopalians who asked to maintain a fraternal union and elements of their Anglican heritage within the Catholic Church. This mission of conscience was well received by the Delegate who personally carried these aspirations to Rome.

For several years the possibilities and ramifications of so unique a request were discussed in Rome and in sessions of the National Conference of Catholic Bishops (N.C.C.B.) in the United States. Bishop Law represented both the bishops' conference and Rome's Sacred Congregation for the Doctrine of the Faith in conversations which came to include not only the S.S.C. but also other Episcopalian groups with similar hopes. The death of two Popes occurred during the years of consideration, and often the petition seemed void of hope, yet I personally never doubted that the Catholic Church would find a way to meet the need. The steadfast purpose of the growing numbers who expressed a desire to be part of the request was full communion with Rome; the constant hope was to be accepted for active ministry as priests in the Catholic Church. It was a faith pilgrimage like few others in modern Church history.

In 1980 the Sacred Congregation for the Doctrine of the Faith announced the Holy See's favorable decision in response to the initial requests of the individual Episcopalians which had been formally put before the Holy See as a petition of the N.C.C.B. The Sacred Congregation's Public Statement said:

"In June 1980, the Holy See, through the Congregation for the Doctrine of the Faith, agreed to the request presented by the bishops of the United States of America on behalf of some clergy and laity formerly or actually belonging to the Episcopal (Anglican) Church for full communion with the Catholic Church. The Holy See's response to the initiative of these Episcopalians includes the possibility of a pastoral provision which will provide, for those who desire it, a common identity reflecting certain elements of their own heritage.

"The entrance of these persons into the Catholic Church should be understood as the reconciliation of those individuals who wish for full Catholic communion, of which the Decree on Ecumenism (no. 4) of the Second Vatican Council speaks.

"In accepting former Episcopalian clergy who are married into the Catholic priesthood, the Holy See has specified that this exception to the rule of celibacy is granted in favor of these individual persons, and should not be understood as implying any change in the Church's conviction of the value of priestly celibacy, which will remain the rule for future candidates for the priesthood from this group.

"In consultation with the National Conference of Catholic Bishops, the Congregation for the Doctrine of the Faith has appointed the Most Reverend Bernard F. Law, Bishop of Springfield-Cape Girardeau, as Ecclesiastical Delegate in this matter. It will be his responsibility to develop a proposal containing elements for the pastoral provision in question to be submitted for the approval of the Holy See, to oversee its implementation and to deal with the Congregation for the Doctrine of the Faith in questions pertaining to the admission of former Episcopalian clergy into the Catholic priesthood."

While this may appear to be an entirely new attitude on the part of the Catholic Church which appears to have ecumenical ramifications, it is significant to understand two positions taken by the Church prior to the 1976 request and the 1980 decision.

1. In the Vatican II Decree on Ecumenism, *Unitatis Redintegratio*, the Council Fathers wrote eloquently and sincerely of their desire to promote ecumenical dialogue and charity. They also said:

"However, it is evident that the work of preparing and reconciling those individuals who wish for full Catholic communion is of its nature distinct from ecumenical action. But there is no opposition between the two, since both proceed from the marvelous way of God."

2. Regarding the consideration of married former Episcopal priests for priestly ministry in the Roman Catholic Church, in his Encyclical *Sacerdotalis Caelibatus* dated June 24, 1967, Pope Paul VI anticipated the *Pastoral Provision* when he wrote:

"In virtue of the fundamental norm of the government of the Catholic Church, to which We alluded above, while on the one hand, the law requiring a freely chosen and perpetual celibacy of those who are admitted to Holy Orders remains unchanged, on the other hand, a study may be allowed of the particular circumstances of married sacred ministers of Churches or other Christian communities separated from the Catholic communion, and of the possibility of admitting to priestly functions those who desire to adhere to the fullness of this communion and to continue to exercise the sacred ministry. The circumstances must be such, however, as not to prejudice the existing discipline regarding celibacy.

"And that the authority of the Church does not hesitate to exercise her power in this matter can be seen from the recent Ecumenical Council, which foresaw the possibility of conferring the holy diaconate on men of mature age who are already married.

"All this, however, does not signify a relaxation of the existing law, and must not be interpreted as a prelude to its abolition. There are better things to do than to promote this hypothesis, which tears down that vigor and love in which celibacy finds security and happiness, and which obscures the true doctrine that justifies its existence and exalts its splendor. It would be much better to promote serious studies in defense of the spiritual meaning and moral value of virginity and celibacy" (nos. 42, 43).

The goal had been achieved. We had at last found as individuals what we had so diligently been seeking corporately. The way was open and the hurdles were no more. The great pastoral heart of Pope John Paul II had been moved by the cause of Anglicans formed as Catholics and yearning for the fullness of faith in union with the universal shepherd of Christ's flock.

It was time to move ahead and I did so with a continuing love for Anglicanism, the church of my baptism and the church which taught me the Catholic religion and nurtured me for so long in that faith.

Early in 1981, I resigned from the rectorship of Saint Mark's Episcopal Church, Albany, Georgia, where I had spent perhaps the happiest years of my ministry. Mary Alma and I moved to Springfield where we were received into full communion and where I began work as assistant to Bishop Law who was appointed the Holy See's Ecclesiastical Delegate to implement the *Pastoral Provision*. Some months before our move our two adult daughters were received into the Catholic Church by a priest in Atlanta, who himself was also a former Episcopalian and a classmate from my Episcopal seminary. Being unmarried, he had already responded to God's call to return to Rome.

Twenty-five years before, I had been ordained an Episcopal priest in South Carolina. I was born in 1930 in Charleston where I attended high school at a military academy. I was graduated from the University of South Carolina. After college Mary Alma Cole of Memphis and I were married and I entered Virginia Theological Seminary in Alexandria.

My ordination in the Catholic Church came two weeks before the day that would have been my silver jubilee in Anglican ministry. I had been accepted by Bishop Ernest L. Unterkoefler of Charleston, the diocese of my native state. Though a priest of the Church of Charleston, I continued, by the bishop's kind permission, in the work of the *Provision* and moved with Bishop Law to New England when he was appointed Archbishop of Boston. In 1985 the opportunity came to travel to Rome when Cardinal Law received his red hat.

My story and the *Pastoral Provision* are not the picture of ecumenism most often put before us. Nevertheless, the ways of the Holy Spirit are not man's ways, and He so often answers prayer in ways we least expect so that we all may be one.

Father James Parker *is Director of Catholic Charities in the Diocese of Charleston and Assistant to the Ecclesiastical Delegate. In the latter capacity he assists Bernard Cardinal Law of Boston in the work of the Holy See's pastoral provision concerning former Episcopal priests who seek Catholic priestly ministry. He and his wife live in his native Charleston. They have two grown daughters. Father Parker is knowledgeable in heraldry and designs coats-of-arms for new bishops and institutions.*

The Journey
of a Lifetime

Claire L. Riley

A Spanish priest once said that conversion is a matter of a moment, but that sanctification is the work of a lifetime. My search for Our Lord has led me to the Catholic Church where I discovered that the most important thing in life is to know, love, and serve Him. The best way to do this is through prayer, to seek and obey His will, and to respond to the graces which He wants to give through the sacraments. My spiritual odyssey has taken me from fundamentalist Protestantism to the Roman Catholic Church, with many ups and downs along the way. This was a long and difficult journey for someone who had such a strong and strict Protestant upbringing.

I often refer to my conversion to Catholicism as moving from one house to another, but keeping the same furniture. In other words the basic fundamentals of Christianity—that mankind was created to give God glory and to be holy—were principles that were taught to me by my mother in the church in which I was raised. I have carried these principles with me and, as an adult through my membership in the Roman Catholic Church, have come to better understand them.

I was born in Wilmington, Delaware, in 1951 to two loving parents who wanted their children to have the best in life. In spite of their modest economic resources, they wanted to make sure that we had the intellectual, spiritual, and moral means to be successful in this world. Though my grandparents were not educated people, they had made sure that my parents were college-educated and they, in turn, stressed the value of a good education to us. My mother, who is very religious, believes that a deep faith in God and a life of holiness are the most important things of all. She raised my brother, three sisters, and me to share that belief. I remember that our lives revolved around our family, the elementary school, and most important of all, the Gethsemane Church of God in Christ.

Sunday services were an intense and often all-day affair. It would begin with Sunday School at 10:00 a.m., followed by the main worship service. I remember these services as being very demonstrative, emotional, and above all—long. The gospel music was very lively, and people showed their love of God by making a joyful noise unto the Lord with hand clapping, tambourines, and shouting or the holy dance. Interwoven between the songs were testimonies in which various people proclaimed the marvelous deeds that the Lord had done for them and how He had blessed them. The main event of all worship, however, was the sermon which could last sometimes from 45 minutes to an hour—half of the worship service. The pastor, visiting preacher, or travelling evangelist would preach from a biblical text in such an emotional fashion that most of the congregation would be caught up in the Spirit and "get happy" i.e., more music, hand clapping, tambourine beating, and shouting. I became convinced as I grew older that this form of Pentecostal worship had its origins in the American South, with its roots ultimately reaching back to tribal worship in Africa. As I grew older and, as I progressed further in school, this way of worshipping God appealed to me less and less.

Another feature of my upbringing was the weekly visit to Bible School. We used to go to one mission on Fridays after school and to another on Saturday mornings. At the Bible schools, and in Sunday School, we were taught the Ten Commandments as thoroughly as any Catholic child learning them in CCD class. My perform- ance in Sunday and Bible class rivalled my performance in school. I was one of the best students. When I was eleven years old I participated in a city-wide Bible contest in which we had to answer correctly questions that were posed to us about various Biblical events and characters. I won by being able to identify David as the man after God's own heart. My prize was a brand new bicycle, and my proud parents treated my brother, sisters, and me to a movie. It was one of the high points of my childhood.

My twelfth year was a watershed one for me. As I neared my teens, for the first time I began to question things that I had automatically assumed were true before. As I entered junior high school, I was beginning to be influenced more by the values that I learned in school and by my friends, and less by my family and the beliefs that I was taught in church. It was 1964 and, like many others my age, I had discovered rock and roll—especially the Beatles. This music was still relatively innocent then and stars were not yet generally singing about the glamor of drugs and illicit sex which became so common in the later 60's. It was about this time that I also found out that my church considered all popular music, not just rock and roll, to be sinful. Only religious music was listened to, although classical music was also tolerated in our house. Worse than that I also discovered that members of our church considered going to the movies to be sinful. Most films in those days were downright wholesome compared to what is being shown today. I had loved the movies since I saw my first Walt Disney picture when I was eight. The first seeds of rebellion had been planted as a result of these revelations. I also learned that the church con- demned dancing, drinking, smoking (they were ahead of their time on this one), card-playing and any kind of gambling including bingo, horse racing, and lotteries. The bishop even disapproved of sports and games of any kind. I was beginning to think that the "saints" were forbidden to do anything that was enjoyable or fun. My mother, to her credit, never stressed those teachings and never imposed those restrictions on me. I, therefore, was not yet at the point of abandoning her faith.

The same year, during the period that I now recognize as Lent, I had my first and only Pentecostal experience. I spoke in foreign tongues as the Spirit prompted and, when it was over, I was flooded with a warm, peaceful, joyful presence of God that I had not felt before. For a few months thereafter I tried to live up to the strictest interpretation of the church teachings and, although they demanded perfection, I found myself sorely lacking. I found that living a holy life was still a daily struggle. The church placed such an emphasis on feelings that I was worried and upset because often I did not "feel" saved or holy. Furthermore, I soon found myself ashamed of my faith and afraid that if I continued in it, I would begin to shout and jump about like many of those around me. In spite of my religious training, I had failed to develop any real roots in it and could not explain my faith to others. One day by chance I heard the latest Beatle hit, number one at the time, and discovered that I liked it as much as ever, and found the tune as catchy as I had before my baptism of the Holy Spirit. I then realized that living close to God would not take away my love for rock music or the movies, despite assurances from my mother and others in the church that it would if I were truly faithful. I began to wonder whether these restrictions were made by God, or whether they were merely human precepts. At the age of thirteen, for these reasons, and because none of my friends were religious, I decided that I would no longer follow the faith of my mother. It was the end of my consenting participation in the Church of God in Christ.

Once I had made the psychological break with my mother's church, the question was to which church would I belong? I was still influenced by background and upbringing and, consequently, thought that it would be a good idea to belong to some church. I seriously considered the Baptist and Methodist churches, the ones with which I was most familiar and, as a result, the ones with which I felt most comfortable. My father had been raised as a Baptist, and most of my relatives belong to that church. Whenever we visited my grandparents in my father's hometown near Atlantic City, New Jersey, we would attend the Baptist church where he grew up. Before my grandparents became ill, we would sometimes spend the entire month of August at the shore. I always liked the church of my father, grandmother, aunts, uncle, and cousins better than my mother's. There were several reasons for this. First of all, the service was quiet and dignified by comparison. Second, they always began and ended on time which we rarely did. Third, it was a beautiful building and not a storefront like our local church. Another fond memory I have of Sundays in Pleasantville, New Jersey, is of my grandfather gathering the entire family together for morning prayer which he would lead. By all appearances, I was headed for the Baptist church. My reasons for wanting to be a Baptist, however, were emotional and social; not spiritual.

As a result, because I no longer had any spiritual roots, I began to drift away from Our Lord. Soon I was doubting everything in the Bible. Although I still was willing to admit the existence of the historical figure of Jesus, I denied His divinity, and no longer believed in His mission of salvation. By then I was even questioning the existence of God. By the time I reached the ninth grade, I was on the road from agnosticism to atheism. While I had become an honor student in junior high school, my participation in Sunday School fell to a bare minimum. I did not do any more than I had to. My intellect was thriving and developing while my soul was slowly dying.

In early 1966 I had no particular feelings for or against Catholicism. My best friend in the third and fourth grades was a Roman Catholic. She and I used to watch the children in the Catholic school up the street from our playground, and I used to marvel at their tidy little uniforms. I was awe-struck at the size of her parish church, which was so much bigger than the storefront I attended, or even than Mt. Pleasant Baptist Church. I also used to play with neighbors down the street who were Catholics. One of them even had an older brother who was studying for the priesthood. I knew nothing about Catholics except that they were a lot different from us, sort of like the Jews were. Elementary school children, however, seldom seriously discuss religion. In the eighth grade, several members of my class could not go on the class trip to Washington, D.C., because it conflicted with the date of their confirmation. Boy, did I feel sorry for them! They would have to spend all that time in church while the rest of us were having fun in the nation's capital. I was glad that I was not one of them. By the ninth grade my two closest friends were Catholics and this time it would be different. They were indirectly, unwittingly going to lead me to the doors of the Catholic Church.

On a Wednesday morning in 1966, I went to school as I did every day. There was absolutely nothing unusual or different about this day in my mind. This was not destined to be just any day, however. This was the day that would change my life. My morning custom was to stand around outside the junior high I attended, and to chat with my friends before classes began. I noticed immediately that my two closest friends were not there. I was upset because I had something that I really wanted to talk about. I could understand one of them being absent, but both of them missing was a disaster to a fourteen-year-old. So I began to ask the others if they knew where my friends were. By this time I noticed that their younger sisters, who were in my brother's class, were also missing. Someone told me that it was Ash Wednesday and that they had gone to Mass. "Mass," I thought, "in the middle of the week? Why?" I had no idea that Holy Mass is celebrated daily. I could not understand, but at the same time was intrigued by the fact that they loved God enough to get up early to go visit Him before school, whereas my mother had trouble dragging me out of bed on Sunday mornings. As I now reflect, they had probably been missing on Ash Wednesday of 1965, too, but I had not noticed it then. In any case, I resolved to ask one or both of them about the meaning of Ash Wednesday. They explained to me that it was the beginning of Lent. I had no idea what Lent was, so they told me about the meaning of the ashes and the 40 days of fasting, prayer, and almsgiving in preparation for the joyous feast of Easter. Holy Week and Easter were both already a part of my religious tradition, but the rest was totally new. My curiosity had been satisfied, and that was the end of it—for three days.

The following Saturday I was sitting in the kitchen talking to my mother. On some Saturdays I would turn on the radio and listen to the countdown of the Top 40 hits of the week. This particular morning my mother tuned in one of the religious stations that she likes to listen to. She left the room to do something else, and so I began to read the newspaper. A program then came on that I had not heard before and have never heard since. As I was reading, I became vaguely aware of children's voices in the background praying, "Holy Mary, Mother of God, pray for us sinners now and at the hour of our death, Amen." This was so repetitive that I soon found myself reading the paper less, and listening to them more, until they had my undivided attention. I realize today that I was listening to a priest lead a group of children in the Rosary, but at the time I had no idea what I was listening to. I do remember, however, that this prayer and the devotion of those reciting it, touched my soul. I decided that I had to find out more about this Catholicism, and so the next week I went to the public library to take out several books on the subject. I have always been an avid reader, and was fascinated as I went through them. My interest at this point, however, was mainly intellectual. I thought that it would be a good idea to learn more about the faith of my best friends, but I still had doubts about the existence of God.

One book in particular made an impression on me. The more I read and absorbed information, the better I began to understand the teachings of the Church. I found myself increasingly drawn to Catholicism. It was after reading this that my intellectual curiosity blended into spiritual attraction. It all began to seem so logical. I learned that the True Church was one, holy, catholic and apostolic. I began to see that only the Catholic Church possessed all four of these attributes.

I now began to realize that not only did all of this make a great deal of sense to me, but I was actually starting to *believe* it! If I could believe this, then there had to be a God. Not just a God who was a "prime mover" who created the universe and then left us alone, but a God who loves us so deeply that He would come to live among us in the person of the Son and to die for us. For the first time in almost two years I began to pray. I asked the Holy Spirit to direct my path in the direction that He wanted me to go. I next studied the Sacraments. I was particularly drawn to the beauty of the Eucharist. That Christ would humble Himself to become present in the form of bread and wine so that He could physically, as well as spiritually, be with us was simply amazing. Who could not love a God who would do so much for us? In my mother's church communion was given only occasionally, and was seen merely as a symbol and memorial of His passion and death. I learned that the Mass is a reenactment of that one sacrifice made long ago at Calvary and that, in the Eucharist, Our Lord is the living bread who comes down from heaven to give His flesh for the life of the world.

In spite of this new revelation, I had to pray very hard because I discovered that I had more negative emotions about Catholicism than I had originally realized now that I was getting so close to it. I still did not understand the sacrament of penance, the doctrine of the communion of saints, purgatory, or devotion to Mary. I began asking my friends more and more questions, which they patiently answered as best they could. I think that they were surprised at my sudden interest, and did not suspect that, by this time, I was seriously thinking of converting. During that Lent of 1966, I saw two films on television which, together with my reading, and the work of the Holy Spirit, removed all obstacles and finalized my decision. They are a definite testimony to the power of the media to influence for the good as well as for the bad.

The first of these films was *Francis of Assisi*. I was deeply moved watching the life of this great saint, and it helped me to better understand the graces that the saints possess and how they can help us. During Holy Week I saw the classic, *The Song of Bernadette*. I was filled with reverence by the story of Bernadette of Lourdes, the simple peasant girl, and her visions of Our Lady. After watching this film, I began to appreciate Mary's special place in God's plan of salvation and in the Church. I also began to realize that it was she who had been calling to me on that Saturday which seemed so long ago, for I had travelled a great distance since then.

On Holy Thursday the family went to church for the service of the Lord's Supper. I did not mind going for a change. Once there, however, I found myself staring in the direction of the nearest Catholic Church. I began thinking that, although we were commemorating the night when Christ gave this sacrament to His apostles, it was the Catholics who were actually experiencing His presence in the bread and wine. I wished that I was there instead of where I was. It was at that moment that I realized that I wanted to become a Catholic.

I spent a lot of time on Good Friday, Holy Saturday, and Easter in prayer. I also reflected on my decision and its implications. Although I knew that my father, who is a very tolerant man, would be open to it, somehow I knew that my mother would not be pleased. When I returned to school after Easter vacation, I told my friends about my desire to join them in the Catholic faith. They were delighted, and one of them offered to take me to see a priest at the church near our junior high school. He was very friendly and open, and gave me a catechism book to study. The priest told me that I would need my parents' permission before I would be able to begin instructions. My heart sank because, during the initial euphoria of my decision to convert, I had forgotten about that detail. I was just shy of my fifteenth birthday, and felt that my strongly Protestant mother would be horrified at the very idea, and certainly would not give her consent. In frustration I felt that I had to tell someone in the family of my future intentions. I chose my brother because I considered my sisters to be too young to confide in. It was probably a naive thing to do because my brother and I were on very poor terms at that point in our lives. We fought constantly, and anything that I told him in confidence, would surely be repeated. True to form, he immediately told my mother and an explosion resulted. My mother called for me and asked me if what my brother had told her was true. I told her that it was, and I have rarely seen her so angry and upset. She could not believe that a child of hers would turn to Roman Catholicism, a faith that I think she considered to be semi-pagan. She said that she would have responded more favorably if I had said that I had wanted to join a Protestant church with beliefs closer to hers. I pointed out that I did not want to become a Catholic out of convenience, but because I was convinced of its truths. She raised all the standard fundamentalist objections to Catholicism that I had heard many times and with which I would have agreed a short time before.

She believed that Catholics could do anything they wanted as long as they went to confession. They were not obliged to live a holy life and to walk upright before the Lord. I told her that a person's sins were forgiven only if he or she were truly sorry and had the intention of avoiding sin in the future. I explained that it was Christ who actually was administering the sacrament and that the priest was his vehicle. I also tried to answer her other questions based on what I had so recently learned. In retrospect, I now feel that the task was hopeless because I was too young, and my faith was too new, for me to make an impression on my mother. I had not been through instructions yet, and did not have the proper doctrinal formation, whereas my mother had years of experience and training in her church's beliefs. So, after weeks of heated discussions which got me nowhere, I decided to lie low. My mother, for her part, probably believed my "infatuation" with Catholicism to be a passing fad like a teenager's newest boy- or girlfriend, the latest dance craze, or the current hit record.

I remember well the first time that I attended Holy Mass. One Sunday afternoon the whole family, except for my father, happened to be walking past the Cathedral when it was time for Holy Mass. My mother decided on the spur of the moment that we were all going. We were shocked, but unlike my brother and sisters, I was also delighted and very excited. Once inside the Cathedral, constructed during the first decade of the nineteenth century, I was overwhelmed by its great size and ornate beauty, far surpassing anything that I had seen up to then. I also noticed the reverent attitude of the congregation. It was so quiet and peaceful, not at all like my mother's church. The Mass was still in the process of changing from Latin to English in late 1966. The Eucharistic Prayer, therefore, was still in Latin and, because I did not have a missal, it was difficult for me to follow. When the altar boy rang the bell, however, and the priest elevated the consecrated bread and wine, I knew that something special and very sacred was taking place. It is a memory that I will retain and treasure as long as I live.

Three years passed and I still had a strong desire to become a Catholic, so I continued to pray, read, and study. I left Wilmington, Delaware to attend Brown University in Providence, Rhode Island, in September of 1969, at the age of 18. I was excited and anticipated new intellectual experiences, new friends, and new challenges. Most importantly, I knew that I would now be free to begin my journey to Rome. I had already bought a crucifix for my wall, statues of Our Lord and Our Lady, a Rosary and a Catholic version of the Bible. My parents accompanied me to my first day on campus and helped me unpack. When my mother asked me if I had brought a Bible, I produced my new Catholic one. She looked at it and said that she would prefer for me to have the King James version. She then gave me one that she had carried along. I politely put it on the shelf and, as soon as my parents left, I put it in my trunk, never to look at it again. This was one of my mother's last acts of opposition to my decision.

The first Sunday at college there was no Mass on campus so I went to nearby St. Joseph's, the church that would eventually store my baptismal records. I was so elated with my new found independence that I was walking on air. The next Sunday after Mass, I made an appointment to talk to the chaplain, a Franciscan priest. I poured out my three years of frustration to him and he sat and listened intently to my story without interrupting me. When I had finished he told me that, now that I was 18 and no longer living at home, he saw no reason why I could not begin instructions as soon as I wanted. He also let me know, however, that he could not baptize me before I reached 21 unless my mother gave her permission before then. I thought that it was highly unlikely that she would ever change her mind. He welcomed me to come to Mass as often as I wanted in the meantime and I needed no encouragement.

Through my freshman and sophomore years I gradually became a part of the Catholic community at Brown, and continued to learn more about my chosen faith. I was as active as I could be, and was even put in charge of refreshments after Mass. During vacations, and even during the summer months, my mother continued to let me attend Holy Mass, and I rarely returned to her church. On the few occasions when I did, it was after I had been to Holy Mass. I was now definitely ready to take the final step, but she still refused to consent to my baptism. I had the desire, and was by now a de facto member of both the community on campus, and the parish in Wilmington. I was, nevertheless, still prevented from having full communion with the Church.

By the end of my sophomore year I had become friendly with two exchange students from France (cousins) whom I had met at Holy Mass. They influenced me to major in French. As a result, I decided that I wanted to spend my junior year abroad. This step was to unexpectedly provide me with the breakthrough for which I had waited so long. When my mother learned of my plans, she finally relented and allowed me to be baptized. She explained that she had changed her mind because she wanted me to have the full benefits of my faith while I was in a foreign land and that, by now, she was resigned to the fact that my entrance into the Catholic Church was inevitable. She also acknowledged that perhaps my perseverance was an indication that this was God's will for me after all. I was ecstatic. I had never felt so close to my mother and was very grateful. In a private ceremony on October 19, 1971, I was received into the Catholic Church. At the Mass which followed, for by now I was attending Mass daily, I was the first one to receive communion. In contrast to my baptism, my confirmation on Pentecost Sunday, May 21, 1972, was a big public affair at the

Cathedral. John, a friend of mine who is also a convert from fundamentalist Protestantism, was also confirmed that day. We even had the same sponsor. There was a party on campus afterwards in honor of the two of us. It was the day before my twenty-first birthday.

Two weeks later I left for Paris. In Europe I was blessed to see the Church in all of its majestic splendor. Not only did I visit the great churches of Paris—Notre Dame, Sacrè Coeur, and the Madeleine—I was also able to travel to Rome. At St. Peter's tomb I prayed the Apostle's Creed, as does every Catholic who makes this pilgrimage. I also thanked our Lord for enabling me to come to Rome a second time—the first time spiritually, the second time physically. The biggest thrill of all, however, was being able to see the Holy Father during his Wednesday general audience. I was truly moved, and felt very privileged. I had been a Catholic less than a year, and Our Lord had blessed me to experience things that many of the faithful do not see in their entire lives.

I was graduated from Brown on a beautiful June day in 1974. On that day my parents finally met the two priests who had directed and influenced my spiritual growth and development. Father O'Shea had prepared me for baptism. Father Kehew had prepared me for confirmation. The meeting was warm and cordial. My mother said that she was glad to finally get the opportunity to meet them, because she had heard so much about them. My father later remarked that the two priests looked like brothers. I had never thought about it before, but although their personalities were very different, they did indeed physically resemble each other because of similar coloring, height, and build.

I returned to Brown in 1980 for a summer session in U.S. foreign policy and a computer workshop. While I was there I saw Father Kehew for confession, and as we were talking afterwards, he told me that he was pleased that I had remained in the Church. He said that sometimes when a person comes into the Church with the support of a particular community, the person does not retain the commitment to the life of faith he or she initially made when that community no longer exists. It was almost as if he had been reading my mind for, like the prodigal son, I had wandered away. It would have been more accurate for him to say that I had returned.

Unfortunately, I did not live happily ever after following my graduation from college. I sometimes now refer to the period from 1966 to 1971 as my courtship of the Church, the period from late 1971 to mid-1974 as my honeymoon in the Church, and everything since then as the marriage. There were many pressures and new adjustments to make to life outside of school, where I had spent 17 years. I did not know anything else, and making the transition to the business world was very difficult for someone who had really wanted to pursue an academic career. With all of my college friends gone, I found myself totally disoriented socially, intellectually, and spiritually, in spite of the fact that I was living in Boston—college mecca of the nation. The network of support that I had in school from Catholic friends had disappeared, and I found it extremely difficult to make new ones. As a result, my faith slowly began to erode. By the end of 1974, I was beginning to miss Sunday Mass for no good reason. I grew lazy in the practice of my faith so, as a result, I grew weak spiritually and lax morally. I condoned conduct that I would have disapproved of only a short time before, and now I am ashamed of my behavior during that period. Society still considered me to be a "good person," but I was living far away from Our Lord. I became friendly with people who had little or no faith, and whose ideas were very far removed from what I had believed as a Catholic. Things got progressively worse through 1975, '76 and '77 until I hit rock bottom in 1978.

In 1978 I did not go to church on Easter Sunday for the first time in my life. By 1978 the only time that I attended Holy Mass was when I visited my parents, for I would not admit to my mother that my love for Our Lord and His Church had grown cold. So I tried my best to keep up appearances whenever I was in Delaware. I was in a situation similar to the one that I was in at the beginning of 1966. To my surprise, I was succeeding in business, for I was by then a supervisor. My soul, on the other hand, was like a barren and parched wasteland.

I attended a college reunion in June, 1978. Back once again in that familiar, comforting environment I could not believe that so much had changed in so short a time. I saw one of my old friends, who is one of the most devout people I have ever known, and who had been an example for me, and realized how far I had drifted from Our Lord. I attended Holy Mass for the second time that year with old friends for old times' sake—but I felt totally empty, as if I were spiritually dying. The reunion was socially like the good old days, but I was painfully aware that my light of faith was going out, and that there was little oil left in the lamp.

Just as my graduation marked the beginning of my descent into the lowest part of the valley, the reunion marked the beginning of my ascent back up the mountain. Although I had fallen far away from the Church by the summer of 1978, my apostasy was never total. During 1975, '76, and '77, I would attend Holy Mass during the Sundays of Lent and Advent. Even during the first part of 1978, my worst year, I went on Holy Thursday to commemorate that night in 1966 when I first realized that God was calling me to become a Catholic. Furthermore, although I was not living a Christian life, I continued to believe firmly in God—Father, Son, and Holy Spirit. I did not return to agnosticism or atheism. Equally important, I continued to believe in the authenticity of the Catholic faith. Although I was having difficulties with certain teachings and practices of the Church, I remained convinced of the value and effectiveness of the sacraments. I never for one moment considered forsaking the Catholic Church for any other. When I finally returned to Our Lord to ask His forgiveness, it was to the Roman Church that I naturally came without hesitation.

I had been occasionally thinking of returning to the Church since the reunion, but as with all the false starts that I had made over the past four years, I seemed to be unable to be consistent. I was merely observing external practice. I would have to fall in love with Our Lord all over again—and I appeared incapable of doing so. On August 15, 1978, the Feast of the Assumption, I happened to be passing a downtown chapel not far from the office, when I noticed the large number of people going in. I had forgotten that it was a holy day, but since it was time for Holy Mass, and I just happened to be there, I decided to go in. Like Bartimaeus at the moment when Our Lord gave him sight, I could feel Our Lord healing me of my spiritual blindness. Our Blessed Mother had invited me to come visit her Son, just as she had done before on that Saturday in 1966. Once again I responded and, after that day, I returned to the sacraments on a regular basis. I wondered how I could have been so foolish, and went to confession with true and firm resolve to avoid sin and its temptations. Although I had finally returned to the bosom of the Church, my faith did not instantly return to the level where it had been in 1971 or 1972. I had to grow all over again in my interior life.

I was very jubilant at the election of Karol Cardinal Wojtyla as Pope John Paul II in 1979. The Holy Father came to Boston in October of 1979, and I was thrilled at the opportunity to see another Pope. Our manager, who was not a Catholic, although his wife and children were, declared a "transportation emergency" and closed the office for the day. I, therefore, had no trouble getting to the Common early to get a good spot. I had just enough viewing space behind the fence on Beacon Street. As the Holy Father's motorcade passed by, however, a man in front of me, whom I had not noticed before, hoisted his young son on his shoulders, and completely blocked my view. I was so frustrated! I, nevertheless, still remember the Holy Father's words to the young people on that rainy day, "Follow Christ." I have tried with even greater resolve since then to do so.

By this time I was back in the habit of attending Sunday Mass. I was getting up a little earlier to attend 12:30 Mass at St. Paul's Church in Cambridge, where I had moved in 1978. One morning I arrived earlier than usual. The 11:00 Mass had not ended yet, and I heard what seemed to me to be the most beautiful music that I had heard in my life. I stood at the back of the church in silent wonder as the Archdiocesan Boys' Choir sang the communion hymn. The next Sunday I decided to attend that Mass and have become a regular there, or at the 9:30 Mass, ever since. This boys' choir, and the adult one that sings at the 9:30 Mass, gave me an appreciation for the traditional music of the Church. I had previously been familiar mainly with guitars and folk Masses. This marked the beginning of my reintegration into parish life and, in 1983, I discovered a parish community for the first time in nine years. I joined the hospitality committee, and began serving coffee and donuts after the 11:00 Mass. I was placed in charge of organizing refreshments in 1984. At the same time I became a lector. The boys' choir from St. Joseph's Oratory in Montréal visited our church the first Sunday that I read. They had reminded me of St. Paul's choir when I had heard them sing in their church. Seeing them now in our church brought back memories of the first time I had read when the Bishop of Providence had come to Brown. My spiritual life and parish activity were finally returning to that level.

In July of 1984 I came into contact with Opus Dei. This is a Catholic lay association whose main purpose is to, in the words of its founder Monsignor Josemaría Escrivá, "encourage people of every sector of society to desire holiness in the midst of the world." Holiness can be found by maintaining presence of God right in one's station in life in whatever occupation one performs. By sanctifying work, a person sanctifies himself or herself and others. By seeking holiness, sanctifying work, and doing apostolate, a person lives the spirit of Opus Dei. This is the Work of God. Pope John Paul II elevated Opus Dei to the status of a personal Prelature in 1982. By the fall of 1983, as a result of my spiritual regeneration and increasingly active parish life, I was beginning to feel that God was asking more of me and calling me to a closer relationship with Him. I also wanted to know and understand the Church better to be more able to answer the increasingly challenging questions that my family was asking me about Catholicism. I struck up a conversation with a Filipino woman whom I met at a party, and somehow the topic turned to religion. We discovered that we were both practicing Catholics, and she told me of a women's center of Opus Dei where she occasionally went to receive doctrinal and spiritual formation. She also told me that her brother was a priest of "The Work" as she called it. I recalled that I had once picked up a bulletin on Monsignor Josemaría Escrivá at the back of a church, but had never taken the time to read it. She said that if I was interested, she would take me there sometime. I agreed, but our schedules were so different—we neither lived nor worked near each other—that it was never arranged. I soon forgot all about it.

I met another woman at the same party who belonged to another group known as Young Catholics which met every other week in the Franciscan center downtown. She invited me to come with her to Young Catholics and so I did. At a Young Catholics meeting a priest celebrates Holy Mass, and usually a speaker follows who talks about various topics, such as the Shroud of Turin, apparitions of Our Lady, or ecumenism. It was there that I met a woman who had studied at the University of Navarre, a university in Spain administered by the Work, and whose mother had worked at a boys' school in Washington, D.C., run by Opus Dei. I told her about the woman whom I had met at a party the previous fall and, coincidentally, they knew each other. Maria also lives in Cambridge, and we soon became friendly. She thought that since I liked Young Catholics, and had already spoken with someone about Opus Dei, that I might be interested in visiting the center. Maria recently told me that she had a feeling that it would be a good match.

I began to attend meditations with her on Wednesday nights. These are talks given by the priest on a spiritual subject or virtue to help those in attendance to make their prayer in the presence of the Blessed Sacrament. There is also the opportunity to go to confession either before or after the meditation. Although I enjoyed them, I did not think that they were extraordinary. Perhaps this was because from the beginning most of my time and energy were consumed trying to salvage a demanding job that I had begun that same July, but which was already a hopeless cause. In any case, I managed to convince myself that I was too busy to live the spirit of the Work, or to follow its plan of life. Once I began attending meditations on Wednesdays, however, I never returned to Young Catholic meetings on Thursdays.

Maria stopped attending meditations regularly in February 1985, and returned to Young Catholics. With no one to accompany me, I did not continue either. I had recently lost my job, and I did not want to spend a dollar to make a special trip into and out of Boston on Wednesday nights when it was easier to relax at home, have a leisurely dinner, and settle comfortably in front of the television set. Lent came, and as usual, I wanted to do something special for Our Lord in thanksgiving for my original conversion. In spite of my attitude about Wednesdays, my spiritual level was really at its highest since college, and I began attending daily Mass again for the first time in over ten years. Being out of work made it very easy for me to get to St. Paul's at 8:00 in the morning. I subsequently found that I was then ready for the task of looking for a new job bright and early by 9:00. A schedule was returning to my life because, when a person is unemployed, it is easy to slip into a pattern of staying in bed and getting a late start on the day. About midway through Lent I felt that I wanted to do still more, and so I decided to return alone to the Wednesday meditations. Soon I found that I was adopting the practice of frequent confession, going at least once a month. I had previously thought I was doing well if I went from four to six times a year. I also began to pray the Rosary for the first time since I was in college. I began to remain a few minutes after Holy Mass to pray and thank Our Lord for His sacramental presence. It was obvious that, unlike before, the spirit of Opus Dei was beginning to influence me. My interior life had not only approached the level of my college days, it was now surpassing it.

I met Julie on a Wednesday in May after Mass at St. Paul's. She is a member of Opus Dei, and said that she had seen me at meditations. Since that is where we were both heading, it made sense to go together. Julie quickly became one of my best friends and, through her example and apostolate, has brought me even closer to Our Lord and helped me to better understand the spirit of the Work.

Julie works in the Office of the President at Harvard University. In July she told me that her old position in Romance Languages and Literatures was open and that, if I was interested, she would recommend me to the Coordinator of Language Instruction. After seven months of unemployment, I had finally found a job, and started work in August. I now understood the reason why Our Lord had permitted me to go through such a long period of unemployment. While I was out of work, I learned to trust Our Lord as I never had before. My unemployment benefits were scheduled to run out the week after I found this job. Previously in my professional life, success, money, and prestige were the most important things to me in spite of my continuing spiritual growth. But after I left there, my desire to achieve holiness increased to become the most important thing in my life. Our Lord, as a result, has shown me the way to sanctity through Opus Dei. He has even added a bonus which I did not expect. In spite of my success in business, my main intellectual interest continued to be languages and, throughout my eleven-year career in insurance, my heart never left academia. So Our Lord has now placed me in an almost tailor-made job in the middle of Harvard where I have the opportunity to speak French almost every day. I am near my parish church where I can continue to attend daily Mass and make visits to the Blessed Sacrament. I can walk to work, and am also right across the yard from my good friend, Julie.

It is now 1986 and, through Opus Dei, I have become involved in a supplementary education program tutoring girls at St. John's-St. Hugh's parish in Roxbury, a predominately black and poor section of Boston. During the first two weeks of July I was a counselor at a day camp in this same parish which Opus Dei had also helped to organize and run. I am involved there because I think it is important for these children to get a good education so that they can lead productive and worthwhile lives. More importantly, I also hope that, from our example, they will want to know Our Lord better. In the spring I became a cooperator in Opus Dei which means that I donate money and, in my case, time to the Work. I also pray daily for Opus Dei and its intentions and, its members, in turn, pray for me. We are all thus living the communion of saints surrounded by the cloud of witnesses that St. Paul mentions in his epistle to the Hebrews.

I was referred by the pastor of St. John's-St. Hugh's in April to the Daughters of St. Paul, who were interested in talking to me about my views on evangelization in the black community. I agreed to read drafts of materials that they intend to publish, and they asked me to write an account of my conversion to Roman Catholicism. I am honored to do this and thought at first that I would only cover the story up through 1966 when I made the decision; then I considered continuing up through 1972 when the promise was fulfilled. I definitely planned to stop when I reached 1974, because my spiritual life began to deteriorate after that. After consulting with the sisters and praying about it, I decided that, although it would make this account longer, my story could best be understood within the context of my whole life, and the person I am today. As Monsignor Escrivá writes in his book of meditations called *The Way,* "Conversion is a matter of a moment. Sanctification is the work of a lifetime."

Claire L. Riley, *a native of Wilmington, Delaware, became a Catholic while attending Brown University in Providence, Rhode Island. For several years she has been an active member of St. Paul's parish in Cambridge, Massachusetts, and—since 1986—a Cooperator of Opus Dei. A staff assistant in the department of romance languages and literature at Harvard University, Miss Riley is active in programs organized by Opus Dei for underprivileged children and teenagers.*

Crooked Lines

Jeffrey Rubin

Catholics are so eager for Jewish converts, I have found, that they often exaggerate my Jewishness: they tend, for instance, to misspell my name "Reuben," no doubt for its Old Testament pedigree (unless they're thinking of the sandwich), and seem disappointed when I can't tell them what "meshuggener" means ("someone who is crazy"—I just looked it up). They advise me how to prove to my father the fidelity of Catholicism to its Jewish roots—imagining, I suppose, a little bearded man haranguing me in Hebrew from the scrolls of the Torah—and are shocked to discover that I attended my first Seder, celebrated with other converts, the year I was confirmed. My father-in-law sometimes refers to me as "a relative of the Boss" (meaning Jesus), while my mother-in-law worries that ancestral loyalties will someday tear me from the Church; and at gatherings I'm expected to know Jewish songs and dances and perhaps a few wry rabbinical sayings.

In contrast, paradoxically, my family and my Jewish friends regard me as a goy. No matter that I now know more about my heritage than I ever did before my conversion, or that I *believe* more of traditional Jewish teachings, via Catholicism, than even they do: to them, I renounced my Jewishness when I entered the Church. The nature of Judaism is a hotly debated topic even—indeed especially—among Jews: Is it a race, or a set of beliefs and practices? Or perhaps a "people," bound by some common history or tradition? And if the latter, what makes one a member?—one extreme demands strict adherence to the Law and matrilineal descent, while the other seems to require little more than vague nostalgic sentiments and liberal sympathies.

One can't appeal to the rabbis to settle the problem, for few groups recognize the others' authority, and all of them—Reform, Conservative, Orthodox and Hasidic (and their further subdivisions)—disagree on many vital questions, not the least of which is: Who is Jewish? Some of the progressives take this very dissension, this "questioning," as a special feature of Judaism, as if not faith but doubt were the hallmark of their people. Neither do secular Jews wish to be left out, and I've had some tell me that, though they don't believe in God, which I do, and though they regard the miracles of the Old Testament as myth and superstition, which I don't, they are rightly to be considered Jewish as I no longer am. It seems that the one thing that all Jews, however defined, can agree on (excepting, of course, converts like myself) is that one can't be Jewish and believe in Christ.

Well, I trust that God knows who or what a Jew is, and that it really doesn't matter much to Him—I don't expect any special treatment either way. And rather than give offense over something unimportant, and out of particular respect for those Jews for whom belief in Christ is—according to their consciences, however mistaken— infidelity to God, I point out to Jews and Catholics alike that I consider myself a convert not from Judaism, but from atheism.

I wasn't raised an atheist, but my parents were far from religious. My father came from a Reform Jewish family which was "assimilated" enough, even in those days, to have a Christmas tree; and he tells me that his Bar Mitzvah involved the mere phonetic memorization of some Hebrew phrases. More influential, perhaps, was his education in a school affiliated with the Society for Ethical

Culture—a group of mostly Jewish secularists who aspired to distill the "essential values" from the great religious traditions, while leaving behind their supposedly archaic supernatural elements. Indeed, when he married my mother, who had been raised nominally Episcopalian, his anger at a rabbi who objected to the intermarriage (as well as their desire not to give offense to either family) induced him to hire a "minister" of Ethical Culture to perform the ceremony.

Nevertheless, he was concerned that his children should have a sense of their "Jewish identity," and my mother forthwith converted, somewhat unofficially, to Reform Judaism. After four children in five years (and another to come six years later) they moved us to Scarsdale, NY, a community so predominantly Jewish that my older sister once expressed pity for a little Catholic girl in her class whom she imagined to be a part of some tiny statistical minority. We joined a nearby synagogue, attended services on Rosh Hashanah and Yom Kippur, and if any of our neighbors or friends were gentiles, I don't remember them. We lit our Hanukah candles every year— shortly before our rather larger secular Christmas (celebrated "because it's a national holiday," my mother explained)—and I vividly remember my father telling us stories of the Maccabees and the justice of Solomon. Such Jewish achievements and values as he cherished were duly impressed on our minds, as were—forever—the horrors of the Holocaust. And though, as I said, we never had a real Seder, Passover was always recalled by a little matzoh (un-Kosherly buttered) with our dinner.

But having succeeded in passing on to us some sense of our heritage, my parents permitted even these vestiges of Jewish practice to fade. My brother and I, at ten and nine, respectively, were given the choice of whether we wished to be Bar Mitzvahed, so naturally we declined (who *wants* to go to Hebrew school for three years at that age?), and though Reform and some other Jews have a similar rite for girls, I doubt that my parents seriously considered it for my sisters. Hanukah disappeared shortly afterwards (though Christmas still has not); ditto our deficient Passover; and by the time my youngest sister was of age she was even excused from the few years of Sunday School required of her elders. By then, too, we had stopped attending services on the High Holy Days; and except for the occasional wedding or funeral, it was henceforth a rare day that found us near a synagogue.

As I entered adolescence it became clear that in our house the real religion was Knowledge (not a bad one as false religions go), which was itself taken to be, perhaps with some justification, a special province of the Jews: weren't we, after all, the People of the Book? But the father of our faith wasn't Abraham but Freud, and our "Book" was the latter's *Complete Works*, which stood in our library, together with commentary by his disciples, where might have been the Torah and the Talmud. When one day my father noticed a volume I had bought on psychology, he urged me to consult the Master himself; and at the age of fourteen, when other Jewish fathers might be testing their sons' familiarity with the Five Books of Moses, mine was starting me off with Freud's Five Introductory Lectures.

It was a real intellectual awakening, and the beginning of a long and close relationship with my father. Having retired early from his successful business career and returned to school (he is now a professor of political science), he had more time for his children, and I don't think it's immodest to say—since he told me so himself— that I became quite special to him. My brother was worldly and athletic rather than intellectual, while my sisters were not only nonacademic but also, well, not sons. We spent many long nights together in his library discussing a wide range of subjects—mostly in the light of psychology—and he seemed determined to give me early in life a love of knowledge and scholarship which had come to him much later. He instilled in me, most valuable of all, a thirst for Truth and its fearless pursuit—and in so doing, ironically, planted the seed of my future conversion.

At that time, however, for us, Religion and Truth were opposites. Here, too, Freud laid down the law, in his classic *The Future of an Illusion*. According to him, God is a kind of collective fantasy with its roots in ignorance and pathology, an "obsessional neurosis" which must be dispelled if humanity would progress toward complete sanity. A Loving Father, the Afterlife, a Moral Order—such "ideas" are "born from man's need to make his helplessness tolerable and built up from the material of his own childhood and the childhood of the human race"; the wish is father to the thought, as it were. Passionate assertions to the contrary are akin to the desperate denials by neurotics of some unbearable truth: our need for God, in short, is taken as evidence against His existence, as if our need for food and air discredits our conviction that we really eat and breathe.

It's unsurprising, then, that I became an atheist; and I still remember, with some amusement, the moment I made it official. Having learned in ninth-grade history class that the deadly disease "trichinosis" was commonly carried by swine at the time of the early Hebrews, I reasoned that the Kosher laws were "projections" into the divine realm of simple social needs—not considering, of course, that God might Himself have had some interest in the survival of His own People. The whole long story of man's religious wanderings suddenly seemed to me the history of pathetic, if innocently human, delusion.

The year was 1969, the times were out of joint, and I was at the tail end of a generation that fancied itself born, like Hamlet, to set them right. Fueled by the fear of war and the lure of sexual license, our "revolution" seemed to sweep over church, state, school and parental authority with all the inevitability of Destiny, and I had the heady sense of riding the crest of a great wave of the future. With many of my peers, I expected the imminent demise of all religious beliefs, sexual taboos, or any authority that derived its mandate from the "imaginary" realms above Reason—no matter that our own imperatives sprang from realms somewhat below. In the place of God we erected a grisly totem to the Pleasure Principle—fashioned from the filth of illicit sex and drugs—which we duly worshipped. Though Freud might make a case for the roots of religion in desire, never has a world view been so patently the result of "wish-fulfillment"—the wish that the pursuit of selfish satisfaction should have no natural or divine limits.

I have been as unexceptional in vice as I've been in virtue, if more for lack of opportunity than of desire, and probably it was my low standing in the brutal sexual competition of those years, and the erosive power of drugs, that threw me into a deep depression, which by my senior year was serious enough for my father to send me to a psychoanalyst. His name was Dr. Goodman, an appropriate name, for no matter what my current views of psychoanalysis, I will always remember him with respect and affection. Indeed, so awed was I over the next five years by his insight, eloquence and fatherly concern, that I came, much later, to postulate a variation on the psychoanalytical theory of "transference" (which holds that the patient unconsciously invests his analyst with the attributes of his own father, or of other significant figures in his life). My version is this: Our need for Christ is so essential to our nature that, without Him, we will seek His image—written in our hearts—in more earthly fathers, however imperfectly they embody it, and whether that "father" is a psychoanalyst, a guru, or a Hitler.

The following fall I entered Harvard College, expecting to become a psychoanalyst myself, though ironically it was Dr. Goodman who talked me out of it. Like many analysts he was fascinated by artistic talent, and was himself an accomplished amateur opera singer, so he encouraged me to follow the artistic bent I had evinced as an actor in high school. I was too cowed by the competitive harshness of Harvard to get on the stage right away, but I had developed a taste for the visual arts, and so decided to major in Art History. Wholly unaware of it at the time, painting and sculpture functioned for me in those years as they had for the Christian people throughout their great periods of ascendancy in art: as instruction in the Gospel. When I later came to consciously consider Christian doctrine, I was surprised at how much I had already learned of it through the medium of pictures.

Meanwhile, I had made two remarkable friends, a pair of indentical twins, both (in different years) my roommates. The ninth and tenth children in a family of Irish-Slavic background, sons of a Cleveland factory worker, they had been recruited by Harvard as scholarship students. They were also Catholics, though slowly lapsing, but with none of that hostility toward the Faith that characterizes other fallen-aways. Indeed, one of them once reprimanded me for expounding ignorantly on the nature of Christianity, and even briefly considered the priesthood; while the other, a history major, corrected my mistaken impression that all reputable historians were agreed that Jesus never existed. More important, they were unusually humble and forgiving—though hilarious mockers of sham—and were always delighted and amused by the myriad oddities of people. Theirs was a truly Catholic embrace of life and humanity, and whatever prejudice I'd had against their heritage was supplanted with respect.

In the spring of my junior year at Harvard, after my first audition in two years, I enjoyed a wonderful and unexpected success on the stage. Suddenly people were encouraging me to become an actor, which I immediately determined to do, and I almost simultaneously met my first real girlfriend. I won acceptance to the Juilliard Theatre Center, a prestigious acting school, and after graduation moved to Manhattan to begin my training. Things seemed so good that I no longer felt the need for psychoanalysis; and when I encountered the works, during my first year at Juilliard, of a strange and brilliant apostate-disciple of Freud's—Wilhelm Reich—I bade Dr. Goodman goodbye.

The career and ideas of Wilhelm Reich are impossible to summarize here, but suffice it to say that the rigor of his method, or the starvation of his soul, led this passionate materialist to the sphere of the cosmic, where his colleagues would or could not follow him; and it is said by some of his detractors—as if it proved his madness, as if he had caught the disease he was supposed to cure—that he died believing in God (for his sake, I certainly hope so). His inspiration may have been as much demonic as divine, so strange a brew of dangerous falsehoods and lucid truths did he concoct, but his effect on me at the time was to persuade me (to paraphrase Hamlet again) that there are more things in heaven and earth than are dreamt of in Freud's philosophy.

For the first time I had a genuine interest in spiritual things, though still convinced, with Reich, that their roots lay in material phenomena. I brushed through some works on Eastern mysticism, and at the same time began serious discussions with an Evangelical Christian classmate at Juilliard, even troubling to attend one of his prayer sessions (where I nevertheless declined to bow my head). I also took more seriously my brother's devotion to Transcendental Meditation, which had alienated him somewhat from our family some years before (and about which he remains as serious as I am about the Church). I fancied, I suppose, like so many fools before me, that I could find an "explanation" for religious beliefs in something other than God Himself.

It is a truism of science that there is no such thing as absolute proof—only a perfectly controlled experiment repeated infinitely can demonstrate beyond doubt any "law"—and this applies equally to proofs—or disproofs—of God's existence. Even Freud admitted as much, and like him I suppose I always had this crack in the door of my mind. That door was opening wider now, and I was aware that science itself (especially physics) was nervously discovering evidence of God. Meanwhile, even my experience as an actor began to play its part.

After I graduated from Juilliard I flew west, for the second summer, to the Utah Shakespearean Festival. I was to play Duke Vincentio, an immense and difficult role, in *Measure for Measure*, one of Shakespeare's most profoundly Christian plays (the title echoes the Sermon on the Mount). Our director, however, blind to its spiritual meanings, set out to conform it to his own fashionably cynical vision, and—worse still for me—to reduce the role of the Duke, the very model of a Christian ruler, to that of a nasty and selfish manipulator. Convinced that the play would fail unless done on its own terms, I tried to persuade him that he mistook its nature, sending him 60 pages of my own scholarly analysis during the short rehearsal period—even finding myself accusing him of "dogmatic atheism." That he finally relented, and that the production was a smashing success, were not the only happy results: in the process, I learned how wise and beautiful the Christian vision of society and morals could be.

That same summer saw the wedding of my older sister, and suddenly the issue of marriage, which I had long ignored, invaded my thoughts. How could I or my siblings, I wondered, make special and permanent any particular union when we had long since forfeited our sexual innocence? My parents' own exemplary marriage could only be envied, not imitated: they had met and married very young, cultivating through their long years together a devotion to each other and to their children that already, in their comparative youth, yielded a rich harvest of shared life and love, proving the truth of

Shakespeare's words: "Ripeness is all." But like so many of their generation, their growing liberalism made them see marriage as only one of many "life styles" which they happened to think the best; and though they desired nothing less than marriage for their children, there was nothing in their creed that upheld its purity and sanctity—in short, they didn't preach what they practiced. The traditions that once favored their own happiness had waned, and I suspected that their children would have to find the basis of marriage in something deeper even than tradition.

But the more I yearned for that "Golden Age" my parents' symbolized for me, the further I was carried away from it. In the fall of that year I joined the Acting Company, a traveling repertory ensemble, and embarked on an exhilirating two-year tour of the U.S., leaving behind the last of two "relationships" that had both developed in the same disillusioning manner: premature intimacy, cohabitation, decay, dissolution and angry recrimination. Lonely and bored, I took it as an opportunity to leap into the kind of sexual intrigues that only actors and actresses, trapped together in buses and motels, could possibly devise. A life of rootless, irresponsible freedom that once had only been my fantasy was now a sordid reality, and I began to despair of ever finding genuine and lasting love.

Two actresses in the Company were Christians, and rode together on the bus in seats we referred to as the "Bible Belt." I initiated some good-natured sparring on the subject of their religion which was to last throughout that first year (after which they left for other jobs). Though poor debaters, they did some lasting good: one of them induced me to read—aloud—the Suffering Servant passage in Isaiah, and as I recited it, I found myself, never easily moved, too choked up (and mortally embarrassed) to continue. They also persuaded me to read the Gospels—which I did, though only to better refute them.

Last and best, they convinced me to say a kind of conditional prayer to God, asking Him, if He existed, to reveal Himself to me. (I was certain He would not.)

Given the convenience of unbelief, and the contrasting difficulty of the life of faith, I might have kept questions of religion forever undigested, a sort of mental cud for pleasant, endless rumination. But as I often need to be reminded, God is more than an intellectual puzzle, and it is only in weakness that the strength of Christ is found. I had to be brought low, and that humbling began with a rebuff, in favor of another actor, by a new actress I had "targeted" in the Acting Company. Devasted, jealous, finally and totally disgusted with sexuality, I became a kind of misanthropic, misogynistic puritan—not unlike the character I was playing, Shakespeare's comic villain Malvolio (whose name suggests "ill will"). Disagreeing with the characterization imposed on me by my director, I hated even my own performance, and looked forward to the next year on the road with dread. As our bus rolled through the deserts of the Southwest I sat alone in the back, sullen and spiteful, the dryness of the climate matching the dryness of my soul.

Longing for some lost wholesomeness, I called my parents every week (I had never felt homesick before); and blaming my troubles on the moral and political liberalism I had always espoused, I began to read conservative books and journals, though I sensed that the answers I was seeking lay beyond the sweep of any merely earthly political pendulum. In one such journal I found an article on the Shroud of Turin, and I can't exaggerate the impact, however slow, it had on me: wasn't this the kind of evidence of God—*physical* evidence—that I, rational materialist that I was, had always demanded? Though still not final proof, it shattered my prejudice that the evidence was on the side of unbelief. With a rising sense of possibility, and the lifting of my foul mood, I said a few more prayers, and even bought and read *The Imitation of Christ*.

But I still had not hit bottom—that came when we returned to New York. Receiving the mediocre reviews I had expected for my performance, and having quit the Company, I found myself, exhausted and demoralized, back on the first rung of a career I no longer cared to pursue. The puzzle of existence I had so many times struggled to assemble still, it seemed, lay in pieces around me, and the strands of my own life had become completely unravelled. In my despair, I began to read *The Gods of Atheism* by Fr. Vincent Miceli, S.J., who effectively obliterated and swept away the crumbling remains of the many false idols I had worshipped, leaving room for the One True God, Whom he so thrillingly affirmed. In the deepening darkness of my soul, the Light of Christ, like the stars at twilight, began to glimmer.

For the next few months, while taking some classes at Harvard's American Repertory Theatre, I lodged in the home of an elderly woman who offered rooms to students in exchange for work—which included, for some, the care and supervision of her 35-year-old, autistic and mentally retarded son, Richard. I deliberately chose this situation because it seemed appropriate to thoughts of Christ: sleeping in a sparsely furnished cellar storage room at night, while by day cleaning toilets, making beds, and scrubbing floors for this burly innocent and his devoted mother enforced a kind of humility and poverty on me of which I had little experience. But I was also privileged to see close up a deeply loving mother-son relationship that, for all the suffering it entailed, utterly belied the view that his was a burdensome, worthless life and hers one of avoidable, unnecessary sacrifice. The calculating creeds of our loveless age seemed measly and mean compared to the boundless love of a God Who would make such as these the first in Heaven.

One day, as I was vacuuming the living room, Richard returned with one of his attendants from his morning walk. Even as my mind was hesitating on the verge of faith, this childlike man—whose mind and speech raced in wild free-association, never stopping on an idea and rarely making sense—began to loudly repeat, as if mocking the only alternative to the commitment I was timidly avoiding: "Oh, *go* to the devil, go to the devil, go to the devil. Oh, *go* to the devil, go to the devil, go to the devil..."—on and on and on. I was as much amused as amazed that Richard might be a bearer of heavenly challenges; and when, that weekend, I contacted one of my actress friends and was baptized at her Manhattan "Church of Christ," I hardly had this in mind. But two days later, as I troubled over unexpected misgivings, he sang out, quite distinctly, to the barely discernible tune of the Beatles' song *Hey, Jude*, this corruption of its opening verse (which goes "Hey, Jude, don't make it bad / Take a sad song, and make it better"): "Hey, Jew, don't make me [*Me*?] sad. Do better, do better. Hey, Jew—begin." A remarkable coincidence, probably, though one might forgive my suspicion that God was telling me, through the agency of this special, uncomprehending child of His, to take up my cross and continue on the road of faith.

The source of my unsteadiness, of course, was that I had stepped from the waters of Baptism directly into the shifting sands of Protestantism; indeed, after a few months' experience of it I nearly sank back into unbelief. Another Jewish convert I had met some years before came to my rescue and quickly persuaded me to enter the catechumenate of his Jesuit parish as an "inquirer." There, however, my catechists' highly selective presentation of Catholic doctrine, and their frequent equivocal invocations of the "primacy of conscience," frustrated my attempts to resolve issues I deemed crucial to any responsible decision; and the Church they presented—with such a developed hierarchy yet such uncertain authority—seemed worse to me, than even the disunited churches of Protestantism. Fortunately, however, my inde-

pendent reading saved me from mistaking this counterfeit
Catholicism for the genuine article.

G. K. Chesterton writes in *Orthodoxy* that "a man is
not really convinced of a philosophic theory when he
finds that something proves it. He is only really convinced when he finds that everything proves it. And the
more converging reasons he finds pointing to this conviction, the more bewildered he is if asked suddenly to sum
them up." Accordingly, I can only sketch how, in this final
phase before my Confirmation, even the "stumbling
blocks" I had encountered in my journey toward the
Church became the very "rocks" of my growing faith.
Wasn't the Successor of St. Peter, I reasoned, rather than
some earthly barrier to Christian knowledge and unity,
nothing less than the sole guarantee of coherent, consistent doctrine and worship, the visible sign of the One
Shepherd and the One Faith? And didn't the example of
our present Pope (who bestrode the world, it seemed to
me, like some moral Colossus—battling Satan, teaching
and exhorting with all the humility and courage of Christ
Himself) prove the matchless potential of his great office
for world spiritual leadership?

And what of the charges—and the promises—of "enlightened" secularism, of the believers in a society "liberated" by unbelief? Hadn't those regimes where atheism
had ruled—Nazi Germany and the Communist nations—
killed more people, in a single century, than all the religious wars since Christ? And what could they offer to
compare with the many charities, hospitals, orphanages,
the great art, music, literature and accumulated wisdom
that was the legacy of the Catholic Church?—nothing but
lies, terror and despair. And in our own decadent West,
what had *we* to show for our rejection of the Church's
"hard teachings" on sexual ethics, contraception, abortion, divorce and remarriage?—nothing but broken families, fatherless children, and what Paul VI, in *Humanae
Vitae*, had long since predicted: a mountain of slaughtered

innocents. The Church had stood firm against all this insanity with the fury of a prophet—and prophecy, it seemed to me, was a mark of Holiness. When the Easter Vigil arrived, and I was given the words to speak that even my instructors and fellow catechumens found embarrassingly absolute, I was by then so convinced of their truth that I fairly shouted them to the congregation: "I believe everything that the Catholic Church teaches to be revealed by God."

"God writes straight with crooked lines," my mother-in-law is fond of saying, and mine has certainly been a twisted path—not too long and confusing, I hope, for the reader to have followed it. I am something less than a theologian, and something lesser still than a saint (though I keep struggling), so I doubt my story offers anything in the way of Catholic instruction or example. But, if nothing else, it may help prove the truth of a maxim my father used to quote—unaware, I think, of its derivation—when one of us children had lost some toy or book or article of clothing:

"Seek, and ye shall find."

Jeffrey Rubin *is currently living in New York City with his wife, Johanna, and son, Michael Joseph. While working at a law firm and pursuing a doctorate in theater, he is engaged in several writing projects.*

Encounter with Light

Sheldon Vanauken

Dedicated to Davy,
The ''One dear person''

This is an account of a spiritual journey, told of necessity from the changing points of view of the traveller. There may have been an invisible Someone (God the Spirit) to help and an invisible Enemy to hinder, but their action was not suspected at the time. And yet, they may have been the real protagonists and my role the modest one of that which is fought for, the guerdon or the maiden in the tower. But not that only; for, however greatly I may have been helped, in the end I had to choose—and abide the consequences.

The Light Obscured

The beginning of conversion was, I suppose, the moment that I abandoned my childhood Christianity and became a small, fierce atheist—in the name of truth. There seems to be in the lives of many rather thoughtful and independent persons a progress of three steps: first, abandonment, often rebellious, of an imperfectly understood, childish Christianity, held only on adult authority; second, reacceptance, very gradually, of many of the moral principles and some of the insights of Christianity; and, third, conversion to the faith. But of course, each step may be one's last. The necessity of this process is explained by the aphorism: 'To believe with certainty, one must begin by doubting.'

By doubting, then, and by abandoning a seemingly inadequate Christianity that I had never, so to speak, believed on my own, I had taken a first step towards real belief. Perhaps any belief that one has not thought one's own way to is inadequate. But, in addition, there were four specific inadequacies in the only Christianity I knew: it was not exciting, not positive, not big enough, and not related to life.

It was not exciting: The Greeks in history, with their passion for truth and beauty, lucid as a sunlit Doric temple above the wine-dark sea, were exciting; astronomy, with its blazing stars and icy distances, was exciting; poetry, reaching for beauty in words of splendour, was exciting; but this Christianity, with its fragmented accounts of dark and incomprehensible deeds in Palestine and its solemn, humourless voices, was too stuffy for excitement, too dull for tears.

It was not positive: The Christians dying in the Roman arena had died *for* something; the crusader knights riding under the cross of gold had fought *for* something; but this Christianity did not preach the crusade—the cross led only to respectability. Indeed, the message seemed to be, mainly, that one was bad if one did any of quite a long list of things, such as saying 'Damn!' or missing church or drinking any of the joyous, sunny wine that Our Lord had made at Cana—indeed, the churches 'improved' on the innocent Jesus by rejecting the glowing wine that was His chosen symbol of the Eucharist in favour of solemn tinned grape juice. It was all negative and on the whole repressive; one was not working *for* something, except perhaps new chairs for the Sunday School and, of course, a rather dull Heaven—though the occasions when someone presumably attained Heaven were ones of unmitigated gloom.

It was not big enough: This Christianity was simply not big enough to include all the worlds that swing about our sun and all the worlds that might swing about a million racing suns in the chilling immensities of space; how could the redemption of Earth, in so far as it was redeemed, be related to Aldebaran or the spiral nebulae? This Christianity, then, was too little to be *the* truth.

Finally, it was not related to life: Outside the church doors beat the turbulence and crookedness and splendour of life. What had the churches got to say about it? With repect to war and arms, the voice of this Christianity was a feeble mutter. It was against sin, to be sure; but the businessmen who practised a dog-eat-dog ethic six days a week were well received at the altar rail—and at the collection plate. Nor was anyone ever rebuked for coming to the altar when she was well known not to be on speaking terms with someone else in the church. Nor was anyone ever turned away for pride. On the other hand, to be fair, it was clear that one oughtn't to say 'Damn!' And there *were* some people who would not be welcomed at the altar rail: the dark-skinned. Who could believe that here in this stuffiness, with all the beauty and laughter and pain of life held at bay outside the church—who could believe that *here* were the truths of life and death? I could not, and I doubted whether anyone else did. I turned away from this religion and declared for atheism.

Such a relief! What freedom! And atheism was exhilarating: if the gods were dead, then man was the highest. Glorious! And it was a belief totally opposed to that impossible Christianity—a strong, bold creed. But *what* had I said? A belief? A creed? There was the flaw in atheism: one must *believe* in no-god. It, too, is a faith. There is no evidence and, certainly, no revelation; and, by the nature of the case, there can be none. So—I renounced atheism.

The next step was agnosticism: not knowing and sceptical about the possibility of knowing. And yet, at almost the same time, I began to think that perhaps one could know a little. Geometry with its unprovable but self-evident axioms provided a clue. Were there any axioms having to do with the meaning of things? I decided that *something* had created the universe: this was self-evident, *axiomatic*. Then I applied myself to the consideration of whether there were any self-evident indications of the nature of this 'first cause', and I perceived order. These were, of course, well-worn ways I was treading, but they were new to me. It began to seem axiomatic that the power that made the universe was intelligent and infinite: order must .be a function of intelligence; and only infinite intelligence could comprehend the infinities of space and time. A very great awareness of beauty coupled with the recognition that everything was beautiful, except where marred by man, persuaded me that beauty was a reflection of the beauty of the Power. (It was much later that I read Plato with excited recognition.) For a long time I wondered whether good might not be, like beauty, an axiomatic attribute of the Power. But good did not exist in nature; it existed in man and was countered by evil, and I could not attribute it, self-evidently, to the Power, which remained impersonal. I did not believe in prayer, providence, or judgement; and my ethics were unrelated to my god. I had thus reached, while still in boarding school, a kind of cold theism, which I was to hold for many years.

Once, in my first year of college, I wavered, needing help that could only come through the miraculous intervention of a personal god; I offered up a few urgent and desperate prayers. When, as expected, no great Hand reached down, I was confirmed in my non-Christian theism. In subsequent years I was dedicated, almost religiously, to beauty and to the love of one person; and, having youth and good fortune, I was happy, mainly through that love. In general I attempted goodness, feeling it to be, like love and beauty, part of the *Tao* or Way. It was, in fact, a fairly high sort of paganism, and the inadequacies of such a position are much less obvious than those of materialism.

Meanwhile, Christianity, which I made no pretence of having the slightest connection with, continued to appear to me as a delusive religion that made quite incredible claims about a brave and fanatical Jew—a religion to be outgrown like one's childish belief in elves and fairies. While there was a sort of beauty in the Christian story (as there was in fairy lore), it did not extend to the churches: they seemed narrow, smug, and complacent, quarrelling obscurely about alleged truths they couldn't agree on; they spoke in clichés with a fruity unctuousness that was incredibly revolting about 'mountaintop experiences' and 'fruitful fellowship'; they sang sticky and horrible hymns and built a good many horrible buildings. I not only disbelieved in Christianity, I disliked it heartily; and a person dropped like a stone in my estimation if he confessed to being a Christian. But I could quite easily keep my distance, and I did so.

Encounter with Light

One wakeful night, standing upon the bridge of a ship in tropical waters, a shimmering moonpath reaching from my toes to the horizon, I fell to thinking a most dangerous series of thoughts: It's odd (the thoughts ran) that otherwise-intelligent people, like T. S. Eliot, the brilliant poet, and Eddington, the famous physicist, and Dorothy Sayers, the novelist and essayist, with her caustic wit and keen intelligence—it's very odd that they apparently actually believe in this Christianity that I saw through in my teens. Could there possibly be more to it than I saw? No, certainly not! Still, it *is* odd. I wonder how they *can* believe it. There must be something. Could it be, perhaps, that I, possibly, ought to have another look, sometime? Not that it's true, of course—quite impossible!—still, one is supposed to be intellectually honest and hear what the other side has to say. Obviously it's not true, but, Good

Heavens! it wouldn't hurt me to look at it. Yes, I'll do that, sometime.

Next day, while I didn't renounce the resolve, I thought with a touch of regret that it all looked like rather a lot of dreary work, and for what? Just to be intellectually honest. Whatever had put such an idea into my head? Naturally, Christianity wasn't *true*: it was precisely incredible and almost all Christians were horrible. At all events, the second look was not then possible, nor for a long time to come. Still, as months and years went by, I never quite forgot the resolve; possibly Someone at my elbow saw to it that I did not forget.

But I was occupied with 'important' things, studying history at the Yale graduate school and doing a little teaching. I became concerned about the tendency in so many parts of the world to erect the state, or the state-disguised-as-the-people, or the community, or the organization, into a soulless monster more important than the individuals that comprised it. I recognized that the Christian Church strongly asserted the importance of the individual, and I became conscious of a faint sense of alliance. At the same time, my interest in history and language prompted me occasionally to attend the Anglican Church, of which nominally I was a member, just to hear the lovely and ancient words of the liturgy: it is possible that, in spite of myself, some of the meanings sank home. Once I actually took the sacrament (I can't think why)—and if, as the Apostolic churches believe, the Eucharist is a means to grace, my action may have had an incalculable effect. But, certainly, I was not a believer—not a Christian.

The next influence was that of place: England and Oxford. At this ancient University, mellowed by the strong intellectual life of a thousand years, many things that seem anachronisms in the hustle of American academic life—cap and gown, gothic spires, Latin inscriptions, and Greek ideas—seem almost to be of the essence. In this city of the dreaming spires the University, despite the modern laboratories, is still, in fact, 'breathing the last enchantments of the middle ages': This wall was part of a great abbey; the Benedictines built the long, lovely buildings that are part of one college quad; the narrow passage where one bought tea things has been called Friars Entry for centuries; the Colleges bear names like Christ Church and Mary Magdalen and Jesus and Corpus Christi—and from them and from half a hundred churches the singing bells sent their lovely clamour across the city. All of a sudden, the ages of faith, when men really believed, when the spires carried their eyes up to God, became real. The great bells still spoke with their strong faith (as perhaps the weakly pretty chimes of modern American churches suggest enfeebled faith). I had seen lots of unbeautiful churches and heard mushy hymns and tired religious clichés—but now I knew there was also a terrible splendour, in the spires and cathedrals and the ancient, glowing glass, in the great music of the plainsong and the masses, and in the superb language of the liturgy. To be sure, such splendour didn't mean that Christianity was true; but, then, dull, horrible churches didn't mean that it wasn't. And perhaps I vaguely felt that the splendour *did* hint at a validity.

At all events, one evening, as I walked back across the meadows into Oxford, hearing the singing of the bells and seeing the tremendous, soaring uprush of the spire of St. Mary the Virgin in the dusk, I thought (or Someone at my elbow murmured) that now, perhaps, was the time for that long-postponed second look. I did not resist. I resolved that I should plunge straightaway into the question of Christianity. I even stopped at a bookseller's then and there and came in late to tea with an armload of books.

There were half a hundred books that autumn and winter. I became interested right at the start and neglected all else, though at first it was only an interesting *study,* not something that might turn out to be true and compel my life into other courses. By good fortune the first thing I read (because it looked easiest) was a science-fiction trilogy [*Out of the Silent Planet*; *Perelandra*; & *That Hideous Strength*] by an Oxford don, C. S. Lewis. This had the effect of showing me that the Christian God might, quite reasonably, be big enough, after all, to include the stars and the spiral nebulae; it wasn't proof, but for me an insuperable difficulty had, in fact, been overcome when I recognized that Christianity was not necessarily a *local* religion of earth. G. K. Chesterton, with wit and no pompousness, presented a brilliant, reasoned case for Christianity [*The Everlasting Man*, &c]. Charles Williams, theologian and novelist, opened up realms of the spirit I hadn't known existed and suggested that God's view of history might be very different to man's—and quite as possible [*The Descent of the Dove*; *The Place of the Lion*; *All Hallows' Eve*; *Descent into Hell*]. Graham Greene showed—terribly—what sin was, and what faith was—also terrible [*The Heart of the Matter*; *The End of the Affair*; &c.]. Dorothy Sayers [*Creed or Chaos*; *The Mind of the Maker*; &c.] preached the crusade, attacked complacency and dullness like a scorpion, and made Christianity dramatic and exciting. I began to see what T. S. Eliot was really saying in *Ash Wednesday* and *The Four Quartets*—and it scared me, rather. His description of the state of being a Christian lingered in my mind: 'A condition of complete simplicity / (Costing not less than everything)'. Everything! Above all, there was C. S. Lewis of Magdalen College, a classicist and a great authority on English Literature; he had been an atheist and was now a Christian, and he could talk the language of the sceptic—my language. His was perhaps the most brilliant and certainly the most lucid mind I had ever encountered; he wrote about Christianity in a style as clear as spring water without a hint of sanctimoniousness or vagueness or double-talk—simply straightforward, telling argument laced with wit. I wrote in my Notebook at the time: 'No one who has not honestly faced up to the overwhelming question—is Christianity possibly false?—can resolve for someone else the counter-question—Is it true?' I read every book of his, particularly *The Great Divorce, The Problem of Pain, Miracles, The Screwtape Letters, Pilgrim's Regress,* and (later) *Surprised by Joy.* I also read a number of the Christian classics, including St. Augustine, *The Imitation of Christ, The Flight from God, Apologia Pro Vita Sua,* and the *Practice of the Presence.* And—of course—the New Testament in numerous translations along with several Catholic and Protestant commentaries. I approached the Testament with reluctance—a legacy of boredom—even though I knew it related what was in fact earth's chief historical event, but the reluctance vanished as all came together into meaning.

Quite as important as the books, or more so, were Christians. Chance (perhaps) had thrown me with several Christians, who became close friends: there were two physicists, one English and the other American; there was a girl studying history, and others were reading English and classics; there was a Benedictine monk, not yet priested, reading history and theology. The American physicist was a Southern Baptist; the Benedictine was Roman Catholic; others were Anglican, Methodist, and Lutheran. I was not only more conscious of their being Christians than physicists or historians, but, for the first time, I was more conscious of what united Christians, that is, faith in Christ, than of the sects that divided them. I was rather impressed that brilliant nuclear physicists and advanced scholars in other fields should be at once competent, civilized, *and* Christian. I was even more impressed with what seemed to be the quality of joy that came to these people through their faith. Non-Christians were often gay and funny and happy when all was going well, but I had not often encountered this quiet joy. Here is an entry from my Notebook of that time:

The best argument for Christianity is Christians: their joy, their certainty, their completeness. But the strongest argument *against* Christianity is also Christians—when they are sombre and joyless, when they are self-righteous and smug in complacent consecration, when they are narrow and repressive, then Christianity dies a thousand deaths. But, though it is just to condemn some Christians for these things, perhaps, after all, it is not just, though very easy, to condemn Christianity itself for them. Indeed, there are impressive indications that the positive quality of joy is in Christianity—and possibly nowhere else. If that were certain, it would be proof of a very high order.

Besides the books and the Christian friends, I had another, tremendous advantage: I did not suppose I *was* a Christian. I was quite outside the fold, and I did not think for a moment that I was in it. Thus I was perfectly aware that the central claim of Christianity was and always had been that the same God who made the world had lived in the world and been killed by the world, and that the (claimed) proof of this was His Resurrection from the dead. This, in fact, was precisely what I couldn't believe. But, at least, I knew that it was what *had* to be believed if one was to call oneself a Christian; so I did not call myself one. But in later years I have met people who no more believe in this central claim than they believe in the Easter bunny, yet they call themselves Christians all the same, on the basis, apparently, of going to church and being nice: I submit that these people prove that there *can* be smoke without fire. At all events, I, being outside Christianity, was not too close to see it—thus it is that my conversion could be said to have begun when I abandoned Christianity and started to put as much distance as possible between it and me. Now I was not so close that I mistook the foothills for the mountain. I saw it there only too clearly, solitary, vast, ice-capped, and apparently unscaleable by me: I knew I had to *believe*. Christianity was a *faith*.

And by now I knew that it was important. If true—and I admitted the possibility that it was—it was, very simply, the *only* really important truth in the world. And if untrue, it was false. No halfway house. I wrote in my Notebook: 'It is not possible to be "incidentally a Christian." The fact of Christianity must be overwhelmingly *first* or nothing. This suggests a reason for the dislike of Christians by nominal or non-Christians: their lives contain no overwhelming firsts but many balances.'

Not only could I see the shining mountain that was the Christian Faith, I could see that Christianity claimed to be, precisely, an *answer*. Not a problem, not a hunting ground for professional 'seekers' who would not wish to lose their seekers' status by finding: Christianity offered an answer to all the eternal questions—a *consistent* answer, my physicist friends kept murmuring. The seeker's quest was over—if he could scale the mountain. I liked the prospect of an answer; I wanted an answer. In so far as I had become a seeker, it was in hopes of an answer. The only trouble was I could not believe the Christian one. Finally I decided to write to C. S. Lewis; excerpts from my letters and his replies follow:—

To C. S. Lewis (I)

I write on an impulse—which in the morning may appear so immodest and presumptuous that I shall destroy this. But a few moments ago I felt that I was embarked for a voyage that would someday lead me to God. Even now, five minutes later, I'm inclined to add a qualifying 'maybe.' There is a leap I cannot make; it occurs to me that you, having made it, having linked certainty with Christianity, might, *not* do it *for* me, but might give me a hint of how it's to be done. Having felt the aesthetic and historic appeal of Christianity, having begun to study it, I have come to awareness of the strength and 'possibleness' of the Christian answer. I should *like* to believe it. I *want* to know God—if he is knowable. But I cannot pray with any conviction that Someone hears. I can't *believe*.

Very simply, it seems to me that some intelligent power made this universe and that all men must know it, axiomatically, and must feel awe at the power's infiniteness. It seems to me natural that men, knowing and feeling so, should attempt to elaborate on that simplicity—the prophets, the Prince Buddha, the Lord Jesus, Mohammed, the Brahmins—and so arose the world's religions. But how can just one of them be singled out as true? To an intelligent visitor from Mars, would not Christianity appear to be merely one of a host of religions?

I said at starting that I felt I was treading a long road that would one day lead me to Christianity; I must, then, believe after a fashion that it is the truth. Or is it only that I *want* to believe it? But at the same time, something else in me says: 'Wanting to believe is the way to self-deception. Honesty is better than any easy comfort. Have the courage to face the fact that all men may be nothing to the Power that made the suns.'

And yet I *would* like to believe that the Lord Jesus is in truth my merciful God. For the apostles who could talk to Jesus, it must have been easy. But I live in a 'real world' of red busses and nylon stockings and atomic bombs. I have only the record of *others'* claimed experiences with deity. No angels, no voices, nothing. Or, yes, one thing: living Christians. Somehow you, in this very same world, with the same data as I, are more meaningful to me than the bishops of the faithful past. You accomplished the leap from agnosticism to faith: how? I don't quite know how I dare write this to you, a busy Oxford don, not a priest. Yet I do know: you serve God, not yourself; you *must* do, if you're a Christian. Perhaps, if I had the wit to see it, my answer lies in the fact that I did write.

From C. S. Lewis (I)

My own position at the threshold of Xtianity was exactly the opposite of yours. You wish it were true; I strongly hoped it was *not*. At least, that was my conscious wish: you may suspect that I had unconscious wishes of quite a different sort and that it was these which finally shoved me in. True: but then I equally may suspect that, under your conscious wish that it were true, there lurks a strong unconscious wish that it were not. What this works out to is that all the modern stuff about concealed wishes and wishful thinking, however useful it may be for explaining the origin of an error which you already know to be an error, is perfectly useless in deciding which of two beliefs is the error and which is the truth. For (a.) One never knows all one's wishes, and (b.) In very big questions, such as this, even one's conscious wishes are nearly always engaged on both sides.

What I think one can say with certainty is this: the notion that everyone *would like* Xtianity to be true, and that therefore all atheists are brave men who have accepted the defeat of all their deepest desires, is simply impudent nonsense. Do you think people like Stalin, Hitler, Haldane, Stapledon (a corking good writer, by the way) wd. be pleased on waking up one morning to find that they were not their own masters, that they had a. Master and a Judge, that there was nothing even in the deepest recesses of their thoughts about which they cd. say to him: 'Keep out! Private. This is *my* business'? Do you? *Rats!* Their first reaction wd. be (as mine was) rage and terror. And I v. much doubt whether even you wd. find it *simply* pleasant. Isn't the truth this: that it wd. gratify some of our desires (ones we feel in fact pretty seldom) and outrage a great many others? So let's wash out all the wish business. It never helped anyone to solve any problem yet.

I don't agree with your picture of the history of religion—Christ, Buddha, Mohammed, and others elaborating an original simplicity. I believe Buddhism to be a simplification of Hinduism and Islam to be a simplification of Xtianity. Clear, lucid, transparent, simple religion

(Tao *plus* a shadowy, ethical god in the background) is a late development, usually arising among highly educated people in great cities. What you really start with is ritual, myth, and mystery, the death & return of Balder or Osiris, the dances, the initiations, the sacrifices, the divine kings. Over against that are the Philosophers, Aristotle or Confucius, hardly religious at all. The *only* two systems in which the mysteries and the philosophies come together are Hinduism & Xtianity: there you get both Metaphysics and Cult (continuous with the primeval cults). That is why my first step was to be sure that one or other of these had the answer. For the reality can't be one that appeals *either* only to savages *or* only to highbrows. Real things aren't like that (e.g. *matter* is the first most obvious thing you meet—milk, chocolates, apples, and also the object of quantum physics). There is no question of just a crowd of disconnected religions. The choice is between (a.) The materialist world picture: wh. I *can't* believe. (b.) The real archaic primitive religions: wh. are not moral enough. (c.) The (claimed) fulfillment of these in Hinduism. (d.) The (claimed) fulfillment of these in Xtianity. But the weakness of Hinduism is that it *doesn't* really join the two strands. Unredeemably savage religion goes on in the village; the Hermit philosophises in the forest: and neither really interferes with the other. It is only Xtianity wh. compels a highbrow like me to partake in a ritual blood feast, and also compels a central African convert to attempt an enlightened universal code of ethics....

Have you read the *Analects* of Confucius? He ends up by saying, 'This is the Tao. I do not know if anyone has ever kept it.' That's significant: one can really go direct from there to the *Epistle to the Romans*....

To C. S. Lewis (II)

My fundamental dilemma is this: I can't believe in Christ unless I have faith, but I can't have faith unless I believe in Christ. This is 'the leap.' If to *be* a Christian is to have faith (and clearly it is), I can put it thus: I must accept Christ to become a Christian, but I must *be* a Christian to accept Him. I don't have faith and I don't as yet believe; but everyone seems to say: 'You must have faith to believe.' Where do I get it? Or will you tell me something different? Is there a proof? Can Reason carry one over the gulf...without faith?

Why does God expect so much of us? Why does he require this effort to believe? If He made it clear that He is—as clear as a sunrise or a rock or a baby's cry—wouldn't we be right joyous to choose Him and His Law? Why should the right exercise of our free will contain this fear of intellectual dishonesty?

I must write further on the subject of 'wishing it were true'—although I do agree that I probably have wishes on both sides, and my wish does not help me to solve any problem. Your point that Hitler and Stalin (and I) would be horrified at discovering a Master from whom *nothing* could be withheld is very strong. Indeed, there is nothing in Christianity which is so repugnant to me as humility—the bent knee. If I knew beyond hope or despair that Christianity were true, my fight for ever after would have to be against the pride of 'the spine may break but it never bends'. And yet, Sir, would not I (and even Stalin) accept the humbling of the Master to escape the horror of ceasing to be, of *nothingness* at death? Moreover, the knowledge that Jesus was in truth Lord would *not* be merely pleasant news gratifying some of our rare desires. It would mean overwhelmingly; (a) that Materialism was Error as well as ugliness; (b) that the several beastly futures predicted by the Marxists, the Freudians, and the Sociologist manipulators would not be real (even if they came about); (c) that one's growth towards wisdom—soul-building—was not to be lost: and (d), above all, that the good and the beautiful would survive. And so I wish it were true and would accept any humbling, I think, for it to be true. The bad part of wishing it were true is that any impulse I feel towards belief is regarded with suspicion as stemming from the wish; the good part is that the wish leads on. And I shall go on; I must go on, as far as I can go.

From C. S. Lewis (II)

The contradiction 'we must have faith to believe and must believe to have faith' belongs to the same class as those by which the Eleatic philosophers proved that all motion was impossible. And there are many others. You can't swim unless you can support yourself in water and you can't support yourself in water unless you can swim. Or again, in an act of volition (e.g. getting up in the morning) is the very beginning of the act itself voluntary or involuntary? If voluntary then you must have willed it, ∴ you were willing already, ∴ it was not really the beginning. If involuntary, then the continuation of the act (being determined by the first moment) is involuntary too. But in spite of this we *do* swim, & we *do* get out of bed.

I do not think there is a *demonstrative* proof (like Euclid) of Christianity, nor of the existence of matter, nor of the good will & honesty of my best & oldest friends. I think all three are (except perhaps the second) far more probable than the alternatives.... As to *why* God doesn't make it demonstratively clear: are we sure that He is even interested in the kind of Theism which wd. be a compelled logical assent to a conclusive argument? Are *we* interested in it in personal matters? I demand from my friend a trust in my good faith which is *certain* without demonstrative proof. It wouldn't be confidence at all if he waited for rigorous proof. Hang it all, the very fairy-tales embody the truth. Othello believed in Desdemona's innocence when it was proved: but that was too late. Lear believed in Cordelia's love when it was proved: but that was too late. 'His praise is lost who stays till all commend.' The magnanimity, the generosity wh. will trust on a reasonable probability, is required of us. But supposing one believed and was wrong after all? Why, then you wd. have paid the universe a compliment it doesn't deserve. Your error wd. even so be more interesting & important than the reality. And yet how cd. that be? How cd. an idiotic universe have produced creatures whose mere dreams are so much stronger, better, subtler than itself?

Note that life after death, which still seems to you the essential thing, was itself a *late* revelation. God trained the Hebrews for centuries to believe in Him without promising them an afterlife, and, blessings on Him, He trained me in the same way for about a year. It is like the disguised prince in the fairy tale who wins the heroine's love *before* she knows he is anything more than a woodcutter. What wd. be a bribe if it came first had better come last.

And now, another point about *wishes*. A wish may lead to false beliefs, granted. But what does the existence of the wish suggest? At one time I was much impressed by Arnold's line 'Nor does the being hungry prove that we have bread.' But surely, tho' it doesn't prove that one particular man will *get* food, it *does* prove that there is such a thing as food! i.e. if we were a species that didn't normally eat, weren't designed to eat, wd. we feel hungry? You say the materialist universe is 'ugly'. I wonder how you discovered that! If you are really a product of a materialistic universe, how is it you don't feel at home there? Do fish complain of the sea for being wet? Or if they did, would that fact itself not strongly suggest that they had not always been, or wd. not always be, purely aquatic creatures? Notice how we are perpetually *surprised* at Time. ('How time flies! Fancy John being grown-up & married! I can hardly believe it!') In heaven's name, why? Unless, indeed, there is something in us which is *not* temporal....

But I think you are already in the meshes of the net! The Holy Spirit is after you. I doubt if you'll get away!

Yours, C. S. Lewis

These letters from Lewis gave me much to think on, and they frightened me, too—especially that shocking last paragraph. Alarum bells sounded, but I couldn't decide which way to flee. I was still unable to make 'the leap.' Several people were praying for me, and I regarded this activity with uneasiness and suspicion. I felt that they were waiting for something to happen: they gave me pleasantly questioning looks when we met on the street. I was also suspicious of any small upsurges of feeling about the Lord Jesus and gave myself cross warnings about sentimentalism. And yet I recognized that there was a place for emotion as well as reason. I wrote in my Notebook:—

> It would seem that Christianity requires both emotional and intellectual assent. If there is only emotion, the mind asks troubling questions that, if not answered, might lead to a falling away, for love cannot be sustained without understanding. On the other hand, there is a gap which must be bridged by emotion. If one is suspicious of the upsurge of feeling that may be incipient faith, how is one to cross the gap?

My position at this point—on the brink—was something like this: I had taken the 'second look' at Christianity so long before resolved on: and I had found—what had I found? Much more than I had expected, certainly. Christianity now appeared intellectually stimulating, aesthetically exciting, and emotionally moving. I was half in love with Jesus; I yearned towards him and wanted to fall on my knees. Like the woman in Graham Greene who fell into belief as one falls in love, I was falling in love—but my mind was suspicious: Something kept saying, 'Don't be overcome! Keep your head! However delicious and comforting it would be, don't give in!' No longer did the Church appear only a disreputable congeries of quarrelling sects: now I saw the Church splendid and terrible, sweeping down the centuries with anthems and shining crosses and steady-eyed saints. No longer was the Faith something for children; intelligent people held it strongly—and they walked to a secret singing that I could not hear. Or *did* I hear something, high and clear and unbearably sweet? One dear person who had been with me outside the Faith suddenly, in the course of walking across a room, was snatched away, into that singing, into the Company of the Faithful. I was alone, and I felt, sulkily, that I had been betrayed. If I couldn't advance, no one else ought to. Christianity seemed to me *probable*: it all hinged on Jesus—Was he, in fact, the Lord Christ? *Was* he 'very God of very God'? This was the heart of the matter. The claimed proof was the Resurrection; it was belief in Christ's rising from the dead, I knew well enough, that had convinced the early Christians. And I saw clearly that there were really only three possibilities: the Apostles had made up the story after the crucifixion; or Jesus himself had invented the claim to divinity and they had dreamt the rest; or—it was precisely and factually true. I had got over the naive belief that modern science had somehow demonstrated that miracles can't happen or that science, which is concerned with nature, could say anything at all about the possible intervention of Supernature. Therefore, the Incarnation and the Resurrection *might* be true. It was simply a question of evidence, nor did the fact that *I* had never seen a miracle imply that there might not be miracles at the supreme occasion of history. It seemed extremely unlikely that the Apostles had concocted the story: the Gospels ring with sincerity, and, besides, men don't die proclaiming with their last breaths what they know to be a lie—especially when they might save their lives by recanting. Most of these men had been unpleasantly executed, and, had they recanted, the recantation would have been famous. But, equally, I could not accept that Jesus himself had been deluded: A man who goes about forgiving sins, claiming to have existed through all eternity [Before Abraham was, I am], saying that whoever had seen *him* (notice, he did *not* modestly suggest divinity in everyone by saying that whoever had seen old Peter there) had seen the Father—such a man is not merely deluded, he is *deranged*, a rather horrible megalomaniac; or He is speaking the truth. And I could not believe that a lunatic could have spoken the Sermon on the Mount or the parables. So I was faced with the third alternative. It was not impossible; it alone was possible; but it was too enormous to be comprehended. I knew it was a reasonable probability; I suspected it to be true. I suspected that all the yearnings for I knew not what that I had ever felt—when autumn fires were burning in the twilight, when wild geese flew crying in the night, when spring arrived on an April morning—were in truth yearnings for God. But suspicion is not certainty. There was still the gap between the probable and proved; and, if I were to stake my whole life on the Risen Christ, I wanted certainty; I wanted proof; I wanted letters of fire across the sky. I did not get them. And I waited.

One night while reading, deeply moved, Dorothy Sayers' tremendous play, *The Man Born To Be King*, I was struck by the significance of the reply to Jesus's query about faith: 'Lord, I believe; help thou mine unbelief.' A contradiction, a paradox. But could it be the key to that other paradox: 'One must have faith to believe but must believe to have faith'? A paradox to open up a paradox? I felt that it was; and I also felt that this was a significant 'break through.'

A day later came the second intellectual 'break through': it was the rather chilling realization that *I could not go back*. In my old, easy-going theism I had regarded Christianity as a sort of fairy tale, and I had neither accepted nor rejected Christ since I had never—really—encountered him. But now I had. It was not, as I had comfortably thought, merely a question of accepting or not. It was now accepting—or rejecting! My God! There was a gap *behind* me, too! Perhaps the leap to acceptance was horrifying, but what of the leap to rejection? There might be no certainty that Christ was God—but, by heaven, there was no certainty that he was not! If I were to accept, I might and probably would face the thought through the years: 'Perhaps, after all, it's a lie; I've been had!' But if I were to reject, there could be no doubt at all that I should be haunted by the terrible thought: 'Perhaps it's true—and I have *rejected my God!*'

It could not be borne. I *could not* reject Christ. There was only one thing to do. I turned and flung myself over the gap *towards* Christ. On a morning with spring in the air [March 29th], I wrote in my Notebook and to C. S. Lewis:

> I *choose* to believe in the Father, Son, and Holy Ghost—in Christ, my lord and my God. Christianity has the ring, the *feel*, of unique truth. Of *essential* truth. By it, life is made full instead of empty, meaningful instead of meaningless. Cosmos becomes beautiful at the *Centre*, instead of chillingly ugly beneath the lovely pathos of spring. But the emptiness, the meaninglessness, and the ugliness can only be seen, I think, when one has glimpsed the fullness, the meaning, and the beauty. It is when Heaven and Hell have *both* been glimpsed that going back is impossible. But to go on seemed impossible, also. A glimpse is not a vision. A choice was necessary: and there is no certainty. One can only choose a side. So I—I now choose my side: I choose beauty; I choose what I love. But choosing to believe *is* believing. It's all I can do: choose. I confess my doubts and ask my Lord Christ to enter my life. I do not *know* God is, I do but say: Be it unto me according to Thy will. I do not affirm that I

am without doubt, I do but ask for help, having chosen, to overcome it. I do but say: Lord, I believe—help Thou mine unbelief.

The Lighted Road

Two roads seemed to diverge from this point, as I saw it from the one I had chosen. One was rather dark and very smooth, broad and ever broadening until it debouched in a dark desert and ceased to be a road. The other was brilliantly lighted, almost too light for comfort, I felt, though light was needed, for the road was rough and horribly steep and ever narrowing. This, the lighted road, was the one I had chosen, though I was only at the beginning: the obstacles and the wearying steepness and the dangerous narrowness, all lay ahead. Still, I could see where I was going, and that seemed to me to be the great thing.

I was now a Christian. I—a Christian! I, who had been wont to regard Christians with pitying dislike, must now confess myself to be one. I did so with shrinking and pride. Indeed, I felt a curious mixture of emotions; the human embarrassment among non-Christians at deserting their precarious camp; an odd sort of pride, as though I had conferred a great favour upon Jesus, which the light made tawdry and silly; and a great joy that fell upon me with the light. My non-Christian friends shrank away; they would have accepted my becoming an atheist, a communist, or a Buddhist with equanimity, but not a Christian; non-Christians, unmistakably, are uncomfortable with Christians. On the other hand, Christian friends were full of joy. C. S. Lewis wrote:—

> My prayers are answered. No: a glimpse is not a vision. But to a man on a mountain road by night, a glimpse of the next three feet of road may matter more than a vision of the horizon. And there must perhaps always be just enough lack of demonstrative

certainty to make free choice possible: for what could we do but accept if the faith were like the multiplication table? There will be a counter attack on you, you know, so don't be too alarmed when it comes. The enemy will not see you vanish into God's company without an effort to reclaim you. Be busy learning to pray.... Blessings on you and a hundred thousand welcomes. Make use of me in any way you please: and let us pray for each other always.

At first I had a surprising assurance and certainty, despite the doubts that had harried me so long. I think that one is given a special grace—joy and assurance—in the beginning. *After* one has chosen, however feebly, then a shining dress of grace wraps one round—for awhile. Until the new-born Christian has learned to stand and walk a little. Nevertheless, the counterattack came. I wrote in my Notebook:—

Forty days after: The decision made, one begins to act on it. One prays, goes to church, makes an incredibly meaningful first Christian communion. One tries to rethink everything one has ever thought in this new Light. One tries to subordinate self—to make the Sign of the Cross, crossing out the 'I'—and to follow Christ, with something less than brilliant success. C. S. Lewis prophesies the enemy's counterattack, and is right as usual. Feelings surge in that it's lies, all lies, that yonder red bus, the hard pavement under one's heels, the glory of the may tree are the *only* realities. But one remembers that the Choice was based on reason, the weight of the evidence, and is strengthened. But that's not quite all. Not only can the doubts be coped with, not only do prayers go better, but the doubts come less often—and when they do are often met with a surge of inexplicable confidence that the Choice was right. *We* are winning.

By the grace of God, I was surrounded by strong Christian friends, including Lewis who became a good friend. Moreover, the Anglican church of St. Ebbe's was a church that was filled with the Holy Spirit. I tended to take this for granted at the time, but, as a result, I could never take for granted any church less full of the Spirit. At all events, I was strengthened and supported by the sure and lively faith of that church. It was divided up, informally, into little Christian cells; my friends from the University and I were one such cell, which included other Christians, such as the Benedictine monk, as well. For two years there was hardly an evening that some of this group were not together, early or late, reading Christian poetry, studying the Bible, and, above all, talking— holding lively discussions far into the night on every aspect of the Faith and the Faith in relation to everything else. Non-Christians came, too, and some of.them became Christians.

The time came at last when, one by one, we were going down from the University—to London and Devonshire, to Africa and Canada, to Indiana and Virginia. I remembered Lynchburg as a city of churches—not such venerable and beautiful churches, perhaps, but it was the Holy Spirit that was important. And where there were churches, there would be, naturally, the Holy Spirit and a strong, Christ-centered life. There would be constant, lively searching into the meaning of Life in Christ. To be sure, I had not, in fact, noticed this vivid Christian life, doubtless surging all about me, when I had been in Lynchburg—but, then I hadn't been a Christian. Now all would be different.

It wasn't quite as I expected in Lynchburg on the James. There were the churches, true; and everyone attended, but where was the surging Christian life? My parish church, and every church I visited, seemed almost dead to Christ. No doubt there were Christians, but I did not find them. Most of those I talked to seemed mainly interested in the success of the convivial Couples' Club or in the radical racial ideas of the Bishop or in money and membership—but no one talked of Christ. One felt it would be rather bad form to speak of Him or to suggest that the Church, possibly, ought to be more than a social club and symbol of respectability. No doubt Christ was there, somewhere, but so, too, was the world.

Even more dismaying, in other circles, was the watering-down of the Faith to little more than respect for (some of) Jesus's moral precepts. 'Yes,' said these unbelievers who called themselves Christians, 'yes, Jesus was the divine Son of God; so are we *all* divine Sons of God. Of course there was an incarnation; *each* of us is the incarnation of God. If St. John suggests anything else, or St. Paul does, they are not to be depended on. Miracles— well, no, we happen to know God doesn't work that way. There was no Resurrection, except in some very, very spiritual sense, whatever those naive Apostles thought. Of *course* we're Christians—though no doubt Buddhism and Islam and all religions except the Catholic Church are equally worthwhile. Truth?—what is truth? What has truth got to do with it? A Christian is one who follows the more reasonable bits of the Sermon on the Mount, someone who is good. A Christian is a seeker who must *never* find, lest he cease to be a seeker.' All this, to one who held the ancient Christian *faith*, was depressing and dismaying. It was about as far from the strong red wine of the Faith as cold tea. The Faith, like 'alcohol,' (the local name for the divine and lovely wine of Cana), was too strong: the wine must be turned to grape juice in an anti-miracle and the Faith deincarnated. What was left had nothing in common with the Christ I had encountered except a set of words—and they had different meanings. In other ages people who could not believe in Christianity (and, admittedly, it takes some believing) had called themselves Deists or Unitarians, not Christians; but these people, for reasons I could not understand, were intent to reduce the Faith to a mild morality that they, and indeed anyone except a villain, might accept and to call this milk-and-water religion the Christian Faith.

It was at this point that there came into my mind a casual remark at Oxford long ago, when a friend returning from a Long Vacation in Italy remarked with a smile: 'All the Italian country priests believe quite firmly that Protestantism is dying. "Look," they say, "look at the rise of materialism and the weakening of faith in England and America; they care for nothing except getting rich. All their religion is dying. It's the withering of the branch cut off from the True Vine. In another century or two it will be gone—and what is a century or two to The Church?"' We had laughed and wished those Italian priests might see St. Ebbe's. But now, somehow, I didn't feel much like laughing. I began to think seriously of the mother church and to ask myself the question that every Christian must sometime ask: Is that enormous church, so full of faith and learning, so full of variety except in the strong, unchanging faith, is it, after all, *THE* Church? The True Vine? The question, essentially, seems to be: *What is the Church?* Is the Roman Catholic Church itself, *including* the faithful who are outside, *the* Church? Or is it the 'invisible church'—the blessed company of all the faithful? Or is there a third answer? I do not know, I still do not know, though I have studied and talked with priests and nuns and ministers. It is not the purpose of this paper to explore the question; but I acknowledge that, once the earlier question—is Christ God?—has been answered in the affirmative, one must face up to the further question posed by the existence in history and the undeviating assertion of the Catholic Church.

Meanwhile, I was gradually discovering a few Christians and was heartened. A girl came to my house to argue about a chance remark of mine about Christianity; she came again with a friend; and, before long, there was a group discussing Christianity: some of them were or became Christians; and there, sometimes, was a fragment of the Church—two or three gathered together in His name. My parish church, though wanting in vigour of Christian life, was at least a place of beauty, enriched despite itself by the unchanging strength and significance of the liturgy—and at its altar one received the blessed sacrament. This I felt to be essential: the Holy Eucharist celebrated by a priest ordained by an Apostolic bishop—the unbroken chain of the laying on of hands from the Twelve, so like and yet so different to that other unbroken chain of the faithful through which I had received the Faith. I do not say that other communion services may not be means of grace to their communicants: God can limit me, but I cannot, assuredly, limit Him. At all events, I clung to the Sacrament. So the years passed: the student group, prayer, the sacraments.

Then one Sunday afternoon my daughter-in-Christ—another link in that never-ending chain, from her to me to C. S. Lewis to George MacDonald and back, untraceably, to Christ Himself—took me to lunch at the Lodge of the Fishermen—a coffee house operated by the Christian community of the small, ecumenical Church of the Covenant—and we stayed for the afternoon as well. An afternoon of lively talk about Life in Christ. People who were supremely interested in Christ. People who walked to that secret singing. The Holy Spirit hovering in the room 'with warm breast and with, ah! bright wings.' It was like coming home.

The Gap

Did Jesus live? And did he really say
The burning words that banish mortal fear?
And are they true? Just this is central, here
The Church must stand or fall. It's *Christ* we weigh.

All else is off the point: the Flood, the Day
Of Eden, or the Virgin Birth—Have done!
The Question is, did God send us the Son
Incarnate crying Love! Love is the Way!

Between the probable and proved there yawns
A gap. Afraid to jump, we stand absurd,
Then see *behind* us sink the ground and, worse,
Our very standpoint crumbling. Desperate dawns
Our only hope: to leap into the Word
That opens up the shuttered universe.

Epilogue

Encounter with Light was written in 1961, not long
after I came down from Oxford. "The Gap"—one of six
Oxford sonnets—was written even earlier. A thoughtful
critic reading the six, two of which honoured Our Lady
Mary, said that, if he hadn't known otherwise, he'd have
supposed they had been written by a Catholic. And,
indeed, once I'd answered the Question of Jesus—Is
Christ God?—with a firm Yes, the Question of Rome—Is
the Catholic Church *the* Church?—had presented itself to
me, demanding an answer. I had been moved towards
Christ by the "dreaming spires" of Oxford, testifying to
the faith that had raised them; but I knew, too, that that
faith was the *Catholic* faith. I was drawn to it and was a
little doubtful, despite my mentor C. S. Lewis, of the
validity of my Anglican church and of 'mere Christianity.'
Once in a Catholic church in France, I knelt at the communion rail and received the Host—God in the hands of a
wrinkled French priest—feeling that now at least I was
truly eating Christ's body.

At its best Protestantism retains a Catholic understanding of Christ and the Trinitarian God, but what it
has lost is all understanding of the meaning of His

Church. I, though, coming freshly to Christianity from paganism, was not burdened with strong Protestant prejudices, and I was beginning to grasp the meaning of the Church. But my Churching was to be deferred. I was caught up, first, in the illness and death of that "one dear person", my wife, and the ensuing grief (what I've told in my book, *A Severe Mercy*); and then caught up in the wild storm of the '60s. Many years passed. Then God (as I've told in *Under the Mercy*) nudged me back to Himself, and I resumed the Obedience. And the Question of Rome represented itself.

Now, though, the religious scene was very different. Vatican II had happened. The "breath of fresh air" in the Church had become a destructive gale of rebellion. Too many Catholics, including, astonishingly, priests and nuns, were unable to comprehend the vital distinction between discipline and doctrine. *Discipline* (the use of Latin, fish on Fridays, communion in one kind) can change; doctrine (the bodily Resurrection, the male priesthood, the murder of unborn babies) can never change. Moreover, Modernism—*which is essentially the denial of the Supernatural*—that had long afflicted Protestantism was now flourishing among Catholic theologians. But there was a difference. When I looked at my own Episcopal denomination, it seemed to me that it was decaying at the centre; and when I looked at the Catholic Church, I saw that the *centre* was holding; it was like a rock—the strong Magisterium and the radiant faith of a great pope. Suddenly I saw that the Magisterium was the essential *mark* of the Catholic Church, without which the Church would collapse into protestant chaos. If a relatively simple document like the US Constitution needs a Supreme Court as magisterium' to interpret it, how much more does the complexity of Bible and Tradition require the Teaching Authority of the Magisterium and the Chair of Peter.

To be able to see this so clearly is perhaps one of the great advantages of those who come to the Catholic

Church from outside: seeing from afar, they see the essentials. The most charitable judgement on the theologians who are trying to weaken or supplant the Magisterium is that they can no longer see the wood for the trees.

And in seeing this myself—seeing the Magisterium as the *essential* mark of the Church—I was already a Catholic intellectually. But not only was I slightly afraid of Catholicism at the parish level (would it perhaps be full of IRA or Mafia types?) but I was held back by an unhappy love for my decaying Anglicanism. I loved its style and beauty of liturgy and tradition. How could I leave the church where my wife's ashes lay? And my friends. How could I become a *papist*? Even if the Catholic Church was my true mother and Anglicanism my foster mother, still she had nurtured me and I loved her dearly. As I put it to myself: "My mind says go, but my heart says stay."

Still, I had to decide. On my fridge is a fragment of a yellow poster saying: "Not to decide *is* to decide." I knew I had to *decide*, not 'decide-by-drift'. At Oxford I was moved to acceptance of Christ by the realisation that I could not *reject* Him. And now: could I *reject* Holy Church? No. Therefore I was a Catholic.

Decision made me very sad and gloomy, because I must leave my Anglican church, St. Stephen's. Nevertheless, I must. I should be received by my old Oxford friend and confessor, Father Julian Stead, OSB, at Portsmouth Abbey on Rhode Island. All through the years he had patiently answered my questions on Catholicism, never urging me to become Catholic. Now he told me something that awed me. For twenty-five *years* he had prayed every single day that I should find my way to the Church. Now I had.

At the Abbey on the Feast of the Assumption, with Peter Kreeft as my sponsor, I was received by Father Julian and confirmed by Bishop Ansgar Nelson, OSB.

Returning to Virginia, I found my way to Holy Cross Church, and discovered that I was blessed in my priest,

Father Anthony Warner. After my first very meaningful Mass there, I would, I decided, go one last time to St. Stephen's and tell people what I had done and say goodbye. And then, suddenly, I realised what had been hidden from me since my decision three weeks before: there wasn't a reason in the world why, without neglecting Mass, I shouldn't continue to go to St. Stephen's, at least for Matins (morning prayer), *as a Catholic*. A graduate Anglican, as it were. Everybody there including the Rector seemed pleased that I was not to leave them entirely. But it seems to me, remembering my gloom between decision and reception, that I had to be *willing* to leave "mother and father" or, at least, foster-mother before she could be given back to me in a new way.

The five years since I was Churched have drawn me ever more deeply into the life (parish council) and the sacraments of the Church. And as a writer I've been drawn into the world of Catholic thought as well as into friendship with other Catholic writers. And these years since I brought myself (or was brought by Our Lord the Spirit) to decision have deeply and comfortingly confirmed me in the belief that the Catholic Church is indeed Christ's Church.

Sheldon Vanauken *comes from a country background which included "dogs, horses and books." College, a happy marriage, and service as a World War II naval officer followed. At this point he was a pagan. Conversion to Christ came during his Oxford years, and after his return to Virginia, he became a professor of history and English. Some years after his wife's death he wrote the well-known* A Severe Mercy *and the novel,* Gateway to Heaven. *Following his entrance into the Church, he wrote* Under the Mercy. *He has also authored* The Glittering Illusion, *about the Southern Confederacy. He lives in Lynchburg, Virginia.*

My Path to Rome

Evelyn Birge Vitz

I am a Catholic. I am also an ex-atheist—and I was so staunch in my atheism that, when my husband and I were married, I would permit no reference whatever to God in our vows. Instead, I took the traditional vows of my Protestant background and doctored them: "Dearly beloved, we are gathered here together [in the sight of No one], to join together this man and this woman in [skip the 'holy'] matrimony"; and so on. But would I, even then, have been so surprised to know that one day I would be a Catholic? I'm not so sure....

As a baby I was baptized Episcopalian, as that was the background of both of my parents. But they soon decided to attend the First Presbyterian Church in Indianapolis because that church had a very impressive minister. For many years I attended that church, primarily with my father. Although I went for a year or so to Sunday school, soon I didn't want to be downstairs with the children; I wanted to be upstairs in church, sitting with my father, listening to the sermon, and singing hymns. The most vivid experience of all those childhood hours spent in church was the singing of hymns—and I still sing them today. Even as an atheist I couldn't get away from "Jesus calls us o'er the tumult of our lives' tempestuous sea..." and "When I survey the wondrous cross..." and so many other unforgettable old hymns. I couldn't stop singing them. Sometimes, just to please me, my father—a natural baritone—would force his voice down as far as he could, and sing bass. I remember too taking communion in church: little cubes of wonder-bread and little teeny cups of grape juice, passed around on trays throughout the pews. It was fun, but it had no meaning for me whatever.

We stayed in First Presbyterian until I was twelve or so. I took Confirmation there—in the preparatory class I was so full of questions that when, at the Confirmation ceremony, we each received our Bible and a little card from the minister with a different quote for each child, it was with a twinkle in his eye that he showed me mine: "Ask and it shall be given you, seek and you shall find, knock and it shall be opened to you."

Soon after that the minister retired, and at that point my parents decided to return to the Episcopal Church. We began to attend a church that various of my relatives and friends also attended. It was a very pretty church, unlike the austere Presbyterian one I was so familiar with. I loved the beautiful stained glass windows, but the liturgy itself made me somewhat uncomfortable: it seemed showy, and there was something so dramatic, so emphatic, about the way in which the Eucharist was celebrated that it made me feel the priest didn't really believe it himself.

So I went to the Episcopal church (often, I believe, by myself)—but I still frequently persuaded my father to pick me up from the early Episcopal service and drive down with me to our old Presbyterian church for a later service.

What is interesting about my father's relation to my religious upbringing is that I remember him—so poignantly, as I have said—beside me in church, but I don't think he ever talked much about religion or about his faith, with me. It was his presence that meant so much to me—but I know virtually nothing of what he believed.

I come from exclusively Protestant stock on both sides. (Not all my family was Episcopalian, however. In particular, my maternal grandfather, to whom I was close, had originally been a Baptist, and it was still with some qualms of conscience that he drank cocktails: it was for his health.) Most of my family's friends were of a similar background, with a sprinkling of Jewish friends as well. My parents had only one close Catholic friend—but he had great impact on me. His name was John Ruckelshaus (his son Bill is the one of Watergate fame). He was a very learned man, with a *gravitas* that impressed me. I was once told that when his youngest child, a daughter about my age, had been a toddler she fell out of the upper window of their house and almost died. John "Ruck" made a vow that, if she recovered, he would attend Mass daily for the rest of his life. She did, and (I gather) he did.

Throughout my childhood and early teens, then, I was quite seriously religious: I read the Bible—the one I got at Confirmation—daily. I prayed quite a lot; I recall praying ardently for a miracle that my near-sightedness would vanish; that prayer was not answered—though perhaps contact lenses were the eventual answer to my prayer.... I had all sorts of little altars in my closet—I was just the kind of child who would have loved to have a rosary, but it was simply inconceivable in my family to have one. But I did listen, regularly I think, to the "Ave Maria Hour"—and there was some deep mysterious appeal in all that for me.

What is so interesting, as I think back on all this, is how little my mother was a part of it. She and I are extremely close, and always have been. I think of her as my best and dearest friend—but my religious life went on mostly outside of our relationship. I don't really have any memory of her attending church with me. I imagine in fact that, at that time, she (who is now a committed and prayerful Christian) was if not actually an agnostic, very lukewarm in her faith. Also, our Protestant upbringing seems to have had little impact on my brothers: they were seldom in church with me, and neither is a Christian today.

What happened to my faith? to my involvement in the Bible, in hymns, in prayer? How did the religious child that I was become so fierce an atheist?

My father was a very gentle and kind man, and it always amused me that some of my friends thought him frightening, as he was a big, heavy-set man with large black bushy eyebrows. He always seemed calm and controlled—and in all my life I never saw him lose his temper. (It is far from clear that this was a good thing.) But he had recurrent bouts—fortunately the interval between them was long—of severe, suicidal depression; at one point when I was little—although I have no memory of this—he spent months in a VA hospital recovering from a breakdown he had had in the Army.

When I was sixteen he had another breakdown, his last. For weeks he walked around in a profoundly depressed state—though I, a fairly typical self-preoccupied teenager, was hardly aware of it—and then, on January 29, 1958, he took a shotgun that we owned, went down to the basement and shot himself in the forehead. My mother, having discovered that he had never arrived at the office that day, went home and searched all through the house looking for him; she finally found him down there in the basement....

I was at school. A friend of my parents' and my grandmother came down to get me. I found out what happened and went back to my locker to get my things. In my numbness, I kept praying, "Hail Mary, full of grace...."

I went home and my mother and I fell into each others' arms. Daddy's suicide was a tremendous blow to her. They had been a very loving couple, and the grief, the sense of abandonment, as well as the sense of humiliation and fear for the future almost overwhelmed her; I'm sure that she must have been angry at him, as well, for abandoning her with three teenage children. At that time, she herself was also rather fragile psychologically—

though through it all she came to a new strength and maturity.

Because I was so concerned about my mother—so focused on her needs—I was virtually unable to grieve for my father at that time. So I got through Daddy's funeral with hardly a tear, and with a sorrow so deeply submerged that it was years before I could let myself feel it. I remember when that grief first struck me with unusual force. This was several years afterward, in college, when I was visiting a school where a "Father's weekend" was going on. I came into a crowded room where the first sight that greeted my eyes was a girl sitting on her father's lap. I was suddenly overwhelmed by a deep sorrow, knowing that I would never again have the experience of sitting on *my* father's lap.

I did have at this time one extraordinary experience that helped me, at least for a while, to come to terms with what had happened. The day after Daddy's funeral I had to go down to my high school for a play rehearsal. After being embraced and consoled very lovingly by some friends of mine, I went out and got into my car—Daddy's car. There washed over me, as I sat there, a powerful feeling: that Daddy was all right, that everything was—that *we* were—going to be all right. Somehow this conviction stayed with me through the dark year or so ahead and gave me hope for the future.

In this period after Daddy died I turned to reading poetry—and, unfortunately, the only poets I knew (the only ones we had in the house) who spoke of death, loss, the meaning of life, were Edna St. Vincent Millay and the *Rubáiyát*—both of course being profoundly agnostic. These poems I learned by heart and repeated to myself, as for years I had learned quotations from the Bible.

Soon, I stopped reading the Bible, although I had read it faithfully for some years. I am not sure how conscious I was of my reasoning, but it was pretty clearly thus: if my father no longer exists, if he is dead—so is

God. A God who would allow something like this to happen to a good man—and one who believed in Him—is one I refuse to believe in. When it says in the Bible that you will not be tested beyond your strength—it *lies*. This was my revenge, if you will, against God for Daddy's death. (Was I angry with Daddy himself? I don't think so. I just never thought he had been able to help himself, and I have never surprised in myself any thought of anger at him.)

By the time I got to Smith College, a year and a half after Daddy's death, I was already functionally an atheist. But I was, and remained, an unresolved atheist—and I came close to majoring in Religion. Religious faith was never a subject of indifference to me! The one thing to which I had taken a mysteriously violent dislike was liberal Protestantism, which seemed to focus on Jesus as a great human being, a great teacher—and nothing more. Whatever—whoever—Jesus was, He was not just a nice guy. Basically the only form of Christianity that really drew me was Catholicism, although why this should have been I cannot say. Still, there was a vast chasm between me and it, a chasm that would remain for years.

During my junior year in college, I lived in Paris. There I had a curious experience that stands out vividly in my memory. I was living, along with two other American girls, with an arch-Catholic but not really very prepossessing family. The youngest of their six children was a young man a little older than ourselves with a strangely compelling character. At one point, I got drawn into a game in which he was to give each of us three Americans "psychological tests" to see what sort of character we really had. When it came to my turn, he declared (after I had written down my answers to his questions) that what was revealed was that I was conceited and selfish. I, who had always thought of myself as an exceedingly good person, was very much taken aback. Unlike my comrades, who soon forgot what this young man had said (one mild girl was satisfied to hear that she was meek), I began a sort of examination of conscience with extreme thoroughness and great intensity. And I discovered that, yes indeed, I was profoundly selfish and vain. At the time I was reading Pascal's *Pensées*, and they—combined with my soul-searching—had a deep impact on me. I came to the conclusion that I had, indeed, all the misery of man without God, but that I could not come to a belief in God; that was now impossible for me. The pain of my self-discovery became so acute and obsessive—and the situation in that strange family so unsettling—that I finally told my mother about it in a letter. She had me moved immediately to a more charitable, and more restful, home—but I had seen myself and my moral and metaphysical situation in a new way, and I never forgot it.

I finished Smith with a major in French and went back to Paris for another year on a French government grant. One advantage to spending time in France—I see in retrospect—was that I was able to satisfy my hunger to go to church and my yearning for Catholicism at an unconscious level, without having to confront it head on. During all those years, I would never set foot in a church *qua* church, but as long as the church was a museum, an architectural edifice, part of French history—no problem! And I spent many happy hours in French churches—as an atheist.... On my return, I went on to Yale to do graduate work in French Literature, eventually becoming a medievalist. Perhaps it is not a coincidence that I did my doctoral thesis on *The Testament* of the 15th century poet François Villon, who had an ambivalence about religion that was not unlike my own.

I came to New York University in the fall of 1968, just after the completion of my Ph.D. At the first faculty meeting, in September, I met Paul Vitz. Not only was I very drawn to him; it soon became clear to me that this person, this relationship, was almost alarmingly *possible*. *I had previously tended to fall in love with men whom I met in, and who remained in, far-distant cities: I had thereby (as I theorize now) the advantages of being in love without the loss of privacy and independence that proximity entails. But somehow I felt, soon on, that this was a marriage that was supposed (supposed by Whom?) to happen.* For example, even before we met, I had almost moved into the apartment building where Paul lived. God does seem to have been determined that we meet!

We were married the following summer, in my mother's apartment in Indianapolis, with our tailor-made vows. We found a Protestant minister who was willing to marry us on our terms: no reference to God. I suspect I wanted a minister to marry us because with just a justice-of-the-peace it wouldn't have seemed quite real. Talk of having your cake and eating it too!

For the first couple of years of our married life our non-religious patterns continued: Paul remained an indifferent atheist, I still a fierce but troubled one. But—it is a cliché, and like all clichés, *true*—parenthood does force one to focus one's attention anew on issues that one may have long set aside. Who am I? What do I stand for, believe in? What sort of parent do I want to be? All I know is that by the time Rebecca, our first, was a year or so old, I was ready to stick a toe, at least, back into church. Somehow, I had to start with the Presbyterian Church before I could do anything else, go anywhere else—a little like the (pseudo-?) scientific adage "Ontogeny recapitulates philogeny." The Presbyterian church we attended briefly was unsatisfactory to us (in particular, it was very liberal)—but at least it began the recapitulation process, and I am grateful to the friend who brought us there. I remember weeping just to be back in church after all those years. Then Paul brought Rebecca and me to St. Thomas Episcopal Church, where we immediately fitted in, and where we were very happy. We were on various committees, such as Adult Education, where we gave presentations: I on books such as *The Way of a*

Pilgrim, on the theology of the Eucharist, and on the Devil in Scripture. During these years of my apprenticeship as a new convert, I read many of the books of C. S. Lewis, which were of great help to me (especially, I recall, *God in the Dock*).

But despite our happiness in the church with a small "c"—in that particular church, with its beautiful liturgy, its excellent sermons, its sophisticated fellowship—we both began to have some problems. As I mentioned earlier, I had never truly been drawn to Episcopalianism; to me it was, is, too much of an ethnic Church, a WASP Church, one for Anglophiles—and I am not an Anglophile. I am no Anglophobe, being largely English myself, but I am rather an Anglophilophobe.

For several years, I thought I was ashamed of being a Christian—but then I realized that at least a significant part of my problem was not with being a Christian, but with being an Episcopalian. Moreover, in our Adult Education Committee, I was increasingly finding myself virtually alone—along with Paul, that is, and another friend or two—in my defense of what was, in fact, the Catholic (or the orthodox Christian) position on a number of subjects. For example, I believed in the reality of the Devil (he's not just a "myth"); I was opposed to abortion; I was even against contraception—pretty unheard of in Anglican circles. I was also stymied by the fact that I couldn't discover what the official Anglican/Episcopalian position was on any given issue—even on something as central as the Eucharist. There simply *is* no Church teaching. I became disillusioned with the notion of the Episcopal Church as a "via media": it was in the middle simply in that it wobbled incoherently between Catholicism, Presbyterianism /Methodism, and liberal Protestantism—anywhere between them that the individual believer chose. One believed what one pleased. I found such a theology conceptually frustrating and personally unsatisfying.

Even the history of Anglicanism disturbed me: Henry VIII never was a hero of mine.

Paul and I were also disturbed by the failure of the Episcopal Church to confront the problem of homosexuality—or of contemporary heterosexual mores for that matter. And the ordination of women further weakened our commitment to Episcopalianism. We were teetering on the brink of a move in the direction of Catholicism. Such a move had long seemed impossible, Catholicism being so alien (if desirable). But it is true that Episcopalianism is a training ground for Rome, and Rome seemed closer, more attainable than it ever had. And yet....

About this time—the spring of 1978—I was sitting and reflecting on all this, and on what I ought to do—when I had a very vivid experience. I don't know that it should be called a mystical experience, but the thought came to me with great clarity and force: "You have no business not being a Catholic!" That was it: the next day I called to go for instructions to a priest who was also instructing a dear friend of ours. Soon—*mirabile dictu*—Paul too was in instruction.

We entered the Church in June of 1979, just a few weeks before our fourth child was due. We also received our first Communion, and were married and confirmed in one extraordinary ceremony.

It's now a little over seven years since we were received into the Church—and I consider myself very blessed to be a Catholic. I am very aware that I am just beginning—just *beginning* to begin—to appreciate adequately the riches of Catholicism, just beginning to understand what it really means to be a Christian. I have completed my journey to Rome, but that is, of course, not the final destination. I am deeply grateful to the many wonderful priests and nuns—and other Christians (not just Catholics)—that we have known, and who have kept us in their prayers, and I hope they will continue to do so! I am grateful too to the saints for their example and their prayers. But above all I am grateful to God for having reached out His hand and plucked me out of the desert—of meaninglessness, of metaphysical loneliness, and anger at Him—in which I languished for so long. It is of course a true miracle of grace that Paul and I—such a pair of opinionated, individualistic academics!—should have been brought together along the long road from atheism to Catholicism.

Evelyn (Timmie) Vitz *is a professor of French at New York University, where she is head of the medieval and renaissance studies program. In addition to publishing extensively on medieval literature and culture, she is well known as the author of a family and Christian oriented cookbook: A Continual Feast. She lives in New York City with her husband, Paul C. Vitz, and their children: Rebecca, Jessica, Daniel, Peter, Michael and Anna.*

A Christian Odyssey

Paul C. Vitz

Though I have no memory of the event, I suppose the story of my conversion properly begins with my baptism as a boy of about twelve in Cincinnati, Ohio. When I was in the middle of the 5th grade, we moved from Minneapolis to Cincinnati. After a few months, the family began attending a Presbyterian Church there. I went to the Sunday School with modest regularity, and during these years my parents often went to church as well. And it was here that I was baptized.

My father, the head of the Cincinnati Public Library, was urged to go to church by my mother. She felt that Dad's position in the community required such attendance. My father acquiesced without much resistance, though he actually seems to have been rather a skeptic or agnostic. In all the years I knew him, I never spoke to my father about religion, nor do I ever remember his saying anything about his beliefs. In part this was simply an expression of the fact that religion was not a central aspect of our family life. I didn't learn of my father's agnosticism until after his death when I asked my mother about it. Nevertheless—in spite of his lack of belief—Dad eventually became an elder in the same church some time after I had gone off to college and was no longer living at home.

I have always loved and admired my parents. This has been easy because they were good parents—and very strong and impressive as people, but they did tend to neglect religion.

To the best of my recollection religion came up in our house in only three quite different contexts. For reasons that are obscure Dad always said grace before dinner or other formal meals. We children accepted this family ritual without discussion as simply the way things were done at the Vitzes.

There were also occasional criticisms of the Catholic Church; thus, anti-Catholic attitudes were a regular though minor part of the family talk. My father, like many no-longer-believing Protestants, kept his hostility to Catholicism intact after his own faith had faded. The third way religion came up was when my father talked about his family. Somehow he never tired of reminding us, with pride in his voice, that his grandfather, Peter Vitz, came over from Germany in 1853 to become a minister. After some seminary study in America Peter Vitz became a minister in the German Evangelical and Reform Church. Thus, Peter Vitz was a kind of pioneer minister to the new German communities in the Mid-West (Ohio, Indiana, Minnesota). Rev. Peter Vitz had nine children: the five boys all became ministers and the four girls all married ministers. So Dad, who was born in 1883, was both the son and the grandson of ministers. Yet, somehow he rejected his faith. How this happened no one seems to have known.

Dad's father, Rev. Martin Vitz, died shortly after I was born in 1935. Dad once or twice suggested that his father's faith had weakened so that near the end of his life he was himself in doubt. Perhaps this was true. However, shortly after my father's death (he died in 1981 at the age of 97) I came across a letter written to him by his father at the time my dad and my mother were married in 1934. (My father's first wife had died a few years earlier—leaving him to raise five children. He was 51 at the time of his second marriage, and my mother was 36; I was the eldest of—eventually—a second family of four boys.) To his son now in his 50's Rev. Martin Vitz wrote a moving letter that ended in a presumably heart-felt "Yours in Christ." (One of his last official acts was to marry my parents.)

My mother's background was English: she was a Clayton. As she would describe it, she came from good English-American pioneer stock. She grew up on a farm in central western Ohio—a farm the Claytons had homesteaded in the early 1800's. The first Clayton came over in 1776 and married an American girl—a Fitz Randolph in New Jersey. (The Fitz Randolphs sold a good deal of land to a then just-starting school called Princeton.) There was always some tension between the Germanic character and background of my father (though he was born and raised in middle America, German was his first language, and he spoke German at home as a child) and the English culture of my mother. (My wife reminds me, however, that her mother-in-law makes a great German "springerle" cookie.) Over the years this tension was largely resolved, but I gather the German character of the Vitz household—Dad plus the five children of his first marriage—was something of a shock for my mother when she first was married.

Mother's religious background was country Methodist —although to her surprise she recently discovered that her early American ancestors were Seventh Day Baptists. However, as I mentioned, she has never discussed her religious beliefs with me—nor with her other children, as far as I know. In Cincinnati, she did go to church fairly often (Presbyterian was apparently the resolution of her Methodism and Dad's Evangelical-Reform background). Her attendance was much more regular, however, in the years after I left for college.

In any case, the religious atmosphere in the house when I was growing up was generally Protestant without any particular clarity or enthusiasm. A modest puritan moral atmosphere, however, was present—more clearly so than any doctrinal or devotional commitment. Neither of my parents smoked, drank or danced and they frowned on all three—but not enough to prevent their children from engaging in all of them! In short, although our parents' way of life was clearly moral, and in many ways impressive, they never explicitly encouraged their children to follow it. A certain American notion of tolerance seems to have kept them from direct "interference" in their children's lives.

At Sunday school I learned parts of the Bible and small amounts of basic Christian doctrine—but precious little of it stayed with me. In fact, Sunday school had little lasting impact on me. We did sing and hear hymns, carols and gospel songs. I suspect these had a permanent effect, and may have been instrumental in my later return to the faith. The positive emotional resonance of these songs, especially Christmas carols, is still with me.

There was also a youth group at church—but its meaning was primarily social, as a kind of introduction to dating, dancing and the early stages of "making out" (as it was more innocently put in those days)!

In retrospect, the problem with the kind of Christianity I experienced was that it was nice—but just not very convincing. (No doubt my father's skepticism influenced my attitude.) Everyone was pleasant and friendly and relaxed. Religion as a deeply serious, challenging thing, however, was something I never ran into. To me Christianity seemed good, idealistic, a little vague—and hard to believe in. Considering how we were brought up, it is not surprising that one of my brothers is either an atheist or skeptic; the other two show no special involvement in religion and are what might be called nominal Christians.

In high school my primary focus had been on extra-curricular activities. I had gone to a good high school, Walnut Hills, but I had treated my studies rather casually. In the fall of 1953, I left Cincinnati to attend the University of Michigan. Here, I chose to be a serious student, and for the first time the life of the mind opened up for me. I plunged in, somewhat surprised to discover that much of the material was easy to master and some of it deeply interesting. Originally I was attracted to the natural sciences, but then soon settled on psychology as my major. It was a field in which I felt comfortable from the start, in part because it contains such a wide variety of intellectual approaches, ranging from natural science to social science, from empirical research to philosophical issues. The breadth as well as the particular subjects within psychology were appealing to me then as they still are today.

In psychology and the rest of the social sciences the attitude toward religion varied from a grudging tolerance —and recognition of its importance in human culture—to active hostility and criticism, the latter being by far the more common. I still remember a course in cultural anthropology taught by a Prof. Leslie White. In it he often made criticisms of Christian positions and offered scathing comments about various aspects of Christianity, especially Catholicism. He was an effective lecturer, and we all laughed at how "foolish" religion was. In retrospect, I see his arguments as brilliant superficialities.

Within the field of psychology it soon became clear to me that all the major psychologists were atheists, from Wundt to Freud to Skinner. Psychology, like most of the other academic disciplines, operated on the assumption that religion was false, indeed rather backward, and in the process of disappearing as science and modern thought advanced toward their inevitable worldwide triumph.

I quickly picked up this general attitude; it appealed to me at once. It allowed me to reject much of my background—to escape from my "provincial" past and to join my new profession without any intellectual or moral liabilities from my nominal Christian up-bringing. Reading Bertrand Russell's "Why I am not a Christian" also facilitated my deconversion. His essay, with its ideal of a non-nonsense stoical pessimism in the face of a meaningless and implacable universe, seemed tough, manly and noble—everything Christianity (as I thought that I understood it) wasn't. Thus, in my sophomore year, appropriately enough, I acknowledged that I was an atheist. There wasn't any big change in my life, since I hadn't been much of a Christian to begin with. My atheism quickly receded into the background of my life to be replaced by a general neglect of the whole subject.

I had always had a deep sense of restlessness, an intense, unfocused searching. This ever-present longing, of *sehnsucht*, is one of my earliest memories. I put much of this restless energy into studying hard to become a professor of psychology. As we would put it today, careerism became the religion of my life. Still, some of this nagging restlessness remained, expressing itself most often in extremely long evening walks, usually by myself. Only after my conversion has the disquiet disappeared.

I was graduated from Michigan in 1957 and entered graduate school in psychology at Stanford that fall. There, the same skeptical attitude toward religion prevailed—indeed, if anything, it was even more pervasive than in Ann Arbor. .

In graduate school my involvement in my career became intensified and my religious indifference continued. Stanford—even all California, from the late 1950's into the 1960's—seems to me to have been primarily a place of sunshine and secularism.

While at Stanford I enjoyed life in many ways, though as the years have gone by I have found myself deeply disillusioned as I reflect on my years there and with the faculty. The psychology department was outstanding then (as now) and was ranked number one in the country. But the faculty members were almost entirely focused on their personal careers. (It was from them that I learned to do likewise—though perhaps original sin could have managed on its own.) The honest search for truth was not high on anyone's list. Subsequently I've learned that this kind of narcissistic careerism characterizes most academics everywhere. It means that much of the university's defense of itself in terms of such concepts as academic freedom, the marketplace of ideas, and the search for truth, etc., is simply empty, and hypocritical posturing.

During my Stanford years I was on the edge of (what was later called) the counter-culture. Richard Alpert was my first faculty research advisor and was a friend for a while. A few years later Alpert and Timothy Leary became famous at Harvard for their infamous LSD capers. Shortly after having to leave Harvard, Alpert became a kind of religious guru and took the name "Baba Ram Dass." At Stanford I lived near Perry Lane, on which also lived Ken Kesey, Alpert and others of similar kind. I visited them fairly often, drove Alpert's motorcycle (before buying my own), etc. This little world would later become something of a national phenomenon in the late 60's. At the time, however, it was already seriously involved in various drugs, and sexual "liberation."

In 1962, I completed graduate school and took a job in the Psychology Department at Pomona College—a fine college in southern California. The next year I married Carol Royce, who had just graduated from Mills College, near Berkeley. Her background was secular and Jewish. In certain respects she was something of a hippie, and she had a good number of friends in the political and artistic counter-culture. Finding Pomona attractive but somewhat limiting, we both wanted to move. I took a one-year postdoctoral fellowship at Stanford (1964-65) that I used to get extra training and to look for a university job. The opening at New York University (NYU) looked promising and I took it. Carol was glad to go to New York because of her own interests, in music especially. So in September 1965, after 8 years in California, I arrived in New York with Carol to take an apartment in Greenwich Village near NYU.

In New York my job at NYU started with research grants and publications developing at a good rate, but in a few years this slowed down somewhat because everything else in my life was falling apart. It was the late 1960's— can you remember (or imagine) it? All around me in the Village and in the university world the new "lifestyles" of the counter-cultere were exploding. Radical politics, LSD and other drugs, the sexual revolution, radical feminism, the Peace Movement, Eastern religions.... The world I had known as a curiosity in California had spread like an infectious disease throughout the country. My marriage began to unravel; Carol and I were legally separated in 1967, then soon divorced.

During this time I saw the peace and radical lifestyle movements up close. Although I had sympathy with some of the ideas involved, my general reaction was revulsion. The personal lives and characters of the people involved contrasted so greatly with their ideals that I was appalled. Their lives were mixtures of self-indulgence, rationalization, and often bitter hatreds derived from personal experiences irrelevant to the issues they espoused. In particular, drugs permeated the counter culture; the result was that illusion and subjectivism were rampant. In time I learned that this new "Land of the Lotus Eaters" was no place to find answers to my underlying and now growing sense of discontent.

On the other hand, the representatives of the status quo—for example, the U.S. government, business, and the universities, came across as deceitful, unthinking and above all as weak and insecure. It was the weakness of the establishment leaders that the opposition sensed, and the counter-culture closed in on them like wolves on old, sick animals. In particular, the university, the community of scholars, showed itself so without standards, so without the courage of convictions, as to be a kind of joke. The last vestiges of my respect for academia collapsed as I watched the university leadership cave in to various social and political pressures. By the end of the 60's and the start of the 70's my secular ideals were in shreds. I kept my career on track, but it was slowed down by both personal and cultural crises—as well as by my growing awareness that a self-centered career was a pretty hollow thing to hold as one's highest value.

One of my concerns was my deepening disillusionment with the field of psychology itself. My research in experimental and cognitive psychology was no longer very satisfying on ethical grounds. This research was aimed at building scientific, testable models of human mental processes, such as pattern perception and pattern learning. The collective purpose of cognitive psychology is, someday, to be able to simulate the processes of the human mind. I came to the conclusion that such a goal was immoral: it was wrong to help create "human minds" to be used by persons unknown. (In addition, the goal itself of simulating the mind—even apart from the issue of who would control and use this "mind"—seemed morally ambiguous at best.) Of course, perhaps the goal was impossible, perhaps the mind cannot be simulated—but then, why waste one's life on such a task?

Even more disturbing was my growing understanding of how other parts of psychology, for example, personality theory and counseling practice, had contributed to the secular madness of what was going on. I couldn't believe that people took such shallow notions as "self-actualization" and encounter groups seriously. Yet by 1970 these ideas that I had first met 10 or 15 years before were being received by millions of Americans with astonishingly wild enthusiasm.

In all this there was one real bright spot. In September of 1968, I met Timmie Birge. (Her given name is Evelyn but she has always been called Timmie.) From the very beginning she seemed right and so she has proven over the years. In early 1969 we became engaged; we got married that August. There was no mention of religion in our marriage vows. We made them up ourselves, carefully leaving out any reference to God. (Timmie was a fiercer atheist than I, who then was mostly just indifferent.) Timmie wore a white mini-dress (this was the 60's!). But in spite of our rejection of Him, God in His mercy blessed us from the start.

When was I first aware of God—or even of the possibility of God's presence in my life? Only looking back does it seem clear that the first fleeting conscious experience occurred in Paris in the summer of 1967. Early the first morning after I arrived I slipped out of the hotel and began wandering through the streets of the Isle de la Cité. (Like so many people, I loved Paris from my first minutes there.) By chance (?) I happened to walk into the Sainte Chapelle. Not knowing its fame, I was totally unprepared for its great—spiritual—beauty. The early light streaming through its windows was a complete surprise. For a brief moment that light told me of Someone else. Then it was gone—and to all appearances forgotten.

Three years later, in the summer of 1970, Timmie and I spent a glorious month in France. After a few days in Paris we rented a car and drove through Burgundy, the Auvergne, Provence, and the Haute Savoie. Continually, I was ambushed by the beauty of France. We spent much of our time visiting French cathedrals and churches. (This isn't strange for Timmie, since she is a French scholar, a medievalist, by profession—but it is strange for a pychologist.) Somehow seeing them, being near and going inside them, was a glorious yet comforting experience.

In the fall of 1971, our first child, Rebecca, was born. (We now have five: Jessica, born in '74; Daniel, in '77; Peter, in '79; Michael, in '83.) Being a father faced me with the concrete issue of what I stood for. The question of what to teach our daughter—what values and ideals—could not be avoided.

By 1972 the collapse of my secular world view and ideals was pretty complete—and the need for an alternative was obvious. One of the symptoms was the frequency with which I got into intense arguments with my universally secular colleagues. More than one dinner party or other social event ended in unpleasantness. (I can still feel Timmie kicking me under the table—generally to no avail.) For example, my academic associates were reliably smug moral relativists—or rather, they were relativists about *my* values, but they were unexamined moral absolutists when it came to their own secular or anti-traditional views. Actually, I have always credited an atheist former friend of ours with being partially responsible for my conversion (he would be much surprised to hear this): once, in the course of a conversation, he exclaimed happily: "Oh, isn't it wonderful to live in an age of decadence!" That remark alone moved me along several steps toward Christianity....

In the fall of 1972, I took my first sabbatical year. Although I had planned to devote it to research and to the further development of my career, the Holy Spirit apparently had other plans. For instead of focusing on my professional goals, the issue of life's meaning, of who I was and what I stood for, pushed its way to the forefront of my concerns. I began talking ever so vaguely about possibly looking into going to some church, maybe sometime, etc.

Once we went to a nearby Presbyterian church where the sermon sounded just like an editorial from the *New York Times*. We didn't go back—but we were launched on our search for a church. In October I recall walking down Fifth Avenue and stepping, briefly, into St. Thomas Episcopal Church. This beautiful Gothic church appealed to me—no doubt it resonated with my experiences in France—but I didn't do anything about it until January 1973. Timmie was in Indianapolis with the baby, visiting her mother. I was alone for the weekend and on Sunday for reasons that I can't even recall I went up to Saint Thomas for the 11:00 o'clock service. I loved it. The gospel was preached clearly, indeed eloquently, in the context of an extraordinarily beautiful liturgy.

Words like "Evensong" and "Advent" brought back some of my English heritage. The people were familiar, reminding me of friends in Cincinnati (two of my closest had been Episcopalians and our boy scout troop met for years in the local Episcopal church). The following week Timmie also agreed to come—and our return to Christianity had begun. At first, our faith was weak and we felt strange, even embarrassed, about it. We hid it from our friends and relatives, as though it were a kind of left-over adolescent activity. I called us "closet Christians."

During this time certain books were critically important, especially the writings of C. S. Lewis and G. K. Chesterton. It was an enormous surprise and relief to me to discover that Christianity was intellectually not only defensible but really very powerful! Indeed, I soon found that its intellectual variety and riches were so much deeper and more sophisticated than any secular framework that there was simply no comparison. As a consequence, my mind—my intellectual understanding—soon went through a really momentous conversion. I began to grasp the essential character of Christian thought and to see clearly the weaknesses of modern secular positions.

I found deep satisfaction in the fact that the Christian view with its firm acceptance of physical, psychological and moral reality, allowed me to understand why I had been so disillusioned with contemporary ideology. Modernism is in its *essential* nature subjective, arbitrary and nihilistic. Thus, it was a joy to steep myself in the wisdom and truth of the Scriptures and of the countless great Christians who have written over the centuries.

As my Christian intellectual life grew, I knew that I must change my professional and public life—not just my personal or private life. Exactly what this would mean was most unclear to me—but I knew I had to become a "Christian psychologist," whatever that meant. I had to give up my professional friends, my status in the department, my understanding of who I was. This realization was extremely painful for it really meant jettisoning all of my career, as it then existed. For example, I had to give up cognitive and experimental psychology and move into the fields of personality and motivation. Granted my original interest in psychology had been in these fields, but I hadn't published on them—and of course none of my career had ever had anything to do with Christianity. Except for my maintaining a modest continued professional involvement in psychology and art, all else was changed. To add to the difficulty, at the time I didn't know one other person who was—much less had become—a Christian psychologist; all I knew of were people who moved the other way, away from faith into secular psychology.

This giving up of my previous career and professional involvement began in early 1973. It was a slow business, with occasional brief regressions, but by 1978 this "move" was largely completed. It was much helped by the publication of my first book *Psychology as Religion: the cult of self-worship* by Eerdmans, in 1977. This book began as a short presentation in 1975 to a small group of Anglo-Catholic Episcopalians. It was a critique of humanistic psychology, the kind of psychology so immensely popular at the time. The group liked the paper, so I expanded it somewhat and sent it off to some Dutch Reformed Christians that I hadn't even met. To my eternal gratitude, they responded very positively and sent it to Eerdmans. Before I knew it I had a contract and not long afterwards the book was published. From the start, the book was popular—and from the start it changed my life. I received all kinds of support in letters and in personal contacts from fellow Christians all over the world. Although to this day I remain isolated in a secular psychology department at NYU, these contacts have kept my intellectual development and much of my spiritual life going for years.

Meanwhile, as my understanding of Christian theology deepened, I quickly came into conflict with liberal Christian theology, most of which was Protestant in origin. It was obvious to me that liberal theology was at best a compromise with anti-Christian modernist thought, and at worst a thinly disguised denial of Christ. No doubt in the past the primary challenge to the Faith has been rigid pharasaical theology, but today the moral danger is modernist self-indulgent mush: liberal theology. Having been intellectually formed in the heart of the modernist and secular world view—that is, in contemporary social science—it was easy for me to recognize these assumptions and ideas when I saw them creeping into Christianity.

Unfortunately, the Episcopal Church was dominated by liberal thought, indeed so dominated by it that many couldn't even see it. As far as they were concerned, liberal theology was the only possible way of understanding things. It was then that I first experienced the rigid, narrow-minded character of liberal thought and of so many liberals. I still remember the remark made to me by a young Episcopal priest—his voice dripping with condescension—"You mean you believe in the *bodily* resurrection of Christ?" My awareness of the prevalence of liberal theology in the Episcopal church brought increasing dismay. In spite of its beautiful liturgy and the many fine individual Christians that I had come to know and love, it became clear to me that its basic Christian character was seriously compromised. I knew first hand the hollowness of liberal, secular thought and values; to find them enthusiastically imported and on display in a Christian church was more than I could take. Emotionally the breaking point came the morning I read in the *New York Times* that the Episcopal bishop of New York had just ordained his first woman "priest"—a practicing lesbian. In the very depths of my being, I felt the faith betrayed, and the heart went out of my relationship with the Episcopal Church.

Already, to our surprise, Timmie and I had often found ourselves taking what would be called the Catholic position on issues under discussion. We found ourselves defending the bodily resurrection of Christ, arguing for the existence of the devil, opposing abortion—even arguing against the legitimacy of contraception. After the ordination of women, the Anglo-Catholic cause within Episcopalianism looked increasingly lost. By the spring of 1978, it was pretty clear that we were both going to become Catholics—it was just a question of when—when each of us would overcome our remaining personal barriers. To me, the Catholic Church seemed so strange, so ethnic—you know, Italian, Irish, Polish—somehow not even American.

In May, Timmie decided to take the plunge and enter instruction. She was helped in her decision by a good and dear friend of ours, Helen Corbett, who had recently completed instruction and entered the Church herself. In late June or July, I too started instruction. All this was during the last days of the pontificate of Paul VI. Even then I had no illusions that the Catholic Church had escaped modernist infection, in a form that might be called "the American disease." But I knew that the Catholic Church was home, and if one was to fight for the faith, then this is where I wanted to take my stand.

In September, 1978, we began regular attendance at Catholic services, and we were both received into the Church in June, 1979, at St. Thomas More Church in Manhattan. At this Mass at which we took our first Holy Communion, we were also married and confirmed. (Timmie, who was quite pregnant with Peter, thought we might end the day with a baptism as well!) My sponsor was Rev. Benedict Groeschel, a Capuchin monk and priest who helped me greatly at this critical time. Timmie and I have in fact been blessed to know many wonderful and deeply impressive priests, and sisters as well. Their example—and prayers—have meant a great deal to us and our family.

Much of the delay between September of 1978 and June of 1979 was due to the time needed by the Church to resolve the question of my first marriage. On the basis of ancient precedent, Rome annulled this marriage as not having been sacramental. I was an atheist/skeptic at the time, Carol, also a skeptic, had never been a Christian, and the ceremony was conducted by a Unitarian minister. In short, it was essentially a civil contract.

Preceding and leading to my Catholic conversion were a series of religious experiences that caught me completely by surprise and greatly deepened my faith. The first three (of four) occurred in a ten-day period in September, 1977. These dramatic, unexpected experiences were really something like visions, all three occurring during the day. The first one revealed to me the existence, power and majesty of God. Let me describe it to you briefly. I had just awakened—it must have been around 6:30 in the morning. Suddenly I saw myself, as in a vision, looking up and seeing an enormous person with a long robe standing in front of me. By "enormous" I mean like looking up from the bottom at a fifty-story building. I reached up to touch the robe and as I did so it turned into a great, huge curtain. The curtain then seemed to move off to the right, as though it were opening before me. I was overwhelmed by the space before me. It was truly infinite in all respects. At first it seemed completely empty except for a diffuse glowing light which permeated it everywhere. The light seemed to be associated with a very quiet but awesome low hum. Even as I was viewing this great space I knew that I was in the presence of God, that I was being shown, if you will, the existence of God through this deeply moving sign of his omnipotence and majesty. After a few moments I saw, in the very center of this space, a very tiny dot, far, far away. I saw that it was moving toward me. At first it seemed to move very slowly but as it got closer, it also moved faster. At some point, about half way toward me, I saw that this dot was Christ on the Cross: it was a Crucifix. In this form Christ came closer and closer to me and then rapidly moved past me on a curve to my right. Then, I became aware that I was lying in bed and the light was coming in the window. This was the first of my visions.

The other visions would be too long to relate here, but I can simply say that the second revealed to me the futility of purely cognitive inquiry with respect to theological issues; also the existence of Satan—I heard his laughter throughout the vision. The third experience was of the reality of sin, especially mine—and of the justice that sin should be judged. That is, I experienced being convicted of personal sin and evil—but there was, with this, no sense of condemnation; rather, I felt the absolute necessity of responding to the call for holiness.

The fourth and last of these most unexpected experiences occurred on a weekday in late August, 1978, when I was praying in the almost empty Catholic Cathedral of Toronto. There in the mid-morning I experienced in simple, dramatic terms both the reality of the risen Christ and my personal relationship with Him. Along with prayer, reading, and Catholic friends—especially many wonderful priests—these experiences solidified my commitment to the Catholic faith.

One of the features of my conversion has been a changing understanding of the "ethnic" nature of Christianity. Part of the initial appeal of the Episcopal Church to me had been that it helped me recover my English and WASP roots. That is, part of the meaning of Christianity was its capacity to reinstate my ethnic identity in a city and at a time when nothing else did or could. In becoming a Catholic, I further deepened my connection to Western culture and to the general heritage of Christendom both in the West and in the East. (I have come to admire greatly the Eastern Orthodox churches.) Even more, one of the great liberations in becoming a Catholic was to be part of the universal character of the Church. Catholics are all over the world, and in becoming a Catholic I sensed a new kinship with people in countries as diverse as Argentina, Poland and Zanzibar. This is one of the reasons why becoming a Catholic was an experience of freedom and expansion. I was linked to millions of people of all nations, races and cultures. It was exhilarating. A particular form of this freedom was the realization that Catholics cover the complete social spectrum: a Catholic may be a king or a truck driver, a millionaire or a peasant. To be a Catholic is not to be part of a particular social class.

A more recent understanding of the ethnic character of Catholicism has come from my experience of the Jewishness of Catholicism. In December, 1983, Providence provided me with a visit to Jerusalem—I have not yet (alas) been to Rome. In Jerusalem, I was deeply affected by the Old City. Here I grasped the tough Jewish character of Jesus as well as the very Jewish nature of the Church's beginnings. This aspect of the Faith I believe needs to be more widely understood and cultivated.

People sometimes ask if I understood and agreed with every part of Catholic doctrine before I came into the Church. The answer is "no." I believed in the central doctrines but I certainly didn't comprehend all Church doctrine at the time; I still don't. There was nothing I rejected but there were things I didn't actively believe in. However, I was, and am, confident that the Church is right—that she is guided by the Holy Spirit—and I believed that in time I would grasp the basis for all her doctrines. So far, this has certainly proved to be true. Joining the Church is really rather like getting married to someone you truly love. To take a human analogy: When you get married you certainly don't know or understand everything about your bride—God forbid! Instead, you are confident that as you get to know her over the years your love and allegiance will grow.

Throughout my new Christian life I have remained in close contact and cooperation with many conservative Protestants, the kind that are probably best described as Evangelicals. These Evangelicals have been friends and supporters even more than all but a few Catholics. I love them a great deal and owe them much. Being with them strengthens my basic Christianity—and also, in some mysterious way, increases my Catholic commitment. They inspire in me the hope that someday the Catholic Church in America will awaken from its slumber in the secular suburbs; that someday Catholics in large numbers, like these wonderful Evangelicals, will blaze forth with love for Christ and his Church—and transform our society in the process.

Looking back on my conversion I can say that it has been filled with truly great surprises—not the least being that it occurred at all. This is the first miracle; the second is that the same kind of conversion took place, at the same time, in Timmie as well—ours has been, and remains, a shared journey. Frequently in this journey my expectations and plans have been very painfully confounded—but the consequences of these confoundings, or "ego-strippings," have always been blessings. This Christian Odyssey is still quite new to me, and who knows what lies ahead—for in spite of retrospectives, such as this report, the prize lies ahead, and one prays to be able to finish the race.   ·

Paul C. Vitz *is a professor of psychology at New York University. Among his publications are* Psychology as Religion: The Cult of Self Worship; Censorship: Evidence of Bias in Our Children's Textbooks; *and* Sigmund Freud's Christian Unconscious. *He lives in New York City (Greenwich Village) with his wife, the former Evelyn Birge, and their six children.*

A Less Traveled Road to Rome

Dale Vree

"All roads lead to Rome," it is said. One way of understanding that dictum is to say that there are many routes to Rome, some well traveled and some less traveled. I suspect my road is of the latter variety—though some may see that road as more of a maze, but if so, let's hope it is "a maze in grace."

Having been raised an evangelical Protestant (Dutch Reformed/Presbyterian), my path to Rome was long and arduous, for the distance between Calvinistic—*cum*-evangelical Protestantism and Roman Catholicism is immense.

Consider what I was up against: As a small boy in the late 1940's/early 1950's, I was told by some relatives that (centuries ago) Spanish Catholics persecuted Christians in Holland—this being a major issue because all of "my people" were Protestant immigrants from the Netherlands. Moreover, I was informed that Catholic countries in Latin America continued persecuting Christians.

Catholics persecuting Christians? This may sound contradictory, especially to the Catholic ear, but I was reared in a milieu that generally thought that Catholics are *not* Christians (while this view is enjoying a resurgence in the 1980's, I am confident that my relatives abandoned it for good long ago). I was introduced to this view in the deceptively simple terms a small boy could easily grasp: since Catholics call themselves Catholics while we Protestants call ourselves (simply) Christians,

Catholics are not Christians—after all, they don't call themselves Christians! And later I would learn that only we Christians are "saved." Christians believe in Jesus Christ, but Catholics believe in Mary, popes, saints, and worship idols in their churches. Catholicism and Christianity were, you see, different religions.

But even as a small boy I didn't quite believe it. I had noticed that Catholics had crosses (not crucifixes, but *crosses,* with which I as a Protestant was quite familiar) on top of their churches. I even realized that Jesus Christ was the central figure in Catholicism.

Later, in high school, I wandered into Catholic churches a couple times at odd hours. We protestants correctly talked about our church buildings as "God's House," but our church interiors resembled auditoriums, whereas I was immediately struck by a different ambiance inside Catholic churches: there was a permeating "divine presence" (even when no worship service was in progress). Perhaps it was the flickering candlelight, or the occasional pilgrim kneeling and genuflecting, or the statues and the "color" and the altar—I don't know exactly—but being inside a Catholic church elicited my primitive sense of worship and my desire to kneel and pray. (Only much later would I learn about the reserved sacrament.)

In 1960, when I was 16, the Catholic John F. Kennedy contested the Protestant Richard Nixon for the U.S. presidency. Virtually all my relatives and the members of my church were against Kennedy—and the most frequent charge against him was that he was Catholic. But my Father and I were for Kennedy (not that we were pro-Catholic, but we weren't anti-Catholic either). This deviation from the norm was significant and deserves an explanation.

My paternal Grandfather, an immigrant from Holland, began his working life as a mechanic and sheetmetal pressman, and he taught my Father (who didn't graduate from high school, but finished his schooling at a trade school) to respect the common man—his culture, his economic concerns, and his trade unions. My Father passed this "proletarian consciousness" on to me. He taught me always to look at things from the point of view of the "little guy." Seeing society from a working-class point of view was a factor which, although I didn't realize it at the time, set me (as well as, I suspect, my Father and Grandfather) somewhat at odds with my Protestant environment.

As I've indicated, my kinfolk were Dutch Calvinists, and they were part of a wave of Dutch Calvinist immigrants who came to America after the turn of the century and settled in the Midwest. They became overwhelmingly Republican—and not surprisingly. Calvinism, many believe, was the progenitor of capitalism. Certainly it was an ideology well-suited to the nascent bourgeoisie. It is individualistic and oriented to self-improvement. Success is thought to be a result of hard work and a sign of God's favor, lack of success a consequence of laziness and a mark of God's disfavor. The connection between poverty on the one hand and discrimination, exploitation, or inherited financial, social, and educational disadvantages on the other is generally overlooked. To be blunt: the social implications of Calvinism (individual pursuit of prosperity) and proletarian consciousness (the idea that to be disadvantaged is not necessarily shameful, and that the disadvantaged should struggle *together* for a better world) are antithetical.

That my tightly-knit ethnic subculture was so heavily, even so naturally, Republican meant that it took a lot of conviction on the part of my Grandfather and Father to be strong populistic Democrats. The working-class issue was responsible for this. I well remember being instructed by them during the 1948 presidential election that the Democratic Party is the party of the workingman—and so, at the wee age of four I knew that I too was a Democrat. The proletarian consciousness I learned was a far stronger influence on me than the anti-Catholicism of my general milieu. Hence in 1960 it was not hard for me or my Father (my Grandfather then being dead) to have strongly favored a Catholic Democrat over a Protestant Republican.

By 1959-1960, I had become deeply troubled by the lack of concern for social justice in my particular Protestant milieu (then a large middle-class Presbyterian church). Being a Protestant, I was taught to read the Bible. Thank God for that! And from my readings I instinctively picked up a sense of God's "preferential love for the poor" (as many Catholics now call it). One of the most poignant passages in Scripture for me was where Jesus warns the outwardly righteous that they stand in danger of Judgment. To them, Jesus will say when He comes in glory at the end of the world: "Depart from me, ye cursed, into everlasting fire." Why? "For I was hungered, and ye gave me no meat: I was thirsty, and ye gave me no drink.... Verily I say unto you, inasmuch as ye did it not to one of the least of these [my brethren], ye did it not to me" (Matt. 25:41-45 KJV).

Then, I surmised, Christ will often come to us in the guise of the least advantaged of people. To want to aid them is to want to aid Jesus. So in addition to simple "proletarian consciousness," I felt I had another reason to be a Democrat and be concerned for social justice.

Now, this was not merely an abstract matter. In the late 1950's and early 1960's, the civil rights movement—led and supported by many Christians, black and white—was gathering national momentum. Racial justice, which was also a matter of economic justice, was a burning issue for me. But the folks at my church seemed utterly oblivious or indifferent to the plight of "the least" of our brethren.

While my Protestant background gave me a strong sense of the authority of the Bible, the importance of a personal relationship with Jesus, and the value of adherence to traditional Christian personal morality—for which I remain eternally grateful—I sensed something was missing.

As a boy I would swing erratically between my orthodox religious convictions and my political interests—but I could never integrate them. For example, an evangelistic rally would come to town and impel me to put religious pictures on my bedroom wall. But then a Democratic political campaign or a liberal political cause would come along, and the religious pictures would go down and political posters would take their place. Then, after going off to a church summer camp, I would switch the pictures and posters again—*ad infinitum*.

In college I tried to resolve this conflict by becoming an Episcopalian. A side attraction was that, like the Roman Catholic Church, the Episcopalian Church *did* elicit my sense of worship. But the more salient attraction was the social justice witness of Episcopalians. (At the time, it would have been much too large a leap for me to have become Roman Catholic.)

However, the hoped-for integration of orthodoxy and (what is now called) orthopraxy did not occur for me, for being an Episcopalian quickly got me—unintentionally—tangled in the web of modernist theology. My hero of the moment, Bishop James A. Pike, was not only speaking up for social justice, but also publicly jettisoning central Christian doctrines such as the Incarnation, the Trinity, and the physical Resurrection of Jesus Christ.

Through the influence of Episcopalians like Pike, I was led to read Paul Tillich, Rudolf Bultmann, and other theologically liberal Protestants. I noticed that, for some reason, the social action emphasis went hand in hand with doctrinal skepticism. Although I didn't particularly want to surrender my belief in a supernatural God, miracles, and afterlife, and all the rest, that seemed to be the required thing to do if one were serious about social justice. That one could combine theological orthodoxy with working for social justice didn't seem to be an option. I knew of no compelling role models among either Episcopalians or evangelical Protestants for orthodox social action.

In the early-to-mid 1960's, my participation in the civil rights and peace movements deepened. In 1964, while a senior at the University of California at Berkeley, I was arrested for my involvement in the Free Speech Movement. As I drank deeply from the wells of modernist theology, my faith in Christ weakened, and my "proletarian consciousness" was redirected into Marxist philosophy. Then I abandoned Christ and became a Marxist-Leninist.

To make a long story short, in 1965 I traveled to Berlin to make a new life in East Germany—what I thought would be a true workers' state. I was searching for an egalitarian social order and the New (Communist) Man. I didn't find either.

While living in East Berlin in 1966, I was, to my surprise, converted to Christ (for details, see my book, *From Berkeley to East Berlin and Back* [Thomas Nelson, 1985]). The conversion was rather sudden. It occurred on Easter Sunday in a Protestant church as a result of hearing a sermon proclaiming the physical Resurrection of Christ.

There are three salient things that need to be said about this:

(1) I saw first-hand the inadequacy of Communism, which is the preeminent and most determined form of human self-salvation in our time. It was deeply impressed upon me that man cannot save himself. So, when I converted to Christ, I did so on *His* terms. For me, modernist Christianity had been a slippery slope on the way to outright atheism. Modernism's assumptions were atheistic: man need only believe what he finds believable, and nothing miraculous or paradoxical is included. I knew modernism to be a shrouded atheism. I knew that, as a modernist, I hadn't believed in Jesus Christ in any signifi-

cant sense—nor had I had any relationship with Him. So I would have no more of the "pick-and-choose-what-you-want-to-believe-or-not-believe" of modernism. It had led me further and further from Christ; I could no longer trust its subjectivism. I would therefore embrace Christ without prevarication. I would adhere to the Bible—both the teachings I liked and those I didn't particularly like.

(2) Part of what turned me to Christ in East Berlin was the witness of the Christians there. Looking for the Communist New Man, I ran into the Pauline New Man instead. Searching for the dictatorship of the proletariat, I found the primitive church instead (the pre-Constantinian church where Christians are a persecuted minority). In America, I had found Christians to be comfortable, complacent, smug. In East Berlin, it was the Communists who were that way, whereas the harassed Christians were dedicated and willing to suffer hardship for Christ. This was a Christian witness I had never really seen before. In retrospect, it would almost seem that for *me* to really find Christ I *had* to go to a place like East Germany to do so.

(3) In becoming a "born-again" Christian, I did not become anti-Communist, much less anti-socialist; nor did I experience a conversion to capitalism or the American Way of Life. After all, the American Way of Life—and the bourgeois captivity of American Protestantism—had been great obstacles to faith for me, whereas the Communist persecution of religion had shown me another—a more primitive and, I dare say, more authentic—face of Christianity, and had actually ignited my faith.

All three of these factors, I now realize, had a bearing on my eventual turn to Rome. But before getting to that, I need to say something about the 17 years which intervened between my turn to Christ in East Berlin and my becoming a Roman Catholic.

Upon returning to Berkeley later in 1966, I began looking for a church to attend. Since I had been Episcopalian, I picked up where I had left off and looked for an

Episcopal parish. But this time it could not be one infected with modernism. It would have to be orthodox—which I thought then meant evangelical (there is a small contingent of evangelical Episcopalians in the U.S.). But in the Berkeley area I couldn't find an evangelical Episcopal parish. The only satisfactory Episcopal parish I could find was Anglo-Catholic. As with much in my life, I found something I wasn't exactly looking for. Was it grace?

I don't know for sure. But what I do know is that I could never have become a Roman Catholic without a long sojourn in Anglo-Catholicism (which is why I can only be grateful to it). For, among Anglo-Catholics I would learn the Catholic understanding of Christianity: the importance of justification *and* sanctification, of faith *and* works; the value of suffering; the authority of tradition; and the meaning of priesthood, the seven sacraments, Mariology, purgatory, the intercession of the saints, the incarnational principle, etc. As for good works and suffering, I had already had a glimmering of their significance in the Christian life, but the rest was new to me.

The most important new thing I would learn as an Anglo-Catholic was that the corporate Church—through her tradition—possesses teaching authority. The Bible is not our sole rule of faith because the Bible was assembled by the Church. The New Testament did not fall out of the heavens whole. Before there was the New Testament there was the Church. In the early years of the Church, there were numerous gospel accounts and other documents circulating that claimed to be authentically inspired. But not all of them were, and the Church had to determine which ones were to be accepted into the Old Testament canon (as well as determine whether the Old Testament was still to be included in what we call the Bible).

Since the Church was deciding which books were inspired and which were not, it was obvious to me that the Church had to be inspired by the Holy Spirit in this portentous undertaking. Moreover, once this undertaking was accomplished, it was quite natural that the Church would feel competent to make authoritative interpretations of the Scriptures.

As we can see vividly from Christian history, the Scriptures lend themselves to a multitude of theological, ethical, and social interpretations. Their meaning is not transparent—which is why there have been so many quarrels about their meaning. For example, Christians believe in the Incarnation of Christ and the Holy Trinity; but although it certainly implies these doctrines, the New Testament does not even mention these terms (nor does it define these doctrines unambiguously). It was the Church through her tradition which spoke *authoritatively* on theological, ethical, and social matters. So, thanks to the Church we have the Christian Bible, and thanks again to the Church we need not quarrel endlessly about the Bible's meaning.

The Church believed that while the Holy Spirit spoke through the Scriptures, the Spirit would continue to guide the Church in her function of articulating the truth. After all, in the latter days of His ministry Jesus said to His disciples: "I have yet many things to say unto you, but ye cannot bear them now. Howbeit when he, the Spirit of truth, is come, he will guide you into all truth..." (John 16:12-13 KJV). Since the Holy Spirit does not contradict Himself, the on-going teaching function of the Church would not contradict, but rather clarify and deepen and amplify, what was revealed in Scripture. The result, most notably in the first millennium of the Church, was the anathematization of heresies and the formulation of creeds and doctrines—in short, the development of doctrine.

From a purely biblical point of view, the idea of the development of doctrine makes a lot of sense. For example, when one contrasts what seems to be the tribal, vengeful, forbidding, and war-like God of the Old Testament with the universal, forgiving, loving, and peace-loving God of the New Testament, one can easily see how doctrine develops in the Bible itself. (Indeed, because of this contrast, some early Christian heretics held that the Old Testament should be omitted from the Christian Bible. In effect, they could not see that doctrine develops.) T. S. Eliot, an Anglo-Catholic, said with great wisdom that man cannot stand too much reality. God's truth is the ultimate reality, but in His kindness God only seems to show mankind as much of His awesome reality as mankind can assimilate at a particular time in history.

That the Church possesses teaching authority makes sense in another way. When Christ ascended into Heaven, He did not leave behind a book; He left behind the Church. And it was *one* Church He left behind. Moreover, he *intended* to leave behind one Church. Again in the latter days of His ministry, Jesus prayed to His Father: "keep through thine own name those whom thou hast given me, that they may be one..." (John 17:11 KJV). When the new-fangled notion of *sola scriptura* ("Scripture is our sole authority") broke out at the Reformation, the results ran directly—and flagrantly—against Christ's will that His Church be one. The reformation has spawned thousands of churches and sects and cults and conventicles (according to the *Oxford Encyclopedia of World Christianity,* published in 1982, there are more than 28,000 recognizable denominations of Christianity). Most all of them base their beliefs on "the Bible alone." But *sola scriptura,* as a principle of authority, is unworkable and self-defeating because the Bible can be interpreted in thousands of different (and often mutually exclusive) ways.

If Christ willed that His Church be one, it is inconceivable that He would have authorized the principle of *sola scriptura*. Indeed, He never did: that principle is not in Scripture!

Now, the only viable alternative to *sola scriptura* is Scripture-and-tradition. This latter principle makes sense because what Christ left us with was the living tradition which is the Church, and the Church gave us the Bible, as well as herself as the guardian and interpreter of divine truth. So, if one wishes to conform one's will to the teachings of Christ, but if those teachings are not unambiguously presented in Scripture, then one is forced to look toward ecclesial tradition and the teaching authority of the Church's bishops. The Church possesses the authority to teach by virtue of her tradition—which is the life of the Holy Spirit in the Church—and by virtue of the authority Christ gave to the seventy disciples when He sent them forth with these words: "He that heareth you heareth me; and he that despiseth you despiseth me..." (Luke 10:16 KJV).

Until 1976, I was content to remain an Anglo-Catholic while accepting the above understanding of the Church. But by 1976 it was apparent that the Episcopal Church had broken with the apostolic, Catholic faith on two decisive counts. That Church (1) approved the ordination of women to the priesthood, and (2) had by then already adopted a permissive position on abortion.

When I say "broken with the apostolic, Catholic faith," what do (or did) I mean? Anglo-Catholics generally understand Catholic orthodoxy in terms of St. Vincent of Lérins' rule, that it is "that which has been believed everywhere, ever, by everyone." That means that Catholic orthodoxy is that which has always been believed by all Catholic Christians. Anglo-Catholics understand "Catholic Christians" as those Christians who stand in the Apostolic Succession of bishops--primarily Roman Catholics, the Eastern Orthodox, and Anglicans.

I will leave it to theologians far more competent than I—whether Roman Catholic, Eastern Orthodox, or Anglo-Catholic—to explain why the two departures from Catholic faith noted above are violations of Catholic tradition rather than "developments" of it. Suffice it to say that of the two departures, the ordination of women is the more far-reaching for Anglo-Catholics. In one sense of course, abortion is the more grievous departure because it involves something the ordination of women manifestly does not—that is, the killing of innocent human life. But when I say the ordination of women is more momentous for Anglo-Catholics I mean that in a strictly ecclesiological sense. In *this* sense it is more far-reaching for two basic reasons:

(1) If a woman cannot be a priest, then her priestly ministrations are invalid. Hence, when one receives communion consecrated by a woman priest, one is *not really* receiving Christ. It is just make-believe. Moreover, when a woman becomes a bishop, the priests she ordains (whether male or female) are not priests either, and the whole Apostolic line of Succession inevitably becomes hopelessly compromised at a minimum or totally defective at a maximum. One way or the other, the ordination of women puts one on the road to Catholic self-destruction—i.e., to the destruction of the priesthood and episcopate. Of course, Roman Catholics hardly ever worry about such a thing as Catholic self-destruction in some ultimate sense. For them, the Catholic identity of their Church is a given. But for Anglo-Catholics, the Catholic identity of the Anglican Communion is not a given. Anglo-Catholics have had to fight for their Catholic identity ever since the English Reformation—and concomitantly, it is something they have persistently feared they could lose.

(2) While a church's stand on abortion can be reversed, it is inconceivable that after thousands of women priests have been ordained, a church would or could

realistically reverse itself and undo what it has done. It is like squeezing toothpaste out of the tube, and then trying to get it back in the tube. Or, to switch the imagery, if the ordination of women puts one on the road to Catholic self-destruction, it is a road which, once taken, one can't get off or turn around on; one must follow it to the bitter end.

Even if one wishes to withhold an opinion on whether a woman *can* be a valid priest, from an Anglo-Catholic point of view one "branch" of the Church Catholic is not entitled to act unilaterally in the vital area of sacramental theology. Thus, that the Episcopal Church did so essentially places that Church outside the Church Catholic (as Anglo-Catholics understand it). It also meant that in the U.S. the Episcopal Church's *via media* between Protestantism and Catholicism had broken down irretrievably, as the Protestant wing of that Church finally triumphed over its Catholic wing.

From an Anglo-Catholic viewpoint, the only way such a stark departure from Catholic tradition as ordaining women could conceivably take place is if a grand ecumenical council of Roman Catholics, the Eastern Orthodox, and Anglicans (as well as the Old Catholics) jointly agreed to do so—i.e., if it became a practice accepted "everywhere" and "by everyone" (i.e., by all Catholic Christians). Needless to say, that such a council would ever take place and that it would come to such a decision are both extremely unlikely prospects.

So, because I wanted to remain a Catholic (indeed, could not become a Protestant again, if only because of my understanding of the nature of the Church sketched above), "1976" began a process in which I had to consider whether—or how long—I could remain an Episcopalian.

For Protestants the question of Rome is usually framed as, "Good heavens, why *Rome?*" But for Anglo-Catholics, the question is usually, "Why *not* Rome?" Even before 1976, this was a perennial question. After 1976 in the U.S., it became quite an urgent question for many Anglo-Catholics. Over the years, I have known countless Anglo-Catholics who have said, "Someday I may have to cross the Tiber." Many who say that have not crossed over (or at least, not yet), and many of them never will, but since 1976 in the U.S., increasing numbers of them have been crossing over.

The question is "why *not* Rome?" for an Anglo-Catholic because in so very many ways the Anglo-Catholic believes exactly what the Roman Catholic believes, and so—in light of the will of Christ that His Church be one, and the sense of the very word "Catholic" as "universal"—he must ask why he chooses to remain separate from the vast majority of Catholics who owe obedience to Rome. So, I too asked myself, "Why *not* Rome?" and over the years found my qualms about Rome pale in comparison to my qualms about invalid women priests and permissive positions on abortion. It became harder and harder for me to justify my separate existence as an *Anglo*-Catholic. (Anglo-Catholics regard themselves as members of the "Western Church" as opposed to the "Eastern Church," and so the question is seldom, "Why *not* Constantinople?" As such, I will not try to answer that question here.)

Furthermore, the more I thought about Rome and the nature of the Church, the more I realized that if (as stated above) the Church is authorized to teach, the Church must also have an in-tact teaching authority—i.e., a magisterium. Anglo-Catholics, holding to the maxim of St. Vincent Lérins, tend to believe that with the schism between the Western Church and the Eastern Church in 1054, the Church's teaching authority essentially went into limbo for the next thousand years. But could this be? The Catholic tradition is a *living* tradition. Could or would the Holy Spirit take a thousand-year vacation from, as Christ said, guiding us "into all truth"? I can't know the answer for sure, but to my mind, it seemed unlikely.

I also came to realize that a magisterium not only guides us into all truth; it protects the truth we already have. Surveying the wreckage of the Western Christianity of the last couple of centuries, I could see that old and new heresies were running rampant in most of the major Western churches. Indeed, for a time it seemed to me, as an Anglo-Catholic, that Rome herself might one day succumb to the disease of modernism (or what Roman Catholics call "neo-Modernism"). But when Karol Wojtyla assumed the Chair of Peter as John Paul II, I no longer worried about that. Furthermore, I could see that the Roman Catholic magisterium is truly alive—and its new-found vigor was most assuring to me. And more, I could see that the only thing in this modern world of skepticism, false messianisms, relativistic morality, and consumerism—that can safeguard Christian truth is a magisterium. And then I saw that the Anglican Communion's lack of a magisterium is no minor deficiency.

Which brings me to the three salient points about my conversion to Christ in East Berlin (cited above) and how they relate to my turn to Rome:

(1) When I converted to Christ in 1966, I did so on *His* terms. No longer would I set myself up as the arbiter of religious truth. I would submit to Jesus and the truth about Him in Scripture—I would even accept those things in Scripture which weren't particularly appetizing. So, the Christianity I had converted to was a kind of generic orthodox Protestantism. But there was a lingering problem here. Integral to orthodox Protestantism is the belief in the supremacy of conscience. Yes, orthodox Protestants hold that the Bible is the truth—but it is true only relative to the individual's interpretation of it. There is, finally, no authority above the individual who can say *with recognized authority,* "your interpretation is wrong." It was the very lack of such authority which, in my judgment, had led to the modernist erosion in the leading Protestant churches. When I became an Anglo-Catholic, I learned that Anglo-

Catholicism had a different view—but I would later see that without a living magisterium it had no credible or durable way of implementing that view.

If I had converted to Christ on His terms, how could I find out what His terms really were? In Protestantism, the individual is thrown back upon himself and his fallible and highly subjective judgments—or upon the ersatz (and, from a strictly *sola scriptura* point of view, illegitimate) traditions of Calvin, Luther, Wesley, and a multitude of others, or worse, upon the ersatz and elusive authority of the modernist theology professors and their shifting opinions. In seeking the living faith of Christ's Church, I was compelled to consider seriously the Roman Catholic magisterium.

Now, there were a few things which Rome taught which didn't much appeal to me (to be sure, they were minor compared to my reservations, as an Anglo-Catholic, about women priests and abortion). But ironically, my qualms about Rome made Rome attractive in a way that seemed fitting. That is, it seemed that if Rome were the authority I thought her to be, I *should* have some qualms. For it would be awfully arrogant of me to think that my own natural preferences would be in perfect harmony with the will of Christ. If the quest for Christian truth had driven me to *submit* to Christ and the revealed word of God in East Berlin, then it might also drive me to *submit* to the magisterium. Christ asks us to believe and do things we might not really want to believe or do, and so it seemed symmetrical that Christ's teaching authority in the Church would do so too. A Bible-believing Christian doesn't "pick and choose" from the Bible what he wants to accept—no, he is under authority. The same applies to the magisterium. If, in accepting Christ in 1966, it was necessary for me to accept even Christ's hard sayings, then if the necessity of the magisterium became apparent to me, I would have to accept even its hard teachings.

So, the very difficulty of "submitting to Rome" made such a submission seem appropriate—as well as consistent with my original decision for Christ in 1966.

(2) In East Berlin I ran into the Pauline New Man and the heroic primitive church. What attracted me to Christ was, in part, the selfless witness of Christians. Is persistent hardship therefore indispensable to authentic Christian living? I hope not, but I don't know for sure. Be that as it may, my experience in East Berlin gave me a profound appreciation for Christian suffering and mortification—themes I saw more powerfully represented in the Roman Catholic Church than in any other Western church. The Protestantism I had been exposed to as a youth stressed the "blessings" (often quite self-centered, even materialistic) which follow from accepting Christ. What was lost sight of was the potentially greater blessings which follow from adversity and suffering. Seldom in Protestant churches did I hear about these inconvenient words of our Lord: "Blessed are ye, when men shall revile you, and persecute you...for my sake" (Matt. 5:11 KJV).

St. Teresa of Avila said, "We always find that those who walked closest to Christ our Lord were those who had to bear the greatest trials." Protestants often overlook the connection between holiness (or sanctity) and suffering (whether voluntary or involuntary). What Protestants derogate as the "cult of the saints" I saw as just another of Rome's strengths. The saints *are* the New Men, and I came to see that one of the primary purposes of the Roman Obedience is, with grace leading the way, to create this new humanity. Which is not to say Roman Catholicism is an elitist form of Christianity—far from it! Rome has a well-deserved, if often misunderstood, reputation for embracing even the weakest of (repentant) sinners. Nor is it to say Rome believes in creating a Pelagian heaven on earth. Rather, the saints are the very embodiments of Love; in their sacrificial charity they dramatize for us the very nature of God; and by their examples they

point us to the New Jerusalem, which is ultimately beyond this world.

(3) When I accepted Christ in East Berlin, I did not
surrender my "proletarian consciousness" or my concern
about "the least of these my brethren." I did not become a
champion of America (where the church is suffocated
with respectability) against Communism (where the
church lives, as she first lived, in agony). I did not resolve
to join the middle-class merry-go-round, become (what is
now called) a "yuppie," or forget about social justice.

In the balkanized Protestant world, one must usually
choose between embracing orthodox theology and right-
wing politics on the one hand, and modernist theology
and left-wing politics on the other hand. As early as my
teenage years, I couldn't quite make that choice. For
decades I would search in vain for a way of combining
theological orthodoxy and populistic political views. But
the more I studied the Roman Catholic magisterium, the
more I realized that it was offering what I had been
looking for all along, that essentially it taught that unusual mix of convictions—socially "left," theologically
"right"—which I had carried with me since boyhood.
And it did so *with authority*. As a Roman Catholic, my
theological and social views would not seem idiosyn-
cratic—peculiar to me.

So, in Roman Catholicism I found a church in which I
could emphatically affirm both the rights of labor and the
ancient creeds, reject both abortion and the use of nuclear
weapons, affirm both lifelong marriage and the dignity of
the poor, reject both laissez-faire capitalism and do-your-
own-thing morals, and stand apart from both the philosophical materialism of the East and the practical
materialism (consumerism) of the West—and do so in full
harmony with the teachings of my Church.

Finally, I have always felt that if I were a Christian, my
loyalty to Christ would have to transcend my temporal
loyalties—whether to nation, ethnic group, or social class.

Most non-Roman Catholic churches have identities forged by nationalistic preoccupations or affected by national conditioning. Only Rome has been able to stand above nation rivalries and relativities. Moreover, of all the churches, the Roman Catholic is least affected by class and ethnic provincialisms. The Roman Catholic Church is the most "catholic"—i.e., the most universalistic, most international, most all-embracing—of all churches.

When I became a Roman Catholic in 1983, many Roman Catholics greeted me with a "Welcome home!" It was meant in an ecclesiological sense which I understood, but in ways in which my greeters did not know, I would feel *very much* "at home" indeed.[1]

Dale Vree *is editor of the* New Oxford Review *(1069 Kains Ave., Berkeley, CA 94706), a monthly magazine which takes its name from the 19th-century Oxford Movement in England, and which is the primary forum for the new generation of converts to Roman Catholicism. He received his doctorate in political science from the University of California at Berkeley, and resides in Berkeley with his wife, Elena, and their four children. He is the author of* On Synthesizing Marxism and Christianity *and* From Berkeley to East Berlin and Back *and is a contributing editor and regular columnist for the* National Catholic Register.

Reading Oneself into the Church

Kenneth D. Whitehead

I was received into the Catholic Church by means of conditional Baptism at the Church of Santa Susanna in Rome on the eve of Pentecost, 1958. My first Communion took place the following morning, Pentecost Sunday, in the same Roman church. The day after that I received the sacrament of Confirmation in one of the side chapels of St. Peter's Vatican Basilica where, a few months later, my presence there was to experience the sacrament of Matrimony. I was twenty-seven years old, at that time, a career diplomat stationed at the American Embassy in Rome. This assignment accounted for my being received into the Church in the Eternal City. But the journey of faith which had finally brought me to the Church had begun years before, in my late teens and early twenties, when the aimlessness and meaninglessness of a life without God was forcefully borne in upon me, both in my own life and in the lives of others whom I observed from time to time in the same state.

I was born and raised in the west, in Idaho. My parents were religious, and sent me to Sunday school as a small child. Bible stories fascinated me, but I had no structured religious formation. Orphaned relatively young, I gave up the practice of religion entirely at about age thirteen or fourteen. I lived at times in the homes of my older married sisters, who had also given up any active practice of religion. I had no stimulus or example to practice it; its meaning and benefits were far from self-evidently clear to me. Who needed God? My basic belief at the time was probably a belief in my own self-sufficiency. This is a kind of belief that, in the long run, is hard to sustain in the face of the buffetings that life customarily delivers to us all. In my early teens, sometimes the sheer vitality and vigor of youth were more than a match for the adversities encountered, even when doubts and discouragements were also present.

But I was still seeking a purpose in life though spending little time at it. Strongly tempting me also was the hedonistic lifestyle. Yet, I don't think there was ever a moment when I didn't realize in my mind that such an existence was ultimately unsatisfying and empty.

Always an omnivorous reader, especially interested in literature and philosophy, I pondered the great questions, trying to find answers on the purely natural level: Why is there something rather than nothing? Does God exist? If so, is God involved in or concerned with what exists? How can a good God permit evil if He is also omnipotent? Or, rather, since He manifestly does permit evil, He must be lacking in either goodness or omnipotence. What can we know about anything? And what is the point of it all?

I did strongly believe in a moral law. The dimension of morality in human existence did seem self-evident to me, whatever its source was conceived to be. I tried, more or less ineptly, to ground the moral law in reason and nature alone since revelation was not my belief. But I remember being bothered by the dilemma so ably dramatized by the Russian writer whose novels I devoured, Fyodor Dostoyevski: if God does not exist, then all is permitted. The years of my early teens had coincided with the climax of the greatest and most destructive war in human history; and, then when the truth about the Nazi death camps emerged at the end of it, I learned along with the rest of the world that supposedly civilized human societies could act upon the premise that all was permitted. It was far from an academic or hypothetical question. Indeed our present society which permits such abominations as legalized abortion illustrates the same harrowing truth.

At an impressionable age I went to war myself, in Korea. I thus witnessed first-hand the violence and destructiveness of war as well as the kind of behavior to which soldiers away from the constraints of home and family can sometimes abandon themselves. In my considered judgment the Korean War was a just war. I adopted this opinion because by that time I had also learned that the totalitarian state had by no means disappeared with the destruction of the Nazis; rather, as a result of the very same war fought to destroy the Nazis, entire nations had become enslaved by a Communist variety of totalitarianism equally committed to the proposition that all was permitted, provided only that the proper social class thereby was served. In Korea we were helping to defend from that fate a people actively fighting to defend themselves.

The events of my life thus did not allow me to ignore the question of evil, even if I had wanted to. But I do not believe I was ever so naive as to believe that the evil was merely "out there somewhere," residing only in institutions or structures. No: the evil was in the heart of man; in the words of the Old Testament: "the wickedness of man was great in the earth and every imagination of the thoughts of his heart was only evil continually" (Gen 6:5). And I knew from the examination of the thoughts of my own heart that I was all too capable of participating in that evil.

The need was clearly there: "Deliver us from evil." Redemption was necessary. Grace was necessary. Sin and its consequences were all too real. This was true of my personal life, just as it was true of the life of society as a whole. Obscurely I sensed all this. But for a fair number of years I did not recognize that redemption and grace were *available* to me.

One thing that did dispose me to accept Christianity once I came to recognize its true face, however, was authentic Christianity's steady insistence that all moral reform must proceed from within, from out of the heart of the individual. Just as Jesus taught that "from within, out of the heart of man, come evil thoughts, fornication, theft, murder, adultery, coveting, wickedness, deceit, licentiousness, envy, slander, pride, foolishness" (Mk 7:21-22), so a cure could only be effected in a heart opened to allow God to enter into it. So many today mistakenly do imagine, apparently, that virtue consists principally in adopting the correct views on the big issues of the day such as abortion, war, poverty, racism, and the like. Rather, virtue is personal, just as conversion is personal, just as grace is personal, infused into each individual soul. Blaise Pascal had his Jesus declare: "I thought of *thee* during my agony; I shed many a drop of blood for *thee.*"

Recognition of all this still left me far from the Catholic Church, especially since I had no knowledge of the real nature and history of the Church, nor did I have any friendships with practicing Catholics. As will become clear, my conversion took place largely through reading and in the realm of ideas rather than through interaction with flesh-and-blood Catholics. I scarcely knew any Catholics.

Moreover, out of prejudice, I did not at that time have a great deal of respect for Catholics as such. My distorted imagination saw the Church as reactionary, a politicized organization holding its members in thrall by methods not easy for an outsider to understand but surely involving the suppression of their own intellectual independence and moral freedom. This was an absurdly distorted view of the Church, of course, but it was my view for a time. Catholics should understand that people sometimes do hold such views about them and about their faith. Our responsibility of witnessing authentically to the true faith is a heavy responsibility. In spite of my disinformed view of the Church as a whole, I did grudgingly admire many of the artistic and cultural achievements inspired by the Church down through history.

Having returned from the Korean War in 1953, I began studying at the university via the G.I. Bill of Rights, making my study major French. This was to mean that I couldn't help being exposed to some outstanding French writers who were Catholics (as well as to some determinedly anti-clerical ones, to be sure). On the balance, I was able to acquire a slightly greater knowledge of what the faith was all about and what the Church looked like from the inside.

Two encounters with Catholic authors in my years at the university decisively helped advance my knowledge of the authentic Catholic faith; they also created within me a budding sympathy for the Church and for the Catholic outlook. The first of these encounters was with the great modern neo-Thomistic philosopher, Etienne Gilson. I discovered Gilson while studying the history of the Middle Ages.

I had enrolled in a course in medieval history primarily because I had liked a course in ancient history given by the same professor. This professor's method included assignments based upon looking up original source materials in the library. I remember having had to demonstrate from medieval sources that a bishop was the primary minister of the sacrament of Confirmation in the Middle Ages; prior to that I had scarcely known either what a bishop was or what a sacrament was. As a result of this course, the scholar in me began taking the Middle Ages seriously as an important period in the history of civilization.

At the same time I was taking a course in the history of philosophy; this latter course began, logically enough, with the philosophers of ancient Greece; but then casually skipping over the intervening centuries, it moved directly into the era of "modern" philosophy inaugurated in the seventeenth century by such thinkers as Descartes, Spinoza, and Leibniz; it then proceeded on through the British empiricists to the Germans such as Kant and Hegel before concluding with the two principal twentieth-century schools of analytical philosophers and existentialists. Considering the content of my medieval history course about the Middle Ages, I thought it rather odd that a survey course in the history of philosophy could simply pass over the great scholastic philosophers as of no importance. I made a comment about this to a fellow student who, it turned out, was planning to enter a Catholic seminary, and he loaned me a book which he had been reading: *The Spirit of Medieval Philosophy*, by Etienne Gilson.

I understood very little of this book on first reading. What did come through for me, in addition to Gilson's own noble and loving spirit, was the evidence that medieval philosophy represented a formidable exercise indeed of the human mind and spirit—not at all what its omission from the university's survey course in philosophy would have led one to imagine.

I was also enough of a rebel in those days to want to pursue out of sheer contrariness anything that my formal mentors at the university were able to dismiss so easily. I went on to read other books by Gilson, including *The Unity of Philosophical Experience*. His *God and Philosophy* helped me to realize that Scripture contained truth as well as poetry; I had continued, in fact, to respect the Bible as great literature to a degree perhaps surprising in one professing no belief in the Bible as revelation. No doubt this favorable disposition towards what I now know to be God's inspired Word, whatever the reasons for it at the time, helped me considerably on my journey of faith; for I have long since come to realize that Scripture possesses a *power* to inspire assent to the message it conveys.

But it was an essay of Etienne Gilson on St. Thomas Aquinas included in the volume *The Wisdom of Catholicism*, edited by Anton Pegis, that helped me realize how main-stream Catholic philosophy lay essentially, and not just accidentally, at the heart of everything I most valued in the free societies of the West.

In this essay, Gilson pointed out how the threat from Islamic thought that faced Western Europe in the thir-teenth century was every bit as great as the threat to Europe from the Moslem armies that Charles Martel had repulsed at the Battle of Poitiers in 732, more than a half millennium earlier. If Charles Martel had not won that battle, historians agree, Europe would have been quite literally Islamicized. If St. Thomas Aquinas had not won *his* battle, Gilson argued, Europe would have been Islami-cized on the intellectual and spiritual planes.

The problem for the Christian civilization of the day lay in the sophistication with which the Islamic philoso-phers, especially Averroës, had elaborated a philosophy based on the ancient philosopher Plotinus which con-ceived of the world as emanating from an eternal, neces-sary but impersonal divinity, in effect a God indifferent to His own creation.

This was hardly the God Who has revealed to us: "Why, even the hairs of your head are all numbered" (Lk 12:7). On the personal level, the individual was not con-ceived by Averroës even to possess an intellect or soul of his own; rather, according to this medieval Islamic philos-opher, the individual was conceived as somehow partici-pating in a kind of universal intellect or world soul.

This conception of the human person was radically incompatible with the Christian belief that "God created man in his own image" (Gen 1:27). Similarly, the Islamic conception of the world as a deterministic and necessary emanation out of an impersonal divinity was radically incompatible with the Christian idea of a world created out of nothing by a personal God who also created man out of love, who communicated directly with Abraham, Isaac and Jacob, Moses, the Hebrew prophets, and so on, and, finally, tangibly and visibly appeared in the world Himself in the person of His Son, "Whom he appointed the heir of all things" (Heb 1:1). However sophisticated it may have been, the philosophy elaborated by Averroës and the other Islamic thinkers was not only incompatible with Christianity; it only could be abhorrent to Christianity.

The trouble was, however, that the Christian intellectual tradition had not developed to the point where it possessed the philosophical weapons to counter what Gilson called "the fatalism of the Mohammedan world [and]...the necessity of the Greek world." Christian theology had up to that time developed out of the very same Greek philosophers, especially Plotinus, who stood behind the Islamic thinkers who themselves posed such a threat not merely to Christianity but to the Western ideas of personalism and freedom. "The contest being ultimately Plotinus versus Plotinus," Gilson wrote, "Plotinus had to win...at least until Aquinas realized that something was wrong in such an attitude and changed it."

It proved to be the task of St. Thomas Aquinas, according to Gilson, to develop the philosophical framework within which the Christian revelation could finally be justified and defended against the best that the human intellect hostile to Christianity could attempt to establish to the contrary; and, in the process, to lay the foundations for the affirmation of human freedom and dignity which still survive in the West.

"He bore the tremendous task of rescuing European civilization from the Mohammedan peril," Gilson wrote of St. Thomas in the essay that impressed me so profoundly. "When his forces left him, Thomas laid down his pen, and looking at the unfinished *Summa Theologica*, he said to his friend Brother Reginald: 'It is to me as straw.' And what else indeed could even the deepest treatise about God possibly be? But of that straw European civilization was going to make its bed."

What St. Thomas Aquinas taught the world, Gilson made clear, was that, "as a person, man deserves to be considered by other men as an end in himself, never as a means to their own ends"; that, "as individuals we are parts of a whole, and the common good of the whole is above the private interests of its members"; and, finally, that "there is in every one of us something that is even above the state: a person, higher than which there is nothing but God."

I was tremendously affected by reading this essay of Etienne Gilson's on St. Thomas Aquinas. The point about St. Thomas which it brought home to me with special force was that the values from my own Western tradition that I held most dear—the Western belief in the freedom and dignity of the individual human person within a democratic society based on principles of justice and the common good—were a direct legacy of the Catholic civilization of the Middle Ages. These values had become established in the West not in opposition to the Catholic faith but rather as a direct result of the Catholic faith as it was lived in Europe in the Middle Ages. And it was none other than the greatest of the Catholic philosophers and theologians, the Angelic Doctor himself, who had succeeded in grounding these values solidly in reality and truth, henceforth enabling them to be affirmed by any human mind with conviction and commitment.

I did not yet understand what St. Thomas himself understood so well, namely, that by comparison with the kingdom of heaven, civilization itself is straw. I was still enamoured of Western civilization. But now I had to recognize that what I was enamoured of was, in its most impressive manifestations, largely a creation of the Catholic Church. It gradually dawned on me that this was true not only with respect to foundational principles, but also with respect to concrete social institutions such as hospitals, universities, social welfare, rule of law, separation of powers, and other typical Western institutions.

The very fact that the Church herself always and everywhere insisted on maintaining her own freedom in her work of preaching the Gospel and sanctifying souls guaranteed a type of society very different from the monolithic "oriental despotisms" of so much of the rest of the world; state absolutism has never ultimately been able to prevail in places where the Catholic Church was flourishing, as can be seen in Communist Eastern Europe, especially Poland, today; some "separation of powers" is inevitable where the Church is present for the simple reason that she can never allow *her* powers to be exercised or controlled by the state.

Even if it is in fact the case that the West has now strayed far from its Catholic roots, and that the center of gravity for the Church has recently been shifting to the Third World—no doubt because of the loss of faith and the consequent secularization and moral decadence of the West itself—the fact remains that the principles to enable free men to live as upright moral agents in societies based on liberty and justice for all have been established for all time through the historical experience of the Christian West. Neither the Church nor Christianity are dependent upon the West, of course; but the West had the honor of having served as the seedbed of Christianity.

For myself, I was still committed to the West rather than to the Church, and still had almost everything to learn about the Church. But at least I was now in a position to actually learn it because I no longer saw the Church as a foreign body within my own universe. This was a far cry from believing the faith, from being able to "hear the word of God and keep it" (Lk 11:28); but at least it was a start.

It might be thought strange that someone on the road to the Catholic Church, as it turned out for me, was not more concerned about Christ during all this time. For initiates, of course, it is quite true that the ultimate religious question is and must remain: "What do you think of Christ? Whose Son is he?" (Mt 22:41) The fact is, though, that my thoughts rarely turned to Christ at this point on my journey. We should never underestimate how verifiably easy it is for so many in this world that dates its calendars from the birth of Christ simply to put Christ out of their minds—this in spite of what we Christians know to have been Christ's unsurpassed and unforgettable passage through this world and His continuing Presence in it. But we should never forget that it is the Church that Christ Himself left behind that continues to bring Him back to the attention of a world too prone to forget Him. For myself, there was the need to discover the Church first; it was the Church that would then bring Christ to me. At this point in my life, I was still engaged in "reading my way into the Church."

The second Catholic author whom I encountered in my years at the university who influenced me as profoundly as Etienne Gilson was the novelist Georges Bernanos, who was prominent on the European literary and political scene in the pre-World War II years. Known in this country primarily for his novel *The Diary of a Country Priest*—a novel worthy of Dostoyevski—Bernanos wrote a number of other deep and haunting novels, all thoroughly suffused with their author's passionate Catholicism.

These novels impressed me greatly: *La Joie* ("Joy"), about a young girl whom a Russian anarchist emigre finds it necessary to murder for no other reason than that she is a saint; *Sous le Soleil de Satan* ("Under the Sun of Satan"), about a saintly confessor-priest, modeled on the life and career of the Cure of Ars, St. John Vianney; and *Monsieur Ouine* ("Mister Yes-No"), about a sceptical and nihilistic French intellectual, the emptiness of whose life literally comes through as terrifying.

These novels not only moved me; they disturbed me. In a dramatic way they demonstrated how authentic Catholic faith was not just an opinion one held; it required one to *act* on one's belief and try to do good. I *wanted* to do good, and began to glimpse the possibility of how the faith could make that possible for me; but at the same time I had to believe that the Catholic faith was *true*, and I hadn't quite reached that point.

Bernanos was my discovery during about my senior year at the university. It was at that time that I won a scholarship to study at the University of Paris, where I proceeded after a year as a graduate student and part-time freshman English instructor. I was thrilled at the prospect. And going to France proved to be a giant stride in my journey of faith. In an obscure way I was already beginning to understand that. In many ways, modern France is as pagan and decadent as the United States, yet the material remains of the great French Catholic civilization of the Middle Ages greeted me everywhere, an unforgettable impression. The splendid gothic cathedrals of northern France affected me as much as they had affected Henry Adams, whose book *Mont Saint Michel and Chartres* I read at about that same time. And there I was matriculating at the greatest of the great medieval universities, where St. Thomas Aquinas himself had taught!

In France I discovered the political writings of Georges Bernanos. He had been one of the great polemicists of the years of the Spanish Civil War and World War II, denouncing with holy wrath the rise of Nazism and Fascism. Although his own antecedents had been royalist and right-wing, he, through sheer brutal honesty and personal integrity, ended up breaking with a large part of the European right and excoriating its opportunism and its alliance with Nazi and Fascist totalitarianism. Whatever the threat from without, Bernanos absolutely refused to admit that Christians could ever enlist under the leadership of what he called *"le général Moindre Mal"*—"General Lesser Evil"—not even to save civilization, not even to save the Church. As a consequence he soon found himself to be a right-winger estranged from the right and a Catholic estranged from many of his fellow Catholics—those he called *"bien-pensants,"* which might be translated as "right-thinking people."

In many respects Bernanos resembled the British socialist writer George Orwell. Orwell went down to Spain to fight on the side of the Republic in the Spanish Civil War; witnessing at first-hand the horrible realities of war as conducted by the Communists who had by then come to dominate the Spanish left, Orwell ended up denouncing the left and all its works in his book *Homage to Catalonia.* Bernanos went down to Spain to fight on the side of the Nationalists at about the same time, and, witnessing the equally horrible realities of war as conducted on *that* side, penned his magnificent book entitled *Les Grands Cimetières sous la Lune* ("The Great Cemeteries beneath the Moon") in which he denounced the *right* and all *its* works. He was a man who gave up everything he had held dear up to that time for the sake of what he considered simple truth and honesty. And he was a Catholic.

My life to then had not quite prepared me for a man like Bernanos. I might admire the glories of Catholic civilization, but had never realized how the faith could motivate such rock-like personal integrity in anyone. Obviously I hadn't yet learned about the saints! That would come.

It was the Fall of 1956. I was passionately interested in the political events of the day—in the great contest, as I saw it, between the freedom realized within the Western tradition even though our society remained imperfect, and the anthill societies that seemed to be the best that Communism could do even though it had started with an alleged dream of greater well-being and justice. And these were the exhilarating months of the struggle for freedom in Poland and Hungary when it seemed for a time that the irresistible urge to be free would even begin to crack the monolith that was the Soviet Empire. Wladyslaw

Gomulka had come to power in Poland with promises of fundamental reform; Stefan Cardinal Wyszynski had been released from his imprisonment and virtually the entire Polish nation promptly rallied around him, as it would later rally around his protege who was to become Pope John Paul II, demonstrating to the whole world that years of systematic persecution by the Communists had only succeeded in making the Church stronger.

In Hungary another whole nation rose up and almost unanimously demonstrated to the world how eagerly it longed for freedom. It was hard indeed to understand how this small country could possibly have posed a threat to the immense Soviet Union. But that, of course, is not how these things are typically viewed by "the world rulers of this present darkness" (Eph 6:12); nor was it how the Hungarian Revolution in particular was viewed by those "world rulers" then residing in Moscow.

As history records, Soviet tanks were ordered into the streets of Budapest and the Hungarians were summarily and bloodily crushed. In Paris, all these events of the Fall of 1956 affected me much more intimately than if I had been in the United States. It was in Europe that all this was happening; the future and direction of European civilization seemed to be at stake.

And to me the triumph of Soviet tanks over the people's revolution in Hungary came as a deeply disillusioning experience—disillusioning in that up to then I had really believed in what I may, perhaps, call "salvation through politics." If ever a cause was just, it seemed to me that the desire of Hungary to be free was such a cause; and yet the justice of Hungary's cause counted for absolutely nothing in the end. All that counted seemed to be the brute power of the Red Army.

Furthermore, the whole notion of "the West, the bulwark against Communism," a maxim upon which the Church too had seemed to rely in the reign of Pope Pius XII, simply proved to be inoperative. The West was no bulwark against anything; the West sat on its hands while Hungary was crushed. I caught one of my first glimpses of what I recognized as the growing moral decadence of the West. I have since come to realize how the events of the Fall of 1956 helped the Holy See to realize how thin was the reed on which it was relying, how fragile indeed the West had become. This in turn helped bring about the Church's new orientation towards the Third World which has come about with Vatican Council II and its aftermath.

But I scarcely understood the significance of it all at the time. It perplexed me. If there was no salvation through politics, of what and where did salvation consist? If the chances for justice in this world are really so slim, in what can our hope repose? Is it all truly "sound and fury, signifying nothing," in MacBeth's words? These questions weighed upon me. I had long been aware of my own personal inadequacies, but at least had identified with a larger cause. But my faith in secular political solutions was coming unglued. The psychiatrist Viktor Frankl learned from his concentration camp experience that a life without *meaning* is the one deprivation that a human being truly cannot tolerate. Some of what I had considered to be the meaning of life had become badly shaken up; at the same time, without my being fully aware of it, much that I had been reading and thinking was gestating within me in a way that would make me more receptive to God's call.

And some of it came to a head for me through an article on the suppression of the Hungarian Revolution which appeared in the Parisian daily, *Le Figaro*. This article was written by the Nobel-prize-winning French author Franccois Mauriac. Mauriac was another one of those French Catholic authors who influenced me so much in the direction of the Catholic Church.

On November 7, 1956, a group of Hungarian writers and intellectuals had broadcast in desperation a "final appeal" to the West. It was addressed by name to a number of prominent European writers, philosophers, theologians, and intellectuals, including Mauriac. These intellectuals were dubbed "soldiers of the spirit" by the desperate Hungarians. The appeal called upon them to "do something, shake up the horrible inertia of the West, do something, do something...." The Hungarians were dying.

Mauriac's published reply to this appeal was very moving. I read it in a state of great emotion and agitation. As it turned out, it helped crystallize much of what I had been thinking and helped me see the terrible events that were taking place in a more supernatural perspective. Contemplating Hungary, Mauriac pointed out how harrowing it was for anybody to consider the history of what he called "human ferocity." He recalled how as a child he had been scandalized by the number of times even Holy Scripture had described entire peoples, including women and children, being put to the sword. "I was scandalized that such abominations could take place under God's very nose," he wrote. He compared Hungary to the Spain of Bernanos, calling it another "great cemetery beneath the moon." There was no way anyone could come to the material aid of the Hungarians, he concluded, much as one might wish to do so. Hence the final word in Mauriac's response could only be grounded in his own Catholic faith and hope. I have saved the clipping for the last thirty years:

> ...This final appeal from Budapest, and, in a word, the tragedy of our entire destiny, obliges me to declare myself. Given the degradation of our political parties, given the constant anxiety that torments our minds and consciences, our first concern must henceforth be to maintain essential points of contact with all the lost souls wandering abroad today, no matter where they come from. Hope remains even when hopes have been shattered. When Pascal wrote,

"Christ will be in agony until the end of the world,"
the words have no meaning except for Christians. But
when he added, "We must not sleep in the meantime," even an atheist or unbeliever can understand
what is meant. No one has the right to go on sleeping
any longer. "Watch and pray...." If you are among
those who do not pray, then at least "watch"—from
the highest tower you can find.... Each one of us, no
matter how modest or obscure his place, has a responsibility for the salvation of the world—both its
temporal and its spiritual salvation. And each one of
us will be obliged to render an accounting.

Two points became fixed in my mind as a result of my
reading of this article of Mauriac's under the circumstances in which I read it; the two points corresponded to
the two parts of the quotation from Pascal.

"Christ will be in agony until the end of the world." What
St. Paul called "the mystery of iniquity" (II Thess 2:7) will
always be with us. Christ by His holy cross has redeemed
the world, but we are still obliged to live out the human
lives God destined for us when He created the world.
Since it is a world into which, even though it has been
ultimately redeemed, sin has nevertheless entered in
through human free will, we must perforce bear with the
consequent pain and suffering—along with Christ, it is
necessary to add, for Christ came into the world precisely
for the purpose of sharing our pain and suffering—and
death—with us.

"We must not sleep in the meantime." As St. Augustine
remarked, God created us without our leave. We were not
given a choice about whether we were going to come into
existence or not. God made the choice for *His* purposes,
and His purposes are the ones which we are in this world
to serve. Whoever and whatever we may be, whatever
station we may occupy in life, whatever the means we
may be given to serve, this "serving" is what we are in
this world to do. There is in fact no way that we can ever

escape our condition and our destiny, and what God wants is that we should freely and gladly embrace it, in imitation of His Son. As Newman wrote, "God has created me to do Him some definite service; He has committed some work to me which He has not committed to another. I have my mission—I may never know it in this life, but I shall be told it in the next. I shall do good. I shall do His work...if I do but keep His commandments...."

My basic intellectual problems with the faith and its meaning were not entirely solved, but I now saw its basic relevance to me and to my life. Problems such as the future of Western civilization and the justice of the cause of the Hungarian nation I now saw as much too big for me "to handle." God would have to handle them—and I would have to rely on God. This is a very hard thing for modern man to accept. But for my part I was now basically ready to accept it—and to accept the faith.

Yet it was still two years before I requested Baptism, though convinced by then that the faith could possibly be true, that it probably was true. I still did not enjoy the infused theological virtue of faith, but nevertheless was no longer *resisting* the entry of grace. I now welcomed it; indeed, I longed for it ("Like the deer that yearns/ for running streams/ so my soul is yearning/ for you, my God" (Ps 42).

One of the reasons my entry into the Church was delayed even after I had acquired basic favorable intellectual convictions about the faith, however, was that I still found it difficult to pray. I did not have the habit of prayer, and found it difficult to acquire the habit. That too would come as I plunged into a more systematic study of the faith.

During the remainder of my academic year at the University of Paris, I did once have a profound experience of the presence of Christ abiding with me, and somehow knew with great clarity that Christ was calling me, that He *wanted* me. This experience passed without my doing much about it, surprising as that may seem. I still had too many habits of the old self which I didn't really want to break, and, as noted earlier, I still didn't really know how to pray, and that, of course, is essential to a life of faith.

But the direct experience of Christ's presence did help me to put into perspective the real essential of the faith. However God may lead us to the faith, whether through Catholic writers and the appreciation of the achievements of Catholic civilization, as in my case, or through attraction to the witness and the virtues of committed Catholics, as in the case of so many other converts that I have known, we must never lose sight of what the real center of the faith is and always has to be: Jesus Christ Himself, a divine person possessing both a divine and a human nature, who came into this world, "suffered under Pontius Pilate, was crucified, died, and was buried; on the third day He rose again from the dead; He ascended into heaven, and from thence He shall come to judge the living and the dead." It is necessary to believe this before we can go on to affirm also: "I believe in the holy Catholic Church," through which Christ principally remains present to us.

Faith in Christ is primary, then: "If Christ has not been raised, your faith is vain...you are still in your sins" (1 Cor 15:17).

Moreover, faith is necessarily personal and proper to each one of us. It is something that we believe and act upon ourselves within the larger community that is the Body of Christ. Those Catholics who have become especially numerous since Vatican Council II and who believe that our faith commitment now requires us to be out lobbying Congress to provide bread for the world, disinvestment in South Africa, or whatever, have, in my opinion, gotten it precisely backwards. This is a politicization of Christianity (which can be found on both the right and left, by the way), and it represents a distortion of Christianity. It is what we ourselves do in person, to and for the Christ always present to us in the sacraments as well as in our neighbor, which counts the most. I believe I was given the grace to see this clearly precisely because I came to the faith *from* politics....

My journey of faith, as I have described it here, may have seemed unduly bookish to many (even though I haven't even referred to the influence upon me of such writers as John Henry Cardinal Newman after I became a Catholic). Nevertheless, that is the way it all came about. God works in an infinite number of ways. For my part I first became intellectually convinced and then went out looking for the Catholics who embodied the faith in practice. It has been a superabundant gift of God that I, in fact, have found so many who have inspired and sustained me in the nearly three decades that I have been a practicing Catholic. The principal one of these, of course, has been my beloved wife Margaret, whom I married in St. Peter's Vatican Basilica a few months after having been received into the Church. Because of the life that, through God's grace I have been able to lead as a Catholic, I can truly make my own these words of John Henry Newman from the final chapter of his *Apologia pro Vita Sua:*

> From the time that I became a Catholic...I have no further history of my religious opinions to narrate. In saying this, I do not mean to say that my mind has been idle, or that I have given up thinking on theological subjects; but that I have had no variations to record, and have had no anxiety of heart whatever. I have been in perfect peace and contentment; I never have had one doubt. I was not conscious to myself, on my conversion, of any change, intellectual or moral, wrought in my mind. I was not conscious of firmer faith in the fundamental truths of Revelation, or of more self-command; I had not more fervor; but

it was like coming into port after a rough sea; and my happiness on that score remains to this day without interruption.

Kenneth D. Whitehead *was appointed Deputy Assistant Secretary for Higher Education Programs in May, 1986. He is the former director of the U.S. Department of Education's Center for International Education and was also a career foreign service officer with the U.S. Department of State. Active in the Catholic lay apostolate since the 1960s, he is the author of* Respectable Killing: the New Abortion Imperative; The Need for the Magisterium of the Church; *and* Agenda for the Sexual Revolution. *He is co-author of* The Pope, the Council and the Mass *and has also published numerous articles. Married to the former Margaret Mary O'Donohue, he is the father of four sons: Paul, Steven, Matthew, and David. The Whiteheads live in Falls Church, Virginia.*

*VISIT, WRITE or CALL your nearest ST. PAUL BOOK &
MEDIA CENTER today for a wide selection of Catholic books,
periodicals, cassettes, quality video cassettes for children and
adults! Operated by the Daughters of St. Paul.
We are located in:*

ALASKA

750 West 5th Ave., Anchorage, AK 99501 **907-272-8183**.

CALIFORNIA

3908 Sepulveda Blvd., Culver City, CA 90230 **213-397-8676**.

1570 Fifth Ave. (at Cedar Street), San Diego, CA 92101 **619-232-1442;
619-232-1443**.

46 Geary Street, San Francisco, CA 94108 **415-781-5180**.

FLORIDA

145 S.W. 107th Ave., Miami, FL 33174 **305-559-6715; 305-559-6716**.

HAWAII

1143 Bishop Street, Honolulu, HI 96813 **808-521-2731**.

ILLINOIS

172 North Michigan Ave., Chicago, IL 60601 **312-346-4228;
312-346-3240**.

LOUISIANA

4403 Veterans Memorial Blvd., Metairie, LA 70006 **504-887-7631;
504-887-0113**.

MASSACHUSETTS

50 St. Paul's Ave., Jamaica Plain, Boston, MA 02130 **617-522-8911**.

Rte. 1, 885 Providence Hwy., Dedham, MA 02026 **617-326-5385**.

MISSOURI

9804 Watson Rd., St. Louis, MO 63126 **314-965-3512; 314-965-3571**.

NEW JERSEY

561 U.S. Route 1, Wick Plaza, Edison, NJ 08817 **908-572-1200;
908-572-1201**.

NEW YORK

150 East 52nd Street, New York, NY 10022 **212-754-1110**.

78 Fort Place, Staten Island, NY 10301 **718-447-5071; 718-447-5086**.

OHIO

2105 Ontario Street (at Prospect Ave.), Cleveland, OH 44115
216-621-9427.

PENNSYLVANIA

214 W. DeKalb Pike, King of Prussia, PA 19406 **215-337-1882;
215-337-2077**.

SOUTH CAROLINA

243 King Street, Charleston, SC 29401 **803-577-0175**.

TEXAS

114 Main Plaza, San Antonio, TX 78205 **512-224-8101**.

VIRGINIA

1025 King Street, Alexandria, VA 22314 **703-549-3806**.

CANADA

3022 Dufferin Street, Toronto, Ontario, Canada M6B 3T5 **416-781-9131**.